Ma Duncan

Ma Duncan

Jim Barrett

Ivy House
Publishing Group

www.ivyhousebooks.com

PUBLISHED BY IVY HOUSE PUBLISHING GROUP
5122 Bur Oak Circle, Raleigh, NC 27612
United States of America
919-782-0281
www.ivyhousebooks.com

ISBN: 1-57197-384-2
Library of Congress Control Number: 2003092961

Printed in the United States of America

To Roland

THE TRIAL

Foreword

The crime? Murder. The victim? A pretty young nurse, eight months pregnant. The mastermind? The victim's own mother-in-law. The reason? Well, that's explained inside the pages of this book, and what a story it is. I had the privilege of meeting Jim Barrett a number of years ago. At the time, I was lecturing about the case, known locally as Ventura's "Trial of the Century." At that time, I received information about a man who "knew everything" about the case. Intrigued, I called Jim and not only did he know everything, he had written a book on it! I've had the distinct pleasure of reading Jim's manuscript and in doing so, came away even more impressed. This is not just a dry read, not just a rehash of the crime, the criminals and the court proceedings. No, this is a living, breathing story. Through Jim's expert knowledge of the crime, his personal interviews of the victim's family and extensive research into the criminal minds of the three killers, we are transported back to that November day in 1958 when this crime catapulted both Santa Barbara and Ventura counties into the limelight. Through Jim's eyes, you'll know the victim to be an honest, caring, sweet young woman who fell in love with the wrong man and paid the ultimate price for it. You'll know the principals—the son, his deranged mother and the two killers. But it's not such a simple case—this case has all the twists and turns of a Hollywood whodunit—and it's true crime. It was a horrific, calculated, cold-blooded murder. This case stands above all others, not only for the crime itself but because of its historic significance to the state of California—Elizabeth Ann "Ma" Duncan was the last female executed and it was the last triple execution ever performed.

—Glenda Jackson
Historian

Preface

I started this book in 1990, after first becoming interested in the improbable story of Ma Duncan because of a family connection. My wife's uncle was one of Ma's jurors during "the trial of the century." Although he had long since passed away when I began to research this story, that period of jury service was one of the highlights of the man's life. After all, the jury did condemn Ma to death, a once-in-a-lifetime event for any man and no small responsibility. My wife, Judy, frequently talked about the Ma Duncan story because she grew up with it. She remembers, from a very young age, listening to her uncle reciting the bizarre tale of Elizabeth Duncan.

I researched this book for two years. As a former homicide detective, I found my investigation into the doings of the cast of characters fascinating. In a certain sense, rediscovering the lives of the players was as rewarding as the actual writing of the book. I can recall many times shaking my head and exclaiming (usually to myself) "They did what?" as I uncovered event after event in this incredible story.

In the course of my research, I interviewed some thirty people and read through thousands of pages of court transcripts, newspaper accounts, and police reports. This was a daunting task, but one that gave me great satisfaction.

Certain highlights of my research help to further define the story and its impact on the community.

The members of Ma's jury took an oath of silence and (with one brief exception) were true to that oath. None of the jurors, save one with whom I had a quick telephone conversation, would talk to me about the process they went through in deciding the fate of their charge. I traveled to Canada to talk to Bill and Marian Kupczyk, Olga's brother and sister-in-law. The Kupczyks were two of the nicest people I met during my investigation. They gave me a sense of the type of person Olga no doubt was: the salt of the earth and certainly undeserving of her eventual fate.

I managed to interview the Reverend Floyd Gresset before his death. His recitation of how he primed Luis Moya to confess is drama in its purest form. While the actions taken by the police in gaining Luis's confession would certainly not stand in today's legal world, they withstood the scrutiny of the courts of that day.

While reading this book, one must take into account the context of the times in which the events took place. This is especially true when considering the lack, in those days, of much of the legal procedure common in American jurisprudence today. As an example, there was no Miranda Rights admonishment, because the murder occurred prior to the famous Miranda decision. Praying with Luis was considered fair game in order to obtain his confession—a tactic now considered out of bounds. Ma's jury included three individuals who admitted they were prejudiced against her prior to the first day of testimony. The Supreme Court later acknowledged this fact, but said, in effect, that this didn't matter because Mrs. Duncan was so obviously guilty. A modern-day court would certainly never issue such a statement. But it's important not to fall into the trap of "revisionism history" when considering 1959's lack of now commonly accepted due process protections.

This is a story that keeps amplifying. Since the completion of my manuscript, a secret recording of the Ma Duncan trial has surfaced, offered for sale on the Internet. After purchasing the recording, I listened with rapt attention to the actual voices of the players in this drama which lent an even more chilling aspect to their testimony.

Ventura county historian Glenda Jackson gives seminars about the Ma Duncan case in Ventura's old Superior One courtroom. Through Glenda, I had the good fortune to meet Roland Baldonado, one of Gus's twin sons to whom I make reference in the book. Roland has spent years trying to come to terms with the actions of his father and the impact those actions have had on his entire family. Through Glenda, I also met Jody Nigh, a niece of Ma Duncan who has a nearly unquenchable thirst to learn the facts of this story. Jody was kind enough to supply several of the pictures contained in this text.

Regarding this project, I owe thanks to a number of people. First and foremost, I thank my wife, Judy, who not only stimulated the writing of the book because of the family connection but also served as my "chief of quality control" for the prose contained herein.

Sonia Nordenson, who is both a professional copy editor and a good friend, polished this work and ensured the book's readability, which is paramount to whatever success it may enjoy.

Upon its completion in 1993, literary agent, Carolyn Jenks, agreed to carry the book. While Carolyn wasn't able to find an appropriate publisher, she provided invaluable insight for improvements. She and I spent many an hour on the phone kicking around the manuscript.

The manuscript then sat untouched on the shelf for years, largely because of a job assignment that consumed most of my waking hours (or so it seemed). Yet the story has always been out there, begging to be told. Toward the middle of 2001, I discussed the project with an Ojai author named Patricia Fry. Patty read the manuscript and stated matter-of-factly that it needed to be published. She has been working diligently to that end ever since, and I truly appreciate her commitment.

To those people who consented to discuss this case with me, often at a perceived personal risk, (after all this book *is* about murder) I say thank you. The many conversations in which I engaged in during the course of my research served to shape this story and to confirm facts found in news accounts and court transcripts. Importantly, many of the words of the people in this book are taken directly from a variety of official records. However, for the sake of the flow of events, a narrative technique that reasonably expresses the thoughts and actions of individuals was used.

Ma Duncan

Finally, this is the story of Ma Duncan. As such, it is based in fact, but not without my own personal interpretations of those facts. Such interpretations of bare-bones data fulfill the role of the storyteller and are an inherent part of writing an historical novel such as the one you're about to read.

—Ojai, California
June, 2003

For the crown of our life as it closes
Is darkness, the fruit thereof dust;
No thorns go as deep as a rose's,
And love is more cruel than lust.
Time turns the old days to derision,
Our loves into corpses or wives;
And marriage and death and division
Make barren our lives.

−Algernon Charles Swinburne, "Dolores"

Part I
A DEADLY COMBINATION

Code Name "Dorothy"

Now the Wicked Witch of the West had but one eye, yet that was as powerful as a telescope, and could see everywhere. So, as she sat in the door of her castle, she happened to look around and saw Dorothy lying asleep, with her friends all about her. They were a long distance off, but the Wicked Witch was angry to find them in her country; so she blew upon a silver whistle that hung from her neck.

At once there came running to her from all directions a pack of great wolves. They had long legs and fierce eyes and sharp teeth.

"Go to those people," said the Witch, "and tear them to pieces."

—L. Frank Baum, *The Wizard of Oz*

Luis Moya ducked into the Tropical Cafe on lower State Street to get out of the pouring rain. He paused at the front door, allowing his eyes to adjust to the dimly lit bar, inhaling the smell of frying tortillas. When he walked past two old men hunched over their beers, one of them, who had a burnt-out cigarette hanging from the corner of his mouth, recognized the young man and nodded to him. Luis sauntered past, ignoring the recognition, and swung himself onto a barstool. The stool, which had one leg slightly shorter then the others, rocked gently under his weight.

"Hey, Louie. *Como esta?*" Esperanza Esquivel called to him from behind the bar. "Need a draft?"

"Yeah, Chelo, a cold one." Luis scanned the cafe through the drifting blue haze that partially obscured the light coming from an old multi-colored chandelier that hung behind the bar. It was dust-covered and had cobwebs that looped from bangle to bangle. Most of the light bulbs were burned out and had been for as long as he could remember.

Placed at evenly spaced intervals on the dingy walls were identical sombreros with Indian blankets drooping beneath them. Like the rest of the establishment, they were in critical need of a good cleaning. The bar itself had seen years of use and abuse, and its fine finish had been marred by countless spilled drinks, dropped cigarettes, and carved initials. Luis's eyes drifted in the direction of the bandstand, where musical equipment was set up in anticipation of the evening crowd.

Suddenly, the odor of beery breath assaulted Luis's nostrils. He turned his attention to its source.

"Hey, Moya. Hows about buying me a brew?" It was one of the old men he had just walked past, now standing next to Luis, yelling in his ear.

The man stood swaying until he reached over and grabbed the bar to steady himself

He reeked not only of alcohol, but also of that pungent odor of the unbathed. Luis looked into the face of the drunkard, whose spittle-soaked cigarette still hung from the corner of his mouth.

"Get lost, asshole."

"C'mon. Just one lousy beer. I'm broke."

"Get away from me," Luis grunted as he swatted at the old man, not really wanting to touch him.

The derelict staggered backward to avoid the slap. Realizing he wasn't going to have any luck with the younger man, he lurched back toward his table, cursing Moya in a loud, incoherent voice.

Esperanza set a frosty mug in front of Luis. "Is Miguel giving you a hard time?"

Luis glanced quickly over his shoulder at the man. "He needs to crawl back under whatever bridge he's been calling home."

"Well, he's harmless. Just a drunk."

Luis turned his attention back to Chelo, looking into her eyes as she spoke. He observed that the brown irises were hazy and dilated. *Hype's eyes,* he thought.

"You working these days?" she asked while drying a beer mug.

"No, I'm sorta in between jobs right now. But I've been thinkin' about goin' back to the Blue Onion."

"Are you broke?"

"I got a couple of bucks. Why, you worried I'll stiff you for the beer?"

Chelo leaned towards Luis and lowered her voice. "Oh, no. It's just that I talked to a lady who's looking for someone to do a job."

"What kind of job?" Luis asked, also lowering his voice. He began drawing designs on the sweating mug with his finger. "I'm not into digging ditches or shit like that."

"It's nothing like that. She's got this relative who's giving her problems, blackmailing her son or something. She wants to get rid of her." Esperanza raised her eyes and looked over Luis's shoulder, checking to ensure that the two men at the table were not listening.

Luis also looked in their direction. He then swiveled off the stool and walked to the jukebox in a corner of the bar. He dug in his pocket for a coin, inserted it into the antique machine, and made his selections from memory. He waited momentarily until he saw the platter begin to spin, then walked back and resumed his place at the bar. "Who is this person?" Luis asked.

"It's the mother of Marciano's attorney."

"Marciano? Your husband?"

"Yeah. He's been in jail since the cops found some stuff in the back from a burglary. I was arrested too, but I made bail."

"So what does she mean by get rid of her?" Luis asked, his curiosity now aroused while the familiar tunes began to fill the bar.

"She didn't tell me any of the details. But are you interested?"

Luis gave no immediate reply. He watched his mug art begin to run into indiscernible shapes. He was considering starting over on the other side of his glass when he heard a shout from the kitchen.

"Hey, Louie, I'm getting off in a couple of minutes. You got money for beer?"

"Don't she ever pay you, Gus?" Luis called back, looking playfully at Chelo.

"The way he goes through money . . ." Chelo began.

"I'll be out soon as I stack this last load of plates," Gus answered, still shouting to make himself heard over the pounding beat of the jukebox.

"Well, what do you think?" Chelo asked, getting back to the subject. "You could use the cash. Maybe Gus could help you out. I really can't pay him that much, and he's always griping about being broke."

"I don't know," Luis put her off. "How about another beer?"

"It beats doing stickups in L.A.," Chelo joked walking towards the tap.

Gus joined Luis at the bar, clumsily heaving himself onto a stool and knocking over Luis's empty glass. "I'll have one, too," he said hopefully.

"Sure," Chelo responded, drawing another one. She delivered the beers, then busied herself at the other end of the counter.

"It's a good thing that glass was empty. I've killed better men for less," Luis grinned at Gus.

"Oh, yeah. You got me scared now," Gus shot back.

Luis's hand shot out towards Gus's cheek. It was adroitly blocked by Gus, who was expecting the slap. Luis settled back to his beer.

"Hey Gus, did she talk to you about a job?" Luis nodded toward the cafe proprietress.

"Yeah, but she didn't say much about it. I told her I might be interested if you were."

"I guess we could talk to the woman."

"Sure, why not?"

"Hey, Chelo! How do we meet this person?"

"Come in tomorrow afternoon. I'll introduce you," she called back.

"Well . . . okay, maybe we will."

Luis turned his attention back to Gus. "You want to go score?"

"Sure, but I ain't got no money."

"I'll float you, just this once. It's dynamite weed. I had some hits the other night."

"If you're buying, let's go!" Gus said, sucking down the last of his beer.

Luis reached into his pocket and pulled out a crumpled dollar bill. He threw it on the counter, where it landed in a puddle of water. "Hey, Chelo, maybe, we'll see you tomorrow," he shouted at the bar owner. She waved in their direction.

The two men headed for the front door, talking in hushed tones about their anticipated buy.

Esperanza watched them walk out of the bar, a knowing smile upon her lips. *Yeah, they'll be back, those two will,* she thought to herself.

The next afternoon, Thursday, November 13, 1958, Luis made his way down State Street towards the Tropical Cafe. This older part of town was Santa Barbara's busiest police beat with prostitutes, dope dealers, winos, and all manner of street people abounding. Luis saw a patrol car driving slowly in his direction, the cop obviously looking for someone to jack up. Luis Moya was no stranger to police contacts and he could ill afford one now. He'd just popped a couple of bennies and didn't want to get busted for being under the influence.

He gauged the distance to the front door of the Tropical and decided that he could probably make it without quickening his pace so much as to arouse the cop's suspicions. Of course, just walking into the Tropical Cafe didn't mean he wouldn't get to meet this guy. It was an establishment frequently checked by the Santa Barbara Police, especially after three recent stabbings, one of which resulted in a death.

Luis reached the front door just seconds before the patrol officer pulled to the curb.

He opened the door and slipped hurriedly into the cafe in an attempt to minimize his exposure to the officer.

Gus was already in the bar, sitting at a table near the window. "What's the hurry, Louie?"

"There's a cop out there that I don't need to meet," the younger man responded, moving to the window and peering out.

"Shit, man. He's stopped out front," Luis whispered, ducking his head away from the window. "If he comes in, I'm runnin' out the back. Gus, you try to distract him or somethin'."

The mention of a cop caught the attention of Chelo, who was cleaning up broken bottles from the night before.

"If that cop comes in here, you're not going through the back," she said fiercely and began walking toward the front door, trying to decide if she should lock it or try to head the officer off. "I already told you about the problems I got and I don't need no more trouble!" she hissed. "If you run, he'll chase you, and I don't want no cops in the back room." Her voice was now on the edge of panic.

Luis stayed by the window, barely breathing, peeking out the corner, and monitoring the cop's actions. "Okay, he's pulling away from the curb. Yeah, okay, he's leaving. Whew! Now I really need a beer." Luis turned on his heels and walked toward Gus's table.

"You're not the only one," Chelo replied, walking behind the bar to draw the beers.

Luis turned his attention to Esperanza, better known as Chelo to her many customers that frequented the bar. The extremely thin, almost emaciated woman, who had been fighting an ongoing battle with tuberculosis, coughed and hacked as she walked behind the bar. In her late thirties, she had aged considerably beyond her years, the ravaged results of a raucous lifestyle.

"Hey, Chelo, what time is that lady supposed to show up?" Luis called.

"She should be here any time now."

"If she don't get here soon, I'm gone," Gus said. "I got important things to do."

"Like what?" Luis asked sarcastically. "Got a caper planned?"

"Well—" Gus had begun to answer when the front door swung open and a middle-aged woman walked into the room. She stood near the door, holding it open and scanning the room with a slow motion of her head until she saw Esperanza to whom she nodded. Then she fixed Luis and Gus with her eyes, a faint smile curling on her thin, painted lips. She continued to hold open the door allowing a very old, frail woman to walk in behind her. A quick gust of wind followed the two into the bar, blowing dust and leaves under the tables.

The first woman walked toward the bar, her head held high as if she were scenting the air—like a cougar tracking its prey. She seemed to dislike what her senses told her about this place, as her wan smile was replaced by a frown. The old woman walked behind, staying what appeared to be a respectful distance to the rear.

Chelo leaned on a table she had been wiping to watch this grand entrance. When the woman had passed her, she nodded to the boys as if to say, "There she is."

Both women took seats on the barstools, looking noticeably out of place. The younger of the two placed her purse upon the bar, reached into it, and pulled out a black compact. She flipped it open and studied herself in the small round mirror. She patted her brown hair, which was pulled back into a severe bun that fully exposed her face. Her prominent chin, which seemed to overpower the rest of her face, lent her an indomitable appearance. She wore little make-up, just a touch of red on her lips. Upon her face she wore brown framed glasses, the kind with wings protruding above each lens. The glasses greatly magnified her eyes, causing the blue orbs to appear unnaturally large.

Chelo approached the two women, addressing the younger, "Hello, Mrs. Duncan. Can I get you something from the bar?"

"Afternoon, Esperanza. That would be nice. I'd like a cup of coffee, black. And my friend will have the same, with cream and sugar. Right, Mrs. Short?"

The old woman nodded.

"Comin' right up."

Mrs. Duncan returned to her mirror, tilting it so she could gaze at the two men sitting behind her. She appeared to be sizing them up, trying to determine if they were capable of her planned assignment.

The fact that he was being watched was not lost on Luis. He had not taken his eyes off this woman since she had entered the bar. He had an uneasy feeling about her.

Though she had said little since arriving, there was an aura of self-importance about her that needed no verbal cues to be felt.

Esperanza arrived with the two cups of coffee, setting them down in front of the women. She gestured over the shoulders of the two sitting at the bar. "Mrs. Duncan, those are the boys I told you about," she said, giving the men a knowing look.

Elizabeth swiveled around and fixed them with sullen, foreboding eyes. Luis was caught momentarily eye to eye with her, but quickly averted his gaze under her scrutiny. He felt an unexplainable fear clutching at his stomach and sensed that there was something sinister about this woman, something not far below the surface.

Luis focused on the woman's hands, noticing that she wore a solitary diamond ring on her left ring finger. Her dress was simple: solid black with no other color. It reminded Luis of a dress he'd seen his mother wear at his uncle's funeral.

Suddenly, Mrs. Duncan trilled out, "Hello, boys," shocking Luis back to the business at hand.

"Hi," Luis replied, his attention once again consumed by her eyes. Gus, less interested, just nodded.

"Why don't you boys sit over here?"

They slid out from behind the table, clutching their beers, and walked to the stools that Mrs. Duncan had indicated. Luis sat on the woman's left, next to the cigarette machine. The old lady got up and moved over one stool so Gus could sit to Mrs. Duncan's right.

Esperanza continued the introductions. "Mrs. Duncan, this is Louie and that's Gus." The woman didn't offer her hand, which was fine with Luis.

There was an uncomfortably long silence, no one wanting to be the first to speak.

Finally, Chelo broke the quiet by saying, "I'll let you get down to business. If you need anything, just let me know." She walked away, busying herself at the other end of the bar.

Mrs. Duncan directed her comments to Luis, whom she had immediately identified as the boss of these two. Her voice had a slight nervous quake to it, a clue about the topic soon to be at hand.

"Well, I see no need to beat around the bush. Did Esperanza tell you what I want?"

"Sort of," Gus piped in.

"Yeah, but we don't know what it is exactly," Luis added, feeling ill at ease sitting so close to this woman.

"You boys look trustworthy, so I'll tell you right out. I have a problem with my daughter-in-law. She's threatened to throw acid in my son's face if I don't give her a thousand dollars by this weekend. She's a foreigner and she's trying to blackmail me. I told Frankie— that's my son—not to marry the bitch, but he wouldn't listen."

While Mrs. Duncan spoke, she rotated her cup of coffee in the saucer, first pointing the handle toward herself and then moving it toward the wall. She seemed to have a fixed pattern in her mind, while the cup continued to rattle in the saucer. Watching this, Luis decided it was a nervous habit. He also noticed that the initial tension in her voice had subsided. She had worked her way into a very smooth presentation, almost as if she had rehearsed this speech many times before. However, when Gus asked, "Where's she from?" the woman pivoted around on the stool, blasted him with her cold eyes, and snapped, "Canada, but that doesn't matter!"

Gus pulled his upper body away from her as if he was avoiding a blow. "Hey, sorry I asked."

"What exactly do you want us to do?" Luis asked to get the heat off his pal.

"Get rid of her."

"You mean run her out of town or somethin'? Scare her back to Canada?"

"No, I tried that. I want you to kill the bitch! I want you to throw acid in her face and burn her eyes out of her head! I want that woman cold in her grave!" Elizabeth's cup now whipped back and forth, sloshing coffee onto the bar.

"Whoa now!" Gus stuttered, reaching for the bar to help brace himself against the force of her words.

"Yeah, hold on there!" Luis agreed, tipping forward and looking first at Gus and then past him to Chelo, who stood leaning against the bar with a smirk on her lips.

"Did you know about this?" he called to her.

With her smile intact, Chelo shrugged her shoulders and turned away from the man.

"She never said nothin' about no murder," Luis continued, talking mainly to himself while he lifted the beer to his lips.

"That's the job. Plain and simple."

Luis watched as she raised her coffee cup to her mouth. Her hand trembled causing more coffee to slip down the side of the cup. He lowered his head and stared into his half-full beer mug. *This woman's not for real,* he thought to himself. *But let's test the water.*

"How much?" he blurted out.

"Louie, wait a minute!" Gus's strident voice assaulted him.

"Shut up, Gus. What are you willing to pay?"

"Louie, wait—"

"Shut the fuck up!" He turned back to the negotiations, glaring into her larger-than-life eyes. "Well?" *I'm calling your bluff,* he thought to himself.

"Three thousand." She didn't bat an eye.

"Make it six."

"Okay, six thousand. Three thousand after the job is done and three thousand in six months."

"No way! We can't wait that long!"

"You'll have to. If I take too much money out of the bank, the cops'll ask questions. We'll have to do it this way."

"Hmmm . . . " Luis was thinking.

"There'll be nothing to connect us. And a person can't be too careful," Mrs. Duncan added, reinforcing her logic.

"I guess that makes sense," Luis agreed.

"Believe me, I've given it a lot of thought," she replied, obviously proud of herself. "I've been looking to hire someone for a long time."

"Hey, Louie," Gus interrupted the conversation, "we gotta talk." He motioned towards the bandstand.

"Sure. We'll be right back." Luis slid off the barstool and put his arm around his friend's shoulders, guiding him to the rear of the restaurant.

"Okay, pal, what's the problem?" Luis asked in a hushed tone.

"Man, I don't like that bitch. I got a bad feelin' about this and you're going along with her. She's bad news, man. Let's shine her on and get outta here!"

"For once in your life, Gus, think! She's talking six thou. Those kinda bucks will keep us in shit for a long time. Besides, we don't have to do nothin'. Just string her along till we can collect something. Hang with me, brother. Have I ever steered you wrong before?"

"I don't know, Louie. If it gets too serious, I'm gone. Just so you know up front."

Gus looked over his shoulder at the two women sitting at the bar and then looked at the door as if he were sizing up an escape route. His gaze returned to the women.

"Look at her, Louie. She's staring holes in the back of my head. It's like . . . I don't know, man . . . like she's one evil cunt."

"Don't sweat it, man. Just hang tough and we'll do this witch for a few bucks. She's on the hook, not us. She can't go to the cops about this, so we're in the driver's seat. Let's go sit down and let me handle it."

Gus looked at his friend with apprehension. He finally nodded his head and walked slowly back to the bar.

Luis walked behind Gus and resumed his seat on the barstool. "Okay, Gus and I have talked it over. We're in agreement. What's the rest of the deal?"

Mrs. Duncan, who had not taken her eyes off them since they left the bar, replied, "It's got to be done this weekend."

"We'll need some up-front money."

"Okay. I can give you $175."

"Is that all?"

"Yes, for now. That'll be enough to get you started, won't it?"

"If that's all you have," a disappointed Luis answered.

"That's all."

"Okay. So do we grab her off the street or what? We could drive her down to Tijuana and get rid of her there."

Elizabeth had begun to reply when the front door opened and a young woman wearing a tight red dress entered. She scanned the bar, her eyes finally resting on Luis.

She smiled at him, giving him a knowing look. Her high heels clicked upon the floor as she made her way toward him. Mrs. Duncan shot an insistent look at Chelo, who took the hint and spoke up. "Sorry, honey. We're closed."

"You don't look closed to me."

"I said we're closed! Now beat it!"

"Well, okay. You don't have to get nasty!" The woman turned on her heels and winked at Luis over her shoulder. "Maybe I'll see you later, baby." She wiggled out of the bar and slammed the door.

Luis' eyes were fixed on her swaying hips. *I sure hope so,* he thought to himself.

"Now, where were we?" Mrs. Duncan said when she was sure the woman wouldn't return.

"We were talking about throwing this broad in the trunk of the car and driving her to Mexico," Luis informed her.

"She's a nurse and pretty strong. She's bound to fight you. I've got some acid. You could pour it on her face and teeth so the cops won't be able to identify her. You'll need to burn her hands to destroy her prints."

Gus felt a chill go down his back while he listened to this matter-of-fact exchange between his friend and this woman he'd decided was stone crazy. Gus looked over at Chelo and motioned for another beer. He decided this would be a good day to get drunk.

"I don't know about acid," Luis was saying. "I thought you said *she* had the acid. Besides, I have a friend who has a gun. He'll let me use it and a piece would be much easier." Luis leaned forward on the stool and looked at Gus. "Hey, Gus, will Sarah let you use her car?"

"Probably, but not for free," was the unenthusiastic response.

"You boys can use my car. I'll even come along to help, if need be," Mrs. Duncan volunteered.

"That's okay. It's better not to use your car, just in case." Luis knew that even if he had planned to carry out such a scheme, he wouldn't want this crazy bitch along. She would obviously enjoy it too much!

"Well, if there are any problems, my son Frankie is an attorney—"

Luis cut her off. "There won't be any problems."

"Good, that's what I want to hear. Her address is 1114 Garden Street, upstairs, apartment number eleven. You boys can grab her from there."

"Sure, the Garden Street Apartments. I know where they are. Near Valerio Street. Apartment number eleven," Luis repeated to fix the number in his mind.

"When you get her, take her purse and some clothes. Make it look like she went on a trip," Mrs. Duncan continued, obviously enjoying her role in planning the job.

Chelo, who had delivered a beer to Gus, stood next to him and listened to the conversation. When Mrs. Duncan exclaimed, "It's decided, then," Chelo clapped her hands together as if the conspirators had just closed a major land deal.

Caught up in the excitement, Chelo cried, "Yeah, that's good. You boys really need the money." And then, in an effort to celebrate the agreement, she asked if anyone wanted anything further to drink.

But Mrs. Duncan rose to leave, putting some change on the counter for the coffee. Her elderly companion, who had not spoken throughout the negotiations, also stood up.

"What about the money?" Luis demanded.

A smile curled on her lips as she contemplated Luis's tone of voice. "I'm a little short of cash right now. But, to get you boys started, I'll go hock this ring that my poor deceased husband gave me. We'll meet back here in an hour, in the kitchen."

"Okay, in one hour," Luis confirmed, wondering how her husband had met his end. Perhaps an unexpected acid bath, he supposed.

Elizabeth walked towards the front door, reached out for the door handle, and then spun around. "We should have a code name. We'll use it when discussing this job."

Luis looked at her in disbelief, but decided not to push the issue.

"It'll be 'Dorothy,'" she continued, which caused the old woman to titter in the background.

"What?" Luis asked. He'd expected something more conspiratorial.

Gus, who'd stayed out of the conversation, broke in. "Dorothy? Who's Dorothy?" The only Dorothy he knew of was the little girl in *The Wizard of Oz*.

Mrs. Duncan lowered her voice. "You'll understand when the time is right."

Now the old lady had progressed from a giggle to outright laughter.

"What's *your* name?" Gus snapped at her, annoyed that there was a joke he was obviously missing.

"How rude of me. Boys, this is my dear friend, Emma Short," Elizabeth said.

The frail old lady put her hand to her mouth, trying to stifle her laughter. When she brought her hand down, the back of it glistened with saliva. She nodded to Luis and Gus.

"I hope she can keep her trap shut," Luis said, thinking she didn't have all her marbles.

"She can." Mrs. Duncan jerked open the front door.

"Wait a minute!" Gus called to the departing woman. "What's the lady's name?"

"What lady?"

"You know . . . the one . . . " his voice trailed off.

"Olga," the name hung heavy in the room as Elizabeth Duncan slammed the door behind her.

Luis

Hindsight is a hell of a thing. Here I thought I was such a hot-shot! How come I let myself be persuaded? I could have done other things to get money. I've pulled a lot of burglaries. I was handling thousands of dollars at the Blue Onion. I could have walked off with it. I can't understand it myself. I just can't understand it. It's one of the problems I haven't figured out yet.

—Luis on himself, Death Row, San Quentin,
The Hired Killers, Peter Wyden, 1963

Luis steeled himself against what was about to happen. For him, it was a matter of survival, unlike the way it was for some of the guys in this joint who actually liked it. This was a for-profit venture, business pure and simple.

"Hurry up, goddamit!" he hissed over his shoulder, lowering his pants while he talked. "You got the cigs?"

"Yeah," came the curt response. Luis turned and grabbed the carton from the man and stuffed them into the front of his shirt. He pivoted back around to the cold metal table, grasping it with his hands.

"Keep your eyes peeled, Roger!" Luis shouted to a third inmate who was acting as a lookout. Luis bent over the dayroom table, exposing his bare buttocks to the other inmate. He felt the man smear an oily substance on his inner cheeks and caught the familiar scent of vegetable oil when it began to run down the insides of his legs. He closed his eyes, clenched his teeth, and began in earnest to block out what was now happening to him. He forced his mind to an earlier, but not necessarily happier time.

The year was 1949.

"You little son of a bitch!" Luis Moya, Sr. raged at his son. "I don't understand you! Why, why do you get involved in these things?"

The boy of eleven shrugged his shoulders, knowing that he didn't have an answer to his father's question. He didn't know why, so he couldn't begin to explain it to his father. Luis sat mute, afraid to look into the man's eyes, guessing what was coming next.

This only further infuriated his father, who now hurried across the sparsely furnished living room, grasped the boy by both arms, and lifted him off the couch. He shouted into the boy's face, spraying him with bourbon-laced spit, "It's gonna stop, so help me God, it's gonna stop! I won't have a liar in my house!" He shook the child violently, his head snapping back and forth. Then he flung Luis away like a piece of unwanted trash. The child caught his breath, bracing himself against the impact he was about to feel. He crashed against the wall and slid to the floor to a sitting position, dazed by the blow.

While the spots buzzed around in his head, young Luis looked in the direction of his father, trying to focus his vision. Out of the haze he saw a large hand appear, which cuffed him across the left side of his face. His head jerked sideways and a trickle of blood began working its way down the corner of his mouth.

"Maybe that'll teach you! I ain't putting up with your shit anymore!" The man stomped from the room, leaving his namesake sitting on the floor, trying to sort out his feelings.

Luis often replayed this scene in his head. It was one he could readily recall, one of many violent confrontations he had with his father.

It was much harder to remember the good times when he thought back through his past.

The best times were with his sister, Eloisa, who raised Luis, his two brothers, and a sister after a disabling injury to their father forced Mrs. Moya to work in the cotton fields outside their home in San Angelo, Texas. Though Eloisa did her best, by the age of eleven, Luis was beyond her control. He began to run with an older crowd known for troublemaking. It was at this time that Luis Sr. began to beat Luis for disobedience. These beatings did nothing to deter the boy's negative behavior and only reinforced his rebellious feelings, especially since he was the only Moya child ever treated that way.

By the sixth grade, Luis began to use drugs. He experimented with marijuana and by age thirteen was a regular user. Luis soon began to steal in order to support the constant need for the drug. It was also in his thirteenth year when the Mexican police arrested him for attempting to smuggle marijuana back to Texas. He spent two days in a Mexican jail before his parents were able to buy his freedom. However, when they returned Luis to San Angelo, the sheriff arrested him for the burglary of a neighbor's residence. Luis had used the money from the burglary to buy the marijuana he had hoped to bring back across the border.

At the age of fifteen, Luis broke into the F.C. Rice Jewelry Store in San Angelo, obtaining more than $5,000 in loot. He was subsequently arrested in nearby Del Rio, where he was trying to sell the stolen property. He was sent to the State School in Gatesville for that crime.

After his release from the reform school, Moya's behavior turned violent. He became involved in two gang fights. In the second, Luis was hospitalized for ten days, suffering from severe stab wounds. However, he managed to "get his licks in," causing near-fatal knife wounds to participants in both fights.

One year later, Luis was returned to Gatesville for violation of parole on another burglary charge. During this crime, the store owner surprised him. Only a malfunctioning gun saved the lucky proprietor from a young man intent on murder. Moya pointed the weapon at his chest and pulled the trigger three times. The gun failed to fire.

Luis escaped from Gatesville School and returned home. He stayed there only briefly. While there, his mother tried to talk him into returning to custody. When this proved fruitless, she made arrangements for her son to go to Bakersfield, California, where she hoped he could get a fresh start. He worked briefly at the Bakersfield Inn prior to moving to San Diego to stay with a relative.

In San Diego, he began to slip back to his old ways. He worked sporadically and was living off older women, most of whom were prostitutes. In December 1955, Luis was arrested for cutting two sailors in a knife fight in Tijuana. These charges were later dropped.

The San Diego Police arrested Luis in October 1956 for possession of marijuana for sale. He was making frequent trips to Tijuana and returning with large quantities of weed packed in Prince Albert tobacco cans. He was convicted of the charge and, although he was only eighteen, was sent directly to the California Adult Authority. It always brought a smile to his face when he recalled the words of the presiding judge, who stated, "I know he is only eighteen, but I think he has no business at the Youth Authority. He would just give them bad ideas up there. I think he would be a bad influence." Now that was something to be proud of!

Luis was committed to Chino State Prison for a term of six months to ten years. It was here that the young, attractive man soon began to sell himself for the sexual enjoyment of the older cons. And, for Luis, it was always strictly business.

"Hey, the man's walking," Roger called out with quiet urgency, grabbing the broom he was supposed to be sweeping with.

"Get off me!"

Luis felt the still-unsatisfied man pull out. He quickly bent down and hiked up his pants. He hurried to the other side of the cell, just before the guard looked into the dayroom.

"You guys about done in there?" the officer asked.

"Yeah, we'll be about five more minutes," Roger replied, pushing around a small pile of debris with his broom.

"Okay, hurry it up then!" The guard continued his rounds.

"You still owe me, sweet cheeks," the other inmate said to Luis when he was sure the officer was gone.

Luis looked in his direction and winked. "Hey, it isn't my problem. Maybe we can get together when you have more smokes." Luis pulled the carton of cigarettes from his shirt and ripped off the end flap. He whistled at Roger and tossed a pack in the air. "Here's what I owe you," he said, watching Roger snag the cigarettes in mid-air and tuck them into his sock.

Gus

He was a very happy-go-lucky boy . . . a little mischievous at times, but nothing you wouldn't expect. . . . A real goose-with-a-broom character . . . He wasn't the killer type.
— Gus's former friend and employer

While Augustine Baldonado's death would make front-page headlines, his birth was much less newsworthy. On September 11, 1933, Sophia Baldonado lay down on the dirty, uncarpeted floor of her barrio home, groaned, heaved, and pushed out the fifth of her eight children. This son they named Augustine, but because his siblings could not pronounce his formidable name, he soon became known by the nickname T'lene.

T'lene's early years were typical for a youngster growing up in the only low-income Hispanic area in the upper-middle-class community of Camarillo.

The small Mexican population in this Southern California town, located in Ventura County, earned their living by working in the rich agricultural lowlands of the Oxnard Plains, whose innumerable layers of topsoil were the envy of farmers throughout the world, providing lima bean harvests that had no equal. The Baldonado household, situated in the heart of the Barry Street barrio, was well known to local officials. T'lene and his brothers and sisters grew up in filth and neglect. Many times, school authorities and the local sheriff's deputies came to the Baldonado home insisting that Mariano and Sophia clean up and care for their ever-growing brood.

At other times, the local lawmen responded to calls to mediate the many drunken brawls that occurred between the parents in front of the wide-eyed children. More then one of these responses resulted in the arrest of Mariano Baldonado, who was not beyond physically abusing his wife.

By the tender age of seven, T'lene was without effective parental supervision and began a life of mischief which would set the tone for his later years. During one of the many unsupervised acts of his young life, he severely broke his ankle trying to hop aboard a passing freight train.

It is little wonder that at age nine, T'lene had his first run-in with the law. He attempted to burglarize a neighbor's home, but walked in on the startled homeowner. He was quickly arrested and served time in juvenile hall for his escapade.

When Augustine was eleven years old, Mariano abandoned his family and moved out of California. He left Sophia Baldonado to raise the children alone and was seldom seen by them again.

Once more, T'lene, still eleven, tried his hand at stealing. He burglarized the home of neighbor Joe Hernandez, obtaining only $5 for his efforts. Having succeeded at that, he next broke into another neighbor's garage for which he was caught and sent back to juvenile hall in Ventura. He was eventually released to the care of his well-meaning schoolteacher, Onorinda Jones.

Mrs. Jones had little success with Gus, as he was to become known in his later youth. He was constantly in trouble at school and soon earned the reputation of being the town clown. His school pranks were notorious, landing him many times in the principal's office.

As is usually the case, Gus's crime patterns turned more serious when he got older. He eventually wound up in the Los Prietos Boys Camp, sentenced to eighteen months for a sophisticated gas station burglary. While he was at this institution, which is tucked away at the base of the Los Padres National Forest near Santa Barbara, it was learned that Augustine's IQ was seventy-five—considerably below normal.

Upon his release, Gus enrolled in Oxnard High School. Shortly after his enrollment in 1950, he was expelled for starting a "riot" between white and Hispanic youths. This fight was evidence of the many years of frustration and hate towards Anglo people that Gus had accumulated.

At the age of seventeen, and with parental permission, Augustine Baldonado enlisted in the United States Army. He was shipped to Fort Bragg, North Carolina, where he became a member of the elite Eighty-Second Airborne Division. However, Gus's antisocial ways followed him into the military and he was soon in trouble for constantly going AWOL. At one time, he spent six months in the Miami area, living off the streets until he was arrested and placed in the stockade. Upon his release, he was shipped to Korea under armed guard and there he was assigned as a combat medic. His stint in Korea was noteworthy only in that he did not get into trouble and seemed to actually like the excitement of battle.

After his Korean tour, Gus was transferred to Japan, where he was soon arrested for injecting other soldiers with heroin. This arrest resulted in confinement in the army disciplinary barracks in Lompoc, California, a town in northern Santa Barbara County.

Gus was given a dishonorable discharge. He returned to Camarillo, where he soon found himself in a stormy marriage with Carmen Lopez, who was also from the Barry Street barrio. The marriage lasted until March of 1957 and resulted in the births of two children. Although legally divorced, Gus and Carmen continued a sexual relationship, the products of which were twin boys born November 23, 1958.

Psychiatric evaluations of Augustine sounded surprisingly similar to those of his crime partner, Luis Moya.

In his testimony at the sanity hearing for Gus, Dr. David R. M. Harvey, a noted Ventura County psychiatrist, stated, "I concluded that he was a sociopathic personality characterized by antisocial reaction. This term refers to chronically antisocial individuals who are always in trouble, profiting neither from experience nor punishment and maintaining no real loyalties to any person, group, or code. They are frequently callous and hedonistic, showing marked emotional immaturity with a lack of a sense of responsibility, lack of judgment, and an ability to rationalize their behavior so that it appears warranted, reasonable, and justified."

As subsequent events would prove, Luis Moya and Augustine Baldonado's friendship provided the deadly combination that Elizabeth Duncan was searching for.

An Attempted Suicide

SECONAL SODIUM —
WARNING: MAY BE HABIT FORMING—
Seconal is a short-acting barbiturate which depresses the central nervous system. In ordinary doses, the drug acts as a sedative and hypnotic. Overdosage can produce death. WARNING: MAY BE HABIT FORMING.
—*Physicians Desk Reference,* 1985 Edition.

The chain of events that would ultimately lead to the murder of an attractive nurse named Olga Kupczyk Duncan started simply enough with an argument between mother and son. It was on the evening of November 6, 1957, on Victoria Street in the City of Santa Barbara. Elizabeth Duncan sat on the couch in the recently refurbished flat and screamed at her son Frank, "I told you that's not the way I wanted this handled! Damn it all!"

"But, Mother—"

"Oh, shut up, Frankie! You knew my wishes. I never agreed to you signing the annulment waiver!"

"Mother, if you'd let me explain," Frank said, hoping that for once she actually would.

"Well, go ahead."

"When you gave me power of attorney, I just naturally felt it was in your best interest to get this Sollenne matter cleaned up as quickly as possible. I thought—"

"You thought wrong!" Elizabeth crossed her arms and glared at her son. "And I never told you to sign anything on my behalf!"

"But, as I said—" Frank began.

"Son of a bitch, Frank, I don't want to hear more of your foolish excuses. I had plans for Mr. Sollenne and you screwed it up! We could have gotten more money out of Leonard and now you've let him off the hook. Son of a bitch!"

"Mother, I don't care about Sollenne's money, and you're not to talk to me that way!"

Mrs. Duncan's prominent chin thrust out at her son and she glowered at him with such intensity that her eyes smoldered with rage. She jerked her body around on the couch and slapped her arm upon the armrest, as if she had to hit something, deciding upon the couch instead of her son. The blow sent up a small puff of dust that swirled around the lampshade, the dust particles appearing to be sucked toward the lighted bulb.

Frank watched the dust cloud disperse in the air around the light. He leaned forward on the edge of the overstuffed chair, placed his head in his hands, and bent over. He didn't look at his mother. His words were measured, his voice modulated to carry the force of his pent-up emotions.

"Mother, this just isn't working out anymore. I can't seem to do anything right, at least as far as you're concerned. Maybe it's time you moved out. Let me live my own life."

Frank's words and the difficulty he had delivering them softened his mother. Her mood changed from rage to concern.

"But Frank, we've always been together," she said, her voice on the edge of panic.

"You understand, don't you?" Frank now found the nerve to unbend his body and look at his mother.

The expression on her face answered his question. She appeared horrified, as if he had threatened her very existence. He quickly looked away, but the image was still there, burned into his brain.

"Well, if that's the way you feel . . . " Her voice spoke of fathomless disappointment.

"I know we've talked about this before, but I mean it this time, Mom."

"Can I at least spend the night?"

"No, I don't think so. Call Emma, she'll put you up in her spare bedroom."

Elizabeth rose slowly from the sofa and shrugged her shoulders in dramatized resignation. "You know, Patsy would never have done this to me."

"For God's sake, Mom, Patsy is dead!"

"She loved me. She wouldn't kick me out to a life on the streets."

"Oh, Jesus Christ."

"Let me get a few of my things together." She shot him one final compelling look and then walked into her bedroom, gently shutting the door behind her.

Frank sat back and took a deep breath, relieved that he had finally dealt with this issue once and for all. It was the day before his twenty-ninth birthday and this argument had helped him to make up his mind. It was time for him to free himself of his mother's influence and get on with his own life.

Frank stood up and ran his hands through his wavy, black hair. While he wasn't tall, his weight was well within proportion, giving him a slender appearance. His nose was slightly big for the rest of his face and his thin lips betrayed him as his mother's son. But, by any standards, Frank Duncan was an attractive man, especially when dressed in his three-piece attorney suits. Still, there was one detracting feature that Frank hated about himself. When he got excited, he had a very noticeable lisp. This handicap had caused him to be the butt of many jokes, especially in the Santa Barbara Courthouse, where, behind his back, he was referred to as "that wicked wascal wabbit."

Frank walked into the kitchen and opened the refrigerator. He pulled out a beer and popped off the bottle top with the opener tied to the refrigerator door. He took a drink, then walked toward his mother's room to listen at the door. He hoped to hear the sounds of a person packing: a drawer opening, a closet door squeaking. There was only silence.

Frank shrugged, went back in the living room, and sat in his chair. *I'll give her a few more moments,* he thought to himself.

While Frank drank his beer, Elizabeth sat on the edge of her bed, pen and paper in hand, composing her thoughts. Her mind wandered through her life, a life filled with tragedy, especially with the unexpected loss of her daughter, Patsy. And, of course, she had really lost her other three children to a vindictive ex-husband who hid them from her for thirteen years. They really didn't know her, didn't accept her as their true mother.

She was a stranger to them.

And now, the only child she had left was putting her out. Her worst fears were coming true: that she would grow old alone with no one to care for her and protect her.

Tears welled in her eyes when she finally began to write. The first letter was to her mother, who was terminally ill with cancer. Elizabeth stated simply that she loved her, but that she could no longer bear to live.

In the next note, addressed to her son, she penned her deep disappointment at how Frank was treating her. She pointed out that he had always been the apple of her eye and that, like a good mother, she had always considered his future over all else. She also told Frank that it was now obvious to her that he no longer wanted her. She reminded him that she was petrified to live alone or even to stay alone at night. She said that it took a very brave person to do what she was doing; it was not the act of a coward. And, finally, she stated that she loved him in spite of the fact that he was forsaking her and that she hoped sometime in the future he could reconcile her act with his own actions on this night.

Mrs. Duncan took out her jewelry and placed it on the bureau and then prepared for bed. She lay down and opened her bedside drawer. Inside were numerous bottles of a prescription drug commonly known as Seconal. She flipped the top off one of the bottles and, instead of taking her usual nightly dosage of eight to twelve pills, emptied the bottle into the palm of her hand.

She sat up in bed, looking at the pills, tears rolling down her cheeks while she again pondered the misfortune of her existence. Poor, dear Patsy—and imagine that Frank—throwing his mother out after all that she'd done for him. It just wasn't fair! She slapped her hand to her mouth, stinging her lips, gulping the pills down with some water, hurrying before her courage failed her. Elizabeth Duncan took a deep, resigned breath, slid down in the bed, and prepared to worry no more.

By the time Frank had finished his second beer, he had decided that his mother was not intending to leave. He pulled himself out of his chair and prepared himself for another round in the fight. *I'm not giving in this time,* Frank thought to himself while he walked to her room and knocked on the door. There was only silence. Frank opened the door a crack and peered in, the light from the hallway flooded his mother's room. Instantly, he realized something was wrong. His mother's jewelry, which she always kept hidden away, sat on the dresser. In the dim light he could see two notes partially covering the adornments.

Frank threw open the door and rushed to the bedside, immediately seeing the pill bottle clutched in his mother's hand. Her breathing was labored and her color an ashen gray. He grabbed the bottle from her lifeless hand and flung it across the room. Bending over the bed, he shook his mother, calling out to her in a strident voice, pleading for her to respond to him. Her body bobbed up and down under his manipulation, her head sinking deeper into the pillow, seeming barely attached to the rest of her form. There was no response to his panicky cries.

Frank looked at the notes. He didn't have to read the one headed "My Son Frank" to know what it contained. He ran to the telephone, dialed "0" for an operator, and requested an ambulance.

By the time the ambulance delivered Elizabeth Duncan to the emergency room of Santa Barbara's Cottage Hospital, she was close to death.

Frank and Olga Meet

"I Want a Girl (Just Like the Girl That Married Dear Old Dad)"
— Popular song title, William Dillon (composer), 1911

Frank paced up and down in the waiting room of Cottage Hospital while the staff worked on his mother behind closed doors. He sat and looked out the window, then stood and stared at the now familiar paintings. He felt like he had seen them, with their brass-plated inscriptions acknowledging those who had donated them, a thousand times.

When Frank again sat down, an older woman wearing a scarf spoke to him. "Is your wife sick?" she asked.

"No, it's my mother," he replied, noticing her for the first time.

"My husband is here," the woman went on absently. "He fell off the ladder changing a light bulb. Isn't that the silliest thing? I think he broke his leg, at least that's what the ambulance driver said. What's wrong with your mother?" Looking at Frank, her soft brown eyes were filled with genuine concern.

Frank gazed momentarily at her sympathetic expression. He was swept by an odd sensation, realizing that this person, who was about his mother's age, was sincerely concerned about a complete stranger. It was an outreaching, this unpretentious thoughtfulness that he had not experienced often in his life. And, as he thought about it, he wondered if his own mother would care about the health of a total stranger. Somehow, he doubted it.

"I'm sorry. Am I being rude?" the woman asked when Frank had not answered.

"Oh, no. I guess I was just caught up in my thoughts." Frank considered lying to her, not really wanting to divulge what he felt was another of many family secrets. But, for some reason, he needed to tell her. Almost without control, he blurted out, "She took an overdose of pills. We had a fight and I told her . . . "

"Oh, I'm so sorry," the kerchiefed woman replied, avoiding his eyes. "I'm sure she'll be all right. They have very good doctors here."

Frank turned away from her and looked again at the brass plate on an oil painting. "In Loving Memory of Robert T. Glazer," it stated. The painting was of a western scene, in the style of Frederick Remington, with wide-eyed horses, contorted out of shape, the riders dallying bellowing steers on the ends of taut lariats.

"Mr. Duncan?" inquired a young man in a green medical suit.

"Yes." Frank whirled around.

"Shall we step into the hallway?" the doctor suggested.

Frank followed him through the doorway before asking, "Well, how is she?"

"She's had a very close call and is definitely not out of the woods yet. We've managed to stabilize her. I'm sending her to intensive care."

"Can I talk to her?"

"Well, she hasn't regained consciousness, but you're welcome to see her once she gets settled in ICU."

"When will she be able to talk to me?" Frank asked, beginning to understand the severity of his mother's condition.

"That's hard to say. She's in a deep coma and, quite honestly, it could be tomorrow or it could be never. We'll have to run some tests on your mother to determine if there has been significant brain impairment."

"Oh, God," Frank mumbled, looking down at his shoes, fearing that his insensitivity had caused this to happen.

"They'll be moving her shortly. When she gets to ICU, be sure to tell the nurse who her regular doctor is. We need that information for the chart."

"It's Doctor George . . . " Frank began to tell the man dressed in green.

"Just tell the nurse in ICU," the young doctor interrupted, preparing to depart.

"Yes, well, okay. Thank you, Doctor, for all that you've done." Frank reached out and shook the doctor's hand.

"You're more than welcome—and good luck." The doctor turned on his heel and walked back towards the emergency room.

Frank stuck his head in the doorway and waved to the woman that was sitting there. "I hope your husband is going to be okay."

"Likewise with your mother," she answered with a comradely smile. "Good luck."

Frank wandered down the hallway until he found a sign identifying the intensive care unit. Looking into the sterile environment, he was unsure if he should just walk into the area or if he needed to knock first. While he was standing there, a woman in a nurse's uniform noticed his hesitation and walked over.

"You may come in," the nurse said with a smile.

"Oh, thank you. I'm here to see my mother. She was just brought here," Frank responded, walking behind the nurse to her station.

"You must be here to see Mrs. Duncan, eh?" the nurse picked up a chart.

"Yes." Frank looked into the sparkling blue eyes of the woman. While she studied the chart, he quickly looked her over, noting her petite yet attractive figure that was accentuated by the white uniform. Her hair was an auburn color, cut short to fit under the white cap that was bobby-pinned to her head. When she spoke, Frank noticed a singsong accent that he couldn't quite place.

"She's in number three." The nurse pointed out the curtain-enclosed cubicle. "We ask that you not spend more than five minutes, please."

"Certainly." Frank walked to the cubicle and caught his breath when he approached his mother, who looked near death. Her breathing was labored and she had tubes protruding from her nose and right inner elbow. Her color was just slightly better than when he had found her unconscious in bed.

Frank picked up her limp right hand and held it in his own. Looking at it, he saw fresh puncture marks turning to bruises among the familiar liver spots. Frank's thoughts turned despairing and, though he wasn't a religious man, he felt that some type of prayer would be appropriate. But he didn't really know how to go about doing that, so he just stood silently, holding his mother's hand, lost in his thoughts until the nurse glided up behind him.

"Mr. Duncan," she said, almost in a whisper, laying a soft hand upon his arm, "it's time to go."

"Oh, okay," Frank said, also whispering.

He gently placed his mother's hand back on the bed and walked to the nurse's station.

"The emergency room doctor said you would need to know my mother's physician's name," Frank whispered.

The nurse looked at the chart, running a finger down the page. "Oh, yes," she replied in a normal tone of voice.

"It's Dr. George Weston," Frank said, maintaining his hushed tone.

"I'm sorry, I can't hear you. You can talk out loud," the young woman said with a smile, sensitive to his embarrassment.

Frank looked at her sheepishly and raised his voice when he repeated himself. "I said it's Dr. George Weston in Santa Barbara. Will someone contact him? My mother has some special medical needs that you should be aware of?"

"Yes, we'll take care of that right away," the nurse said, making a notation in the chart. She looked up at Frank, whose eyes were downcast. "We'll take good care of your mother, sir."

"Oh, I know you will," he said, looking into her deep blue eyes and seeing that his mother was indeed in good hands. "Well, I guess I'll go now," he added, turning towards the doorway. "By the way, what's your name?"

"My name is Miss Kupczyk."

The "Miss" was not lost on Frank Duncan when he replied, "It's nice to meet you, Miss Kupczyk, and thank you for everything. I'll be back tomorrow."

"Very good then, Mr. Duncan. We'll see you later," she replied in that same melodious tone.

"Yes, later. And, by the way, please call me Frank." He smiled at the nurse.

"Well, if we're to be on a first-name basis, my name is Olga."

"Good-bye, Olga. And thanks again."

She waved an acknowledgment, hurrying to answer a patient's request.

Frank Duncan was a regular visitor at the intensive care unit during the four days that his mother was treated there. He showed up for the allotted two visits a day and always stayed at least five minutes, if not longer.

He would often see Olga, who was working the night shift. He soon learned that her friends and coworkers called her Ollie and he found that he was attracted to her. He felt comfortable around her, even though he saw her only for short periods of time. He liked her gentle manner, especially with people who were critically ill and very difficult.

Frank's mother was progressing nicely. On her third day in intensive care, she began to regain consciousness, blinking her eyes in response to the questions. She could not yet speak, but the doctors were encouraged by her relatively quick progress.

On day four, Elizabeth was moved to a ward. Frank was glad to see her transferred because that obviously meant she was improving. But he was also disappointed that he could no longer easily talk to the nurse called Ollie.

Elizabeth Duncan spent fifteen days in Cottage Hospital before she went home for another month of convalescence.

Frank Duncan began to date Olga Kupczyk and by March they were a steady couple.

A Formal Introduction

. . . Jealousy is cruel as the grave: the coals thereof are coals of fire . . .
—Song of Solomon 8:6

Frank and Olga lounged together on a Sunday morning, not yet ready to face the day. Propped up in bed, they sipped from two steaming mugs of coffee and listened to the chirping of some friendly sparrows that were nesting outside their bedroom window.

Olga finally broke the silence. "Tell me, Frank, when am I going to meet your mother?"

"You already have."

"I know, but not like that. She was so sedated, I doubt she would remember me."

Frank looked at Olga lying in bed next to him and considered how attractive she was. Even the first thing in the morning, when most people are rumpled, she invariably looked fresh.

Throwing back the covers, Frank bounded out of bed and went to the kitchen to get a second cup of coffee. "Ollie, do you want another cup?" he called to her.

"Please."

Frank poured two more cups and returned to the bedroom, a mug in each hand. When he set them on the nightstand, he sloshed a little over the rim.

"Damn it," he muttered to himself, looking for something to mop up the spill.

"You go get the newspaper. I'll clean up your mess," Olga suggested.

"That sounds like a deal."

Frank went out onto the front balcony of the apartment and retrieved the local paper. Snapping off the rubber band, he looked at the headlines: "U.S. Pulling Ahead of Soviets in Space Race."

"Well, it's good to see that we're finally catching up to those communist bastards," Frank muttered to himself.

"What did you say, dear?"

"Oh, nothing. I was just thinking that it's about time we started to show those people in Russia what good old American ingenuity can accomplish," Frank said, walking back to the bedroom and handing Olga the second section of the newspaper, while he climbed back into bed and continued to read about the new Vanguard and Atlas missiles.

Olga gave him a quizzical look and then opened the paper to an article about the planned creation of a manmade lake.

"Lake to Provide Water Needs for West End of Ventura County," the article started. It went on to say that the completion of this project would be the culmination of years of planning and construction in the hills west of Ojai.

"Frank, why don't we drive to Ojai today? We can take the back road and go by this lake site. Let's see, it's called Lake Casitas."

"Good idea. I've heard about a good place to eat in Ojai. We can stop for lunch."

"The drive will be nice, eh?" Olga commented, still reading the newspaper article.

"Sure, why not?" Frank replied, setting down the newspaper. He looked at Olga and reached over to stroke her auburn hair. She tilted her head in his direction.

"Ummm, that feels good," she purred.

Olga dropped the paper to the floor while Frank's hand ran down her body until it reached the hem of her lace nightie. Pulling up the flimsy garment, he slid over and embraced her. As they kissed,

42

he removed the nightie and flung it onto a dresser. She reached down and touched him, stroking him gently, and finally guiding him into her. They moved together slowly, then more passionately, until they finally lay spent upon the bed.

Afterward, Frank asked matter-of-factly, "What'll we name him?"

"Name who? What do you mean, dear?"

"I don't know. I just have a feeling about this time. It'd be good. In fact, it might even make things easier."

"You mean, if I got pregnant?" Olga asked, finally comprehending Frank's meaning.

"Yes."

"Why would it be easier?"

"I know you don't understand, but you will once you get to know my mother," Frank replied, getting out of bed and pulling on a pair of shorts.

"You make her out to be some kind of ogre. She can't be all that bad."

"Well, I guess she isn't all that bad, as you say. But she has a way about her. Let's go for that drive. Later, if we have time, we'll stop by the apartment and I'll formally introduce you," Frank said, watching a naked Olga get out of bed and disappear into the bathroom.

"Okay, give me a couple of minutes to shower. And, by the way, it'll be a her," Olga added, peeking out of the bathroom door and winking at her sweetheart.

They drove the backcountry road to Ojai, whisking past the sign indicating the route as California Highway 150, and pulled over to stop next to a culvert. Nearby was a worn road marker that read 6.95. From that spot they had a remarkable view of the partially filled lake and they could breathe in the fresh spring air. Standing there and taking in the view, neither Frank nor Olga had any idea of the significance this lonely country road would have in their near future. At this time, it simply presented a good place to relax and to appreciate the day and each other. After lingering at the spot for awhile, they continued on to Ojai for lunch.

Early that evening, when they got back to Santa Barbara, Frank took Olga to meet his mother.

They pulled up to the curb and Frank stopped the car, putting it in park. He took a deep breath and looked over at Ollie. "Let's get this over with."

Ollie reached over and grasped his hand, pulling it to her lips. She gently kissed the back of his hand and looked up into his questioning face. "It's not going to be that bad, dear. Just try to relax."

He smiled weakly at her before exiting the car and walking around to open the door for her. He took her hand and led her toward the front door of the apartment. He opened the front door and stepped in, squeezing her hand in nervous anticipation. When they walked into the living room, Frank saw Emma Short sitting on the couch. "Hi, Emma," he said, a little too loudly, startling the old woman who had been listening to the radio.

"Oh, you surprised me! Hello, Frank. Who have we here?"

"Emma, this is my friend Ollie."

"Hello, Ollie. It's nice to meet you. I've heard Frank speak of you."

"I hope only good things," Olga replied, smiling at the older woman.

Emma did not reply, returning her attention to Frank. "Your mother's in the bedroom. I'll go get her."

Olga took a deep breath and gazed about the place. It was a small apartment, probably just two bedrooms, but it was tastefully done with furniture that was obviously new.

Frank motioned for Olga to sit, but he continued to stand, smiling nervously at her.

Olga sat on the couch. While waiting for Mrs. Duncan, she felt an unexplainable chill run down her back. She took a deep breath and tried to relax.

Mrs. Duncan suddenly burst into the room, startling the nervous occupants.

"There you are, Frankie!" she emoted, hugging her son in a consuming embrace.

"Hello, Mom. How are you?"

"Oh, I haven't been at all well. Where have you been? I haven't seen you for two days!"

Frank ignored the question. "I want you to meet someone," he said, still caught in her clutches and talking over her shoulder.

"Oh, really?" she said, looking directly at Olga, who had risen from the couch. "Is this the lady you've been spending all your time with?" Elizabeth asked, sarcasm heavy in her voice.

Frank ignored the barb and continued with the introduction. "Mom, this is my friend Olga Kupczyk. Everyone calls her Ollie."

"Hello, Mrs. Duncan," Olga said, smiling to herself while viewing this unusual scene.

"You probably don't remember her," Frank gasped, trying to extricate himself from his mother's grasp, "but Ollie took care of you while you were in ICU."

"No, I can't say that I do," Elizabeth replied, finally letting go of her son and turning her attention to the girl.

"Please do sit down, Ollie," Mrs. Duncan continued in a travesty of courtesy. "Emma, will you put on a pot of coffee for our guest?"

Mrs. Short, who had been watching this exchange with unabashed interest, walked reluctantly into the kitchen.

"Kupczyk, what sort of name is that?" Elizabeth smirked, seating herself in an easy chair across from Olga.

"Well, it's actually Ukrainian."

"Is that so. Does that mean you're a Russian?" a frown formed on her lips.

45

"Oh my, no. I'm Canadian, originally from the province of Manitoba, but most recently from the Vancouver area, where I did my nurse's training. My father is Ukrainian, from the old country."

"I see." Mrs. Duncan nodded, looking up at her son, who was still standing, his hand resting on the back of her chair.

"Frank, you've brought a foreigner home!" came her forced attempt at humor.

"Mother, she's hardly a foreigner!"

"Canada isn't really a foreign country, if you go to visit. We speak a little differently than you do in the States. I'm told we use the expression 'eh' too much." Olga offered, trying to lighten a tense moment, "but everything else is pretty much the same."

"Really?"

There was an awkward silence, broken finally when Mrs. Duncan shouted towards the kitchen, "How's the coffee comin', Emma?"

There was no answer from the kitchen.

Elizabeth redirected her attention to Olga. "How do you like my new furniture? Frank and I picked it out together and, of course, he's paying for it." She pointed at the end tables. "They're made of genuine marble from Portugal and cost over five thousand dollars."

"Oh, really. He's such a dear," Olga replied, looking at Frank and realizing that this conversation had nothing to do with furniture.

"Come sit down, dear." The younger woman patted the couch next to her.

Elizabeth shot a glance at Olga, then raised her head and fixed her son with a cunning look.

Frank stood by the easy chair, looking at his girlfriend and wrestling with his choice. He finally looked down into his mother's eyes and an instant communication passed between them, which was not lost on Olga.

Frank finally spoke, "Maybe I should check on Emma, see how the coffee is coming." He glanced in Olga's direction, then hurried into the kitchen.

46

After coffee and more uncomfortable small talk, Frank made excuses and escorted Olga out of the apartment. The first meeting had lasted a little over half an hour.

Upon their departure, Mrs. Short would later testify in court that Mrs. Duncan had said, "I'd like to push that foreigner down the stairs. Maybe she'd break a leg!"

Olga's only comment to Frank was, "Now I'm beginning to see what you mean."

A Child's Name

Dorothy: Dorothea is the original form. From the Greek Doros,
meaning 'gift,' plus Theos, meaning 'God,' hence, 'Gift of God.'
—Dictionary of First Names, Alfred J. Kolatch

Frank Duncan stared at the black rotary phone and contemplated the call he was about to make.

The date was June 19, 1958, slightly more than a week after Frank had found out that Olga was pregnant. She had told him in an excited manner, thrilled at the idea of their becoming parents.

"Isn't it wonderful news!" Olga had said. "Let's look at this as a positive experience that we were meant to be together."

Frank had replied with equal enthusiasm, "We'll get married right away, and I promise I'll take care of you. You can quit your job and just get ready to have our baby. I love you, Ollie. Everything will work out fine."

Later, Frank's elation had been tempered by a rush of cold reality while he pondered how he would continue to support his mother and provide for a new wife and baby on his beginning attorney's salary of $1,000 a month. And, though he thought he loved Olga, he wasn't totally positive of his feelings towards her.

One notion which was becoming crystal clear was his mother's obvious dislike for his girlfriend. Every time he mentioned Olga's name, Elizabeth constantly picked at him about their relationship, encouraging him to look elsewhere for a woman more suited to his station in life. Frank tried to ignore Elizabeth's meddling, hoping that she would eventually tire of the game.

He also hoped that the prospect of a grandbaby would soften his mother's view of Olga. However, since her near-successful suicide attempt, Frank had been walking on eggshells. Though he had never discussed the incident with his mother, it seemed to hang over them like a cloud. She would occasionally make obscure reference to it, using it subtly to get her way. This proved effective because, unlike in the past, he now felt that when she talked of death, she meant it.

While steeling himself to use the phone, Frank absentmindedly spread some papers around his large oak desk. He was originally going to call and give her the news over the phone. Later, he had decided that was the coward's way out, that he should face the music and tell her in person. He finally picked up the phone and dialed his mother's number.

The phone rang twice before he heard "Hello?" and recognized his mother's voice.

"Hi, Mom," he replied in his most cheerful tone.

"Frankie! How nice to hear from you. When am I going to see you?" came the predictable response.

"I'll be home for lunch today, and I have something important to tell you."

"Really, now, what could it . . . "

The phone began to make a loud hum in Frank's ear.

"I guess we don't have a very good connection, but I'll be over about noon!" he shouted into the receiver.

"Okay, dear," was all Frank could faintly hear.

He hung up the phone, hoping that this confused conversation was not a precursor of things to come.

At a quarter to twelve, Frank straightened up his desk and pulled on his coat. He walked into the reception area and told his secretary that he would be a little late returning from lunch. He wanted to leave himself plenty of time to deal with his mother's reaction.

He drove to Elizabeth's and parked at the curb. Frank walked directly into the apartment without knocking and immediately saw his mother in the kitchen. She was wearing her familiar pink apron.

"Hello, Frankie," she called to him over her shoulder. "I've made you some lunch. Sit in the usual place."

Frank pulled off his jacket and hung it on the back of the chair. While his mother placed a sandwich and a bowl of soup on the table, Frank took a seat. She then poured herself a glass of iced tea and sat across from him at the tiny table.

"So what's this big news you have? Have you gotten your first promotion?"

"Hardly, Mother," he answered, dipping his spoon into the steaming soup, but not yet ready to try to eat it. "It's about Ollie and me."

"Yes, what?"

Frank sipped slowly at the hot soup, his head bent down. He thought carefully, trying to choose his words precisely, hoping to remember the words he had rehearsed at the office, fearful that no matter how he said it that the news would devastate his mother.

Looking up, he saw that she was playing with her glass, rocking it back and forth in the puddle ring in which it sat. She looked at him anxiously, her thin lips pursed in anticipation. He dreaded that there was no way to make this announcement without upsetting her. He decided to jump right in. "Ollie is pregnant, Mom."

"What?" She sat back in her chair.

He tried another approach, one that he had previously practiced. "I said you're going to be a grandmother."

"I don't want to be a grandmother!" she exclaimed. "And besides, you aren't married. What the hell's the matter with you, Frankie?"

"Mom, this wasn't exactly planned. It just happened. These things do happen, y'know."

His mother glared at him with those piercing eyes, a look of disgust consuming her face. "Well, it can't happen to you! Jesus Christ! How could you do this to me?"

Frank had no reply. He sat staring into his bowl, wishing she would just accept things for what they were. There was a tense silence. Frank set his spoon upon the table, no longer finding the appetite to finish his soup.

Mrs. Duncan's voice finally pierced the quiet. "There's only one thing to do."

"What?"

"Get an abortion."

"Mom," he whined, "Ollie would never do that."

"Well, are you sure this baby is yours?" she asked, presenting a new concept that Frank had never considered.

"Yes, I'm sure."

"I wouldn't be too sure, Frankie. Remember when you had the mumps? The doctor said it might leave you sterile. Maybe she's been sleeping around. It certainly wouldn't surprise me. I've never thought much of that woman."

"Mother!"

"I'm just pointing out a possibility, Frankie. You just don't know these days." She shrugged her shoulders and looked at him inno- cently, hoping that she had planted a seed.

"We've been going steady since April and I would know. Ollie loves me, Mom."

"Loves you, huh? Well, you don't have to marry her just because of this, y'know."

"For Christ's sake, I'm an attorney. Of course I know!"

"Don't you raise your voice to me! I'm only thinking of your best interest. Besides, this would not be a good time to get married, or a good reason. We just bought this furniture and we still owe money on it. I don't see how you can afford to get married," she continued, her voice pitched higher with emotion. "It isn't right, I mean the timing!"

Frank, seeing that his mother was working herself up, tried to calm her.

"I'm sorry I shouted. Please don't get emotional about this."

Rather than calming her, his concern seemed to further agitate his mother. She jumped up, knocking the chair to the floor, and began to pace around in the kitchen, her hands jammed into her apron pockets.

"I can't lose you, Frankie," she moaned. "You're all I have left! You understand that, don't you?" She turned toward him, her arms outstretched, pleading to be taken into his arms.

"I understand how you feel, Mom. But even if I get married, it isn't like I'm going to move away. I'll still be here in Santa Barbara, just like now," he said, deliberately keeping his seat and avoiding her look.

She dropped her arms and turned away from him, leaning against the sink, her head bowed. "I don't like that woman!"

"Why?"

"I want someone who'll like me to be my daughter-in-law. And I'm sure she doesn't."

"Ollie has nothing against you."

"She's not a fit woman for you, Frankie. Look at you, an attorney. You should have someone very special."

"But I think Ollie is special."

Elizabeth whirled around and shouted at him. "She's a whore and now she's found a way to trap you into marrying her! Are you blind? Can't you see what she is doing?"

Frank sat back in his chair, not finding the words to answer his mother's allegations. He briefly considered getting up and leaving, feeling that this conversation was no longer going to be productive. He put the thought behind him, hoping that he could still salvage the moment.

His mother turned back towards the sink, her hands clutching the drainboard. "We've got to get you out of this. I can't be alone. I won't be alone." She began to ramble, looking first at the ceiling, then back down at the sink.

"Oh, go look at this sink, will you? It's a mess."

She reached into a cabinet and pulled out some cleanser, sprinkling it generously in the sink, then began to scrub vigorously.

"Settle down, now, Mother . . . please!"

"That fucking bitch. I can't deal with this," she moaned, throwing more cleanser around and creating a small white dust cloud.

Frank stood up, pushing his chair aside, and caught his mother in his arms, sending the can thudding to the floor in a white puff.

Elizabeth reeled around, returning his embrace. She began to cry, "Oh, Frankie, I can't live alone. You know how I hate to be by myself with no one to care for me. I'm so afraid. You won't leave me to die a lonesome old lady, will you?"

"There, there," he tried to comfort the sobbing woman. "I won't leave you. We can work this out."

"You won't marry her, then?" his mother choked, getting a hold on her emotions. "I'd rather be dead than live without you!"

"No, Mom. I won't do anything right away."

"What do you mean by right away?" she asked, pulling away from him with tears streaming down her cheeks, reddened eyes looking into his.

"Before she got pregnant, Ollie and I discussed getting married in July."

"Oh, really. And why haven't you told me any of this?" Elizabeth asked, wiping away a tear with the back of her hand.

Frank didn't reply, knowing the answer was obvious even to her.

"Sometime in July," he repeated. Frank pulled away from his mother and walked to the kitchen table. He bent down and picked up the tipped over chair and slid it carefully under the table. He turned around and watched his mother pull a handkerchief out of an apron pocket and begin to dab at her eyes. She sighed and walked around him to the table, pulling the chair out and taking a seat where her tea still sat, her manner now subdued.

"Will you do me one favor, Frankie?" she asked, seemingly resigning herself to the inevitable. "When you have this child, if it's a girl, will you name her after your older sister, Dorothy? She was my first born and they took her away from me. Now she's like a stranger to us. She might as well be dead!"

"Sure, Mom, if that'll make you happy," Frank said, ready to agree to anything, hoping to put this ugly scene behind him.

"Thank you, dear. You finish your sandwich. All this excitement has made me exhausted. I'm going to go lie down," his mother murmured, rising and walking toward her room.

"Sure. I'll let myself out when I'm done."

He watched while she walked down the hall, her head slightly stooped. She glanced back briefly at him, giving her son a weary smile before stepping into her room. When she was out of sight, Frank threw his sandwich in the trash, snatched his jacket off the chair, and hurried out the front door.

In her room, Elizabeth sat on the edge of her bed, relentlessly twisting a handkerchief. *That slut Olga might think this pregnancy would get Frank to marry her, but she was wrong, dead wrong!* Somehow Elizabeth would see to that.

The next day, June 20, 1958, Olga Nettie Kupczyk and Frank Patrick Duncan were married in the chambers of Judge Atwill Westwick at the Santa Barbara Courthouse. It was a simple civil ceremony, without frills. In an effort to prevent his mother from finding out, Frank convinced the county clerk to delay recording of the information so that the marriage would not be in the newspaper. However, his efforts to keep the marriage a secret would prove futile.

Frank and Olga Together

I've just got to accept the fact that he'll never be man enough to leave his mother.

—Olga, in a letter to her parents

"I really don't believe this!" Olga glared at her new husband.

"I'm sorry, Ollie. But it would be better if I went."

The newlyweds sat arguing in the front room of Olga's Bath Street apartment. Their marriage was only a few hours old and they were already having their first disagreement over what their relationship with Frank's mother should be.

Olga went on, "We're married now, whether she likes it or not. We can't let her run our lives. And I won't let your mother ruin our marriage before it ever gets off the ground. There's a time for everything and she just has to accept that you and I are together."

Frank nodded his head in agreement, but he thought Olga's assessment to be very simplistic. It was just not going to be that easy.

"I know you're right, dear. But my mother is so paranoid about my leaving her. She has this ridiculous fear of being left alone to die without anyone to care for her. I think that's the reason she's married so often."

"I wish we could convince her that our being married doesn't necessarily mean that she's losing you. Unless, of course, she manages to drive us away with her attitude." Olga had begun to regain her composure, trying hard not to be angry on her wedding night.

"I certainly hope that doesn't happen," Frank said, looking down at his watch. "Y'know mother and I had quite an argument yesterday. I promised her that I wouldn't get married."

"You what?" was the incredulous response.

"Please, let me finish. I told her we wouldn't get married right away. I know, I know. I lied to her. But it was the only way to appease her."

"Frank," Olga's voice began to rise again, "why don't you stand up to her. Tell her that's just the way it is. For God's sake, you're an adult!" Olga rose from the couch, looking down at her new husband, her hands planted firmly on each hip.

Frank sat on the couch looking up at her. "The whole point is that I should go home tonight so she doesn't become suspicious."

Olga walked to the apartment window and gazed into the dark Santa Barbara night.

"Home, Frank, home? This is your home now! I feel like I'm losing you before we even get started, especially if you still call your mother's place home. We should be sharing our bed tonight, instead of having this stupid argument."

"I really am sorry," was all Frank could manage, standing up and pulling on his jacket. "I'll make some excuses with Mom and tomorrow we'll go away for the next couple of days. Maybe we can stay at the beach?"

"Go if you must, but I think it's a sad state of affairs to leave your wife on your wedding night. Especially to go back to your mother!" Olga said, turning and looking directly into Frank's eyes.

He gave her a sheepish grin and brushed her lips with his. "I'll call you first thing tomorrow," he told her, hurrying out the front door.

"Whatever," she replied, pushing the door shut behind him. She crossed her arms and threw herself on the sofa. *Damn her, anyway!* she thought.

Frank Duncan crept into the Victoria Street apartment, hoping he wouldn't disturb his mother. He was heading quietly toward his bedroom door when the hall light snapped on. His mother, dressed in a black nightie, stood in the doorway of her bedroom.

"So where have you been?" Elizabeth's miffed tone was not lost on her son.

"Oh, hi Mom," he replied with false cheer.

"Well, answer me."

"It's really none of your affair," Frank declared, getting his nerve up.

Elizabeth began her usual lecture. "As long as you live—"

Frank cut her off. "Spare me the speech, Mom."

There was a momentary silence, until Elizabeth finally spoke up. "I've been thinking about our relationship of late. We've been at each other's throats since you met Ollie," she said, seeming to soften. "And I want to make things right between us. I just can't stand it when you and I fight."

"Uh-huh."

"I mean it, Frankie." Elizabeth walked down the hall and took Frank's hand. She looked into his eyes and he saw in her expression more than a motherly look. It was a look that spoke of other things, a look he had experienced many times before.

"What is it, Mother?" he asked, knowing that he could guess the answer.

"Let me show you how much I love you," she purred at him.

"No, Mother!" came the panicky reply. "God no, not tonight!"

Elizabeth pressed her body against her son, grasping his arm firmly with her hands. Frank's mind raced, *Oh, Jesus Christ! This can't happen, not on my wedding night!* Elizabeth's hand wandered down Frank's body, touching him intimately. Frank pulled away from his mother.

"C'mon, dear, after all these years I know how to please you," she encouraged him.

"Oh, Mom, not now!"

The woman made no response, but began to tug on his arm, leading him toward her bedroom. He looked desperately at the door, judging the amount of time he needed to act. When he reached the doorjamb, Frank pushed his mother away, screamed "No!" at her, and ran for his bedroom, slamming the door behind him and bowing his back to the door to prevent her from following him into the room. Frank looked down at his wrist and noticed two deep scratches where Elizabeth had been holding him. The blood began to soak through his shirt, but he dared not treat it until he was sure his mother would not enter his room.

Elizabeth reeled backwards into her bedroom, sitting abruptly on her bed. "You son of a bitch!" she screamed at her son, jumping to her feet and rushing to his bedroom door. She tried the door, but was unable to force it open. She slammed her fist against the wood, cursing her son. When he didn't open the door, she finally gave up and returned to her bedroom.

The next afternoon, June 21, 1958, Frank and Olga sat on the verandah of a local beach hotel. They were soaking up the bright Southern California sun and talking of their hopes for the future. At Frank's suggestion, Olga had given notice at the hospital and was determined to take an active interest in her new husband's work. After they had discussed Frank's current criminal case, the talk turned to Olga's pregnancy.

"If it's a girl, like I think it will be," Olga was saying, "then I'd like to name the baby after my mother, Jessie."

"Certainly," Frank replied, taking a drink of his scotch and water, "but I did make a deal with my mother, in that regard."

"Oh, really. Now what would that be, eh?"

"I told her we'd name a baby girl after my sister, Dorothy."

"I've never even met your sister."

"I know. It's not really that important." He shrugged his shoulders.

"Well, it may be real important to your mother," Olga reasoned. "And heaven knows we don't want to do anything else to upset her.

Besides, I have a very good friend named Dorothy. You know, Dorothy Woytko. I've spoken of her often. She was like a second mother to me. She'd be honored if we used her name for our daughter. That's if it's a girl."

Frank drained his glass and looked around for the waiter to order another drink. He waved his arm, getting the man's attention.

"Yes sir, another scotch and water?"

"Please. Do you want another drink, Ollie?"

"No thank you, dear. I think one's my limit, especially now," she replied, patting her stomach.

The waiter walked off to place the order.

"Well, it's agreed then. If it's a girl we'll call her Dorothy. But, if it's a boy, we can still name him Jessie. Jessie works for either sex. What do you think?" Olga asked.

"I think we don't have to cross this bridge for some time yet. Let's not worry about it now."

"I like the idea. Do you think our son would care if he was named after his grandmother?"

"I doubt it," Frank said, having lost interest in this name game.

They sat quietly for many minutes, watching the bright orange sun inch its way into the glittering Pacific Ocean.

"Dear," Olga inquired, noticing the fresh scratches on her husband's wrist, "what happened to your arm?"

Frank looked down at the injury, wanting to tell Olga the truth, but knowing that he would not be able to explain it to his wife's satisfaction. "A damn stupid cat scratched me last night," Frank lied, looking towards the beach while he spoke. "It was on the porch when I got home and I picked it up to move it. I guess I frightened the animal, because it scratched me."

"Can I look at it?"

Frank tucked the wound away from his wife. "It's okay, dear. Not to worry, it's only a slight scratch."

"Well, okay, then—but I am a nurse."

"Really, it's no big thing," Frank cut her off.

They sat quietly for a moment until Frank finished his drink. Then they decided on a walk along the beach and strolled off hand in hand, the ocean breeze ruffling their hair.

Turning Up the Heat

Mother was petrified at being alone. I was always there.
—Frank Duncan, March 7, 1959
Ventura County Star Free Press

Elizabeth Duncan slammed down the phone and let out a long string of curses, attracting the attention of Emma Short, who was normally unheedful of her friend's ranting.

"Well, that bastard went and did it!" the irate Mother Duncan shouted.

"Went and did what?"

"He married the bitch. I can't believe it! He just told me he wouldn't wed that woman! He flat lied to me!"

"Are you sure?" the older woman asked, also surprised at this turn of events.

"You're damned right I'm sure! I just called the hospital and they told me Olga was on her honeymoon and that she may not return to work because she'd married an attorney."

Elizabeth stood in the middle of her living room, fuming at this new threat to her well-being. She felt a need to do something, but had no idea what that should be. She finally walked over to a lamp sitting on an end table and gave it a backhanded swipe. It teetered momentarily and then fell to the floor, the ceramic base breaking into pieces.

"That'll teach the bastard!" she snarled. "I'll break up all this furniture and he'll still have to pay for it!"

When she turned towards the other lamp, Emma intervened. "Now, Betty," Mrs. Short reasoned, "this won't solve anything. It'll just cause us a bunch of cleaning up." To prove her point, she walked over and began to pick up the broken lamp.

The enraged woman stopped, her eyes aflame. "I'm gonna show that bitch she's bitten off more than she can chew!"

"I would've thought your call to her the other night had taken care of the problem. I guess she didn't get the message."

"She ain't seen nothin' yet!"

Emma was referring to a conversation that Elizabeth and Olga had had on the evening of June 19, the day Frank had informed his mother that Olga was pregnant.

After talking with Frank, Elizabeth had decided to call Olga to ensure that she would not entrap her son. She'd found Olga's number in the phone book and dialed it.

Later, in her trial, Mrs. Duncan remembered what she told her future daughter-in-law that evening: "I don't approve of my son marrying a woman of your kind, and when my son marries, I want him to marry someone that will like me and that I can have as my daughter, and I can visit him."

About this same conversation, Mrs. Short testified that Elizabeth actually had said, "I will kill you before you ever marry my son. You are not a fit person to live with my son."

Olga, who had no reason to believe that the woman could be serious, responded defensively. She told the possessive matriarch that she would marry Frank regardless of her wishes, and did so the very next day.

On the day after the wedding, after learning of the marriage, the obsessive mother went straight to Olga's apartment in hopes of finding her son and bringing him home. The newlyweds were not there, but Elizabeth was able to confirm with the landlady that Olga and her attorney friend had gone off to get married.

After spending the weekend at the beach with his bride, Frank Duncan returned to his mother's house and to a woman in the depths of depression. Elizabeth alternately cried and raged at her son, accusing him of the worst form of treachery. While she vented her anger, Frank noticed the missing lamp and figured it had something to do with the tantrum he was now enduring.

Frank tried to explain his actions, but soon realized that there was no reasoning with his mother. He made a hasty exit, returning to his wife.

Frank and Olga decided that his mother needed some time to cool down and get used to the idea of their being married, so they avoided contact with her for three peaceful days.

Both were rudely shocked back to reality on June 25, when Olga happened to be reading the classified advertisements in the *Santa Barbara News Press.* Included in the personals section was an ad that stated: "I will not be responsible for debts contracted by anybody other than my mother, Elizabeth Duncan, on or after June 25, 1958. /s/ Frank Duncan." This discovery of her mother-in-law's handiwork prompted a hasty call to Frank who was at work. He promised his bride that he would straighten out the ad at the first opportunity. Olga informed him that he had better find an opportunity very soon!

Because of this ad, Frank saw his mother for the first time in five days. When discussing the ad, Elizabeth told her son that she had placed it because she was afraid Olga would "run up some bills." Frank advised her that his financial affairs were none of her business and to keep her nose out of his marital affairs.

Frank felt that his mother understood and that she would be more careful about interfering in his life in the future. What he didn't know was that Elizabeth, playing the Good Samaritan, had gone to various stores in the Santa Barbara area and warned the proprietors not to extend credit to one Olga Duncan because she had a history of failing to pay her bills. This was, of course, a falsehood aimed at controlling Olga's expenditures of Frank's money—money which Mother Duncan felt was rightfully hers.

It didn't take long before Elizabeth's lies began to approach the truth. Frank never seemed to have enough money to cover both women's expenses. In spit of his promises, Olga sometimes had insufficient money for food.

She economized the best she could, but soon realized that either Frank had to provide more money or she'd have to go back to work. When she discussed this with Frank, he told his wife that he still felt responsible for his mother's bills, and would continue to pay them, and that he was doing the best he could.

Olga returned to work, taking a position in the emergency room of St. Francis Hospital. She had considered returning to Cottage Hospital, but decided against it. She didn't want to face her old friends after having left with such high hopes. Besides, since the phone calls had begun, she felt it would be too easy for Elizabeth to locate and bother her at work.

In the meantime, a more desperate Mother Duncan decided to turn up the heat in her campaign to break up the marriage. In what Frank would later call a "donnybrook," the jealous mother went to the newlyweds' apartment to bring her errant son home after he failed to show up for dinner.

The argument lasted for several minutes, with Elizabeth again telling Olga that she didn't want her married to Frankie. When the dispute grew more heated, it became apparent to Olga that she didn't have the support of her husband. She finally went next door and enlisted her landlady to help her insist that Elizabeth leave. The obsessively possessive woman eventually did so, taking her wayward son with her.

In her subsequent trial, the matriarch was queried about this argument. The district attorney asked her if she had gone to the couple's Bath Street apartment "to get him to come home."

She answered simply, "Yes."

"From the wife that he had married a week before?"

"From the wife that he had just married a week before."

"You saw nothing wrong in that?"

"Yes, I did see wrong in it, but I did it anyway, I did!"

Next came the incessant phone calls, by day and night. Elizabeth would call and threaten Olga whenever the new bride answered the phone. The message was always short and simple: "If you don't leave him, I'll kill you!" If Olga didn't answer the phone, Elizabeth would let it ring and ring in a blatant act of harassment.

On one day not long after his marriage, Frank received a series of phone calls from his mother and from Olga, each one complaining about the other. When his observant secretary asked if he were having domestic problems, he remarked that his might be the shortest marriage in history.

On July 1, the harried couple moved to 1512 Grand Avenue in order to escape Elizabeth's badgering. While at this address, Frank lived with Olga continuously for three weeks—the longest time they were ever together.

The resourceful mother immediately went to work to find their new address and phone number. Although it took her some time, she was finally able to locate her son and she resumed her crusade of hate.

Once again, the couple decided to move. This time they rented the Garden Street apartment where Olga would spend the last few months of her life. Of course, Frank had their phone number changed. However, Mother Duncan was able to locate them by talking to Frank's insurance agent, who inadvertently allowed her to see their new address on a policy. So, the badgering continued.

Elizabeth also employed another form of harassment against the couple. As she readily admitted in court, she hired acquaintances to move and hide Frank's car. She would seek out his car and give the key to a friend, who would then conceal the vehicle at another location. She did this because she claimed the car was partially hers and she didn't want Olga riding in it.

The stress caused by this constant persecution finally took its toll on the hapless Olga. She developed neuritis of the hands, making it difficult for her to hold surgical instruments at work. This medical problem, coupled with her rapidly advancing pregnancy, prompted her to quit once again. It was also at this time, in August of 1958, that she began to question whether her marriage to Frank was worth the constant turmoil. Frank was only living part-time with her, spending some evenings in her company and then returning home to his mother. In a succinct summation of her view of the bizarre individuals who were now so entwined in her life, Olga told a friend, "Frank has never grown up, and that woman is nuts!"

Indeed, Olga was convinced that her mother-in-law was in need of psychiatric care and suggested to Frank that she should be committed to a mental institution. Olga pointed out that the constant threats and other games Elizabeth played were not the acts of a rational person. However, Frank downplayed his wife's viewpoint.

After an incident in which Elizabeth went to their Garden Street apartment and pounded her shoe upon the glass door while a frightened Frank and Olga cowered inside, Olga wrote to her parents in Canada: "She came to the apartment and threatened to kill me. Life is short and I want to enjoy the rest of it!"

By this time, Olga had seen an attorney in Santa Barbara about the possibility of a divorce. Although she never had time to follow up on that action, the unnamed attorney told her to "dump him."

Mother Duncan's constant demands on her son's time made it impossible for Frank and Olga to maintain any type of normal relationship. Unbeknownst to Elizabeth, these demands, coupled with her campaign of madness, were heading toward a fruitful conclusion. However, this was not occurring quickly enough for Elizabeth, so she concocted some additional schemes that she hoped would accelerate the process.

A Kidnapping Plot

Every person who forcibly steals, takes, or arrests any person in this state, and carries the person into another country, state, or county or into another part of the county, is guilty of kidnapping.
—State of California Penal Code Section 207,
Kidnapping, Enacted 1872

Elizabeth Duncan, Helen Franklin, and Emma Short sat in Mrs. Duncan's Victoria Street apartment, drank coffee, and hatched a most unusual plot.

Predictably, Elizabeth took the lead in the outrageous scheme, explaining the roles everyone was to play as if she were directing a Broadway production.

"Now, Helen," she was saying, "once Frankie is knocked out there'll be no trouble. It'll be easy as pie! We'll tie him up and drive him to Los Angeles. My sister has found an apartment where I'll have some time to talk to him. I only want to keep him there until he comes to his senses over this woman."

An unconvinced Helen, who was an old friend visiting from San Francisco, continued to question the feasibility of the conspiracy. "Now, Betty," she asked, "what good are three old ladies going to be in tying up a strapping young man like your son? After all, I'm seventy-five years old, and Emma here is . . . Emma, how old are you, anyway?"

"I'll just say I'm in my mid-seventies," came the cagey answer.

"And besides," Helen continued, "even if we do get him to L.A., how are you gonna keep him there?"

"All these questions. Now, don't you ladies fret none," the director responded. "When Frankie gets here, I'll slip him a mickey, put it in a warm cup of milk. He used to drink warm milk all the time and I'll convince him to have some tonight. After he's out, we'll tie him up. Once he sees how strongly I feel about this, he won't want to go back to that slut anyway."

"What'll we do after he's knocked out?" Helen asked, twisting around on the sofa to size up the layout of the room. "What if he falls on the floor? We'll never be able to lift him."

Mrs. Duncan, sitting across from the other women, tightened her mouth in an exasperated expression.

"Helen, I've thought of *all* of this. You two will hide in Frankie's closet until he passes out in his bed. Then you can come out and we'll truss him up."

"I ain't gettin' in no closet!" Mrs. Franklin protested. "I get scared in closed-in places, especially if it's dark."

"I agree with Helen," Emma piped in. "Can't we just hide in Frank's bedroom until he passes out on the couch?"

"That means I'll have to keep him in the living room until the drug works," Elizabeth said, thinking out loud and not happy with the proposed changes.

"How do we get him out to the car?" Helen asked.

"Well, Barbara will be here around eight. She's young and strong, and all of us working together should be able to move him."

"Who's Barbara?" Helen asked.

"Barbara Reed," said Elizabeth. She was a close friend of Patsy's and she's supplying the car to drive Frank to L.A."

"I dunno," Helen said, shaking her head in doubt, "but, if you insist on doing this, then I guess we'll give it a try."

"That's the spirit!"

The women continued to discuss their plot, moving to the kitchen so that Elizabeth could prepare dinner for her son.

About a half-hour before Frank arrived home, Elizabeth emptied ten Seconal capsules into a pan of milk she was warming on the stove. She didn't really know how much of the potent drug Frank could tolerate, but ten seemed like a good round number.

Even though Frank had been married for several weeks, his usual routine was to eat dinner at his mother's house. He would then go to his wife's apartment and spend a few hours with Olga, returning "home" around 10:30 or 11:00 P.M.

Emma was posted as lookout and sounded the alarm when she saw Frank walking up the sidewalk. After signaling, she and Helen scurried into Frank's bedroom to begin their vigil. Though they refused to hide in the closet, they did make an effort to conceal themselves in separate corners of the room.

When Frank walked into the apartment, he felt that something was out of the ordinary. His mother was more cooperative than was normal, taking his jacket from him and hanging it in his bedroom closet.

Lately, his life had been a nightmare with the constant feuding between his mother and Olga. Frank was a man caught in the middle. He did what he could to maintain some kind of harmony between the two women in his life. He would later testify in court, "I was going back and forth like a yo-yo, trying to keep them both happy."

He welcomed any sign of cooperation from his mother. However, he was completely taken aback when he sat down for dinner and his mother poured a glass of warm milk from a saucepan. He hadn't drunk warm milk since he was a child, so his natural reaction was to ask, "What's that?"

"I thought you'd enjoy a little change with your meal," Elizabeth replied while setting the liquid in front of him.

He didn't bother to answer, because he didn't want to explain to her how he really felt about warm milk. As a child, he had encountered it only when he was ill, so he had hardly been left with a positive appreciation for the stuff.

His mother sat down to eat and they enjoyed a typically intimate dinner, just the two of them. They discussed Frank's upcoming cases, a topic in which his mother always took an interest. She frequently went to court with her son and could often identify all the players involved in his various criminal trials.

Frank attempted to avoid the milk, but began to feel guilty about it. She had, after all, tried to do something special for him.

Under a watchful eye, he finally decided to try drinking the white fluid. He carefully lifted the glass to his lips, endeavoring not to smell the milk before taking a drink. He tilted the glass and swallowed a small amount. The taste, which was more bitter than he remembered, gagged him. He knew another gulp would cause him to lose his dinner, so he set the glass down on the table, and wiped his mouth with his napkin.

"I'm sorry, Mom, but this milk must be spoiled. It tastes bitter."

"Now, Frankie, you drink it down."

"I can't. It's making me ill."

His mother gave him a dejected look, intended to melt his resistance. But he refused to buckle to her pressure and got up from the table so she'd understand that the conversation was over.

"I suppose you're going over to her house?" Elizabeth spoke, clearing the dinner dishes from the table.

"Yes, for just a few hours is all."

"Well, if you must go, I'll get your jacket," she said, setting down a dish. She began to hurry toward Frank's room. For a split second, Frank thought her actions peculiar, like she was hiding something. He considered following her, but changed his mind. His attorney's logic told him it was better not to know some things.

Elizabeth handed Frank his jacket, which he slipped on. He kissed her, stating, "I'll be home around eleven," and walked out the front door. The frustrated woman slammed the door behind her departing son. He looked back momentarily, shrugged his shoulders, and continued to his car.

"The coast is clear," Elizabeth called softly towards the bedroom. Then, "Son of a bitch!" she shouted when she knew her son was out of earshot.

"What happened?" asked Emma, who was first into the living room.

"He wouldn't drink the goddamned milk!"

"What'll we do now?" Helen asked, secretly relieved that the plan had fallen through.

"I don't—" Elizabeth began, interrupted by a knock at the door.

"Is Frank back?" Helen asked, turning towards his bedroom in order to hide again.

"No, he wouldn't knock," the disgusted woman replied. "See who the hell's at the door, would ya, Emma?"

Emma opened the door and Barbara Reed stuck her head in the door.

"Hi, Mrs. Duncan," Barbara said cheerfully.

The irritated woman only nodded at her, still too mad to even pretend to be courteous.

Barbara walked into the living room. "I can see things didn't go according to your plans. I just saw Frank getting into his car, so I figured it was all screwed up."

"Yes," Elizabeth finally answered in a clipped manner. "I've decided to let Frank solve his own problems."

Barbara looked at Mrs. Duncan, doubting her, but saying nothing to betray her feelings.

"Well, okay then. I hope it works out for you. But I sure could've used the $25 you promised me for this deal. Maybe you'd lend me a few bucks?" Barbara asked hopefully. "I missed a day's work to help you out."

"I can't loan you any money. And this is not a good time to ask. Ever since he married that whore, he's been chiseling me!"

A flash of anger passed over Barbara, but she decided not to push the issue. She began to make her way toward the door, saying, "I'll be seeing you around, Mrs. Duncan," before hurrying out of the apartment. Elizabeth turned on her heels and walked to the table. She picked up the glass of milk and took it to the sink, where she poured it down the drain.

She then walked back to her cronies in the living room, sat down on the sofa, and let out a long sigh, seeming lost in her thoughts, her head down, staring at the floor. A feeling of frustration hung over her like a dark cloud.

"I could strangle that bitch!" she finally exploded. "And maybe that's exactly what I should do!"

"Nowadays, that'll get you the gas chamber," Helen pointed out.

"Only if you get caught," Elizabeth murmured, for the first time seriously thinking about this new possibility. "Nothing else seems to be working," she reasoned, "and now she's taking all of my—I mean Frankie's—-money. When that damn baby gets here, it'll be even worse. They're determined to leave me penniless." Elizabeth threw up her hands in a "what's-a-person-to-do" gesture.

"Maybe that's the answer," she said, looking first at one then the other for some type of approval. Neither of them spoke and Helen looked away nervously.

There was a prolonged silence in the room. Finally Emma piped in, "Have you given up on the annulment plan?"

"No, that's still on."

"Did you find someone to pose as Frank?"

"I called the Salvation Army. They're supposed to send someone over. I told them I needed a man to do some odd jobs around my house."

"It certainly qualifies—as an odd job, that is," Mrs. Franklin chuckled.

Elizabeth shot Helen a glance intended to let her know that this was not a laughing matter. Helen's laughter died on her lips.

"Well, perhaps that'll take care of all your problems," Emma said.

"I hope it does. But that bitch just doesn't seem to get the idea."

"Let's try the annulment before we worry about anything more drastic," Emma suggested.

"We'll see," came the skeptical reply.

✌he Annulment

O, what a goodly outside falsehood hath!
—Shakespeare, Merchant of Venice, I. iii. 102

Hal Hammons pushed himself away from his large oak desk and swiveled his chair so he could see the Pacific Ocean. A wraparound window afforded him a commanding view of the foothills north of Ventura, as well as the sea. Today, the Pacific was a multitude of colors, fading from a dark navy blue near the shore to an off shade of green—in fact, almost turquoise—further out. A southern tropical storm had kicked up the water, causing those familiar whitecaps that pounded the old Ventura Pier. In the morning haze, Hal could just make out Anacapa Island, nearest of the chain of Channel Islands that lies off the California coastline. Anacapa was particularly noticeable with its flattop landscape and distinctive arch on the east end.

Hal squinted at the island, trying to pick out the elusive greenery, which reminded him of an old Chumash Indian saying: "If you can see the Channel Island, rain is soon to follow." But Hal didn't put much stock in fables. It seldom rained in Southern California in August and seeing Anacapa depended more on the absence of fog than anything else.

Hal's intercom startled him out of his thoughts. "Mr. Hammons, I have a Mrs. Duncan on the line from Santa Barbara. She says that Charles Lynch referred her and she's interested in getting her marriage annulled. She'd like to see you as soon as possible. Tomorrow's schedule doesn't look too bad. You have a 9:00 matter in municipal court, which should be over by 10:30, if you wish to schedule her."

"She said she's from Santa Barbara, but wants an annulment here?"

"That's correct."

"Hmm, that's odd. Maybe I'd better have a word with her. Thank you, Martha," Hal said, picking up the phone.

"This is Hal Hammons. How may I help you?"

"Hello, Mr. Hammons. My name is Olga Duncan and I'm interested in having my marriage annulled. Charles Lynch, who is my attorney in Santa Barbara, recommended you. This is an uncontested matter between my husband and myself."

"Well, were you married in Ventura County?"

"No, but I don't want to go through the publicity in Santa Barbara, so I'd like to do this quietly down there," came the measured reply.

Hal thought for a moment then responded, "My secretary says I do have a 10:30 time open tomorrow morning, if you can make it on such short notice."

"That would be fine. We'll be there tomorrow morning."

"You'll be bringing your husband with you, correct?"

"Yes, we'll both come."

"Okay, I'll see you then."

After they had exchanged good-byes, Hal hung up the phone and buzzed his secretary. "Martha, put the Duncans down for that 10:30 slot."

"Yes, Mr. Hammons. Don't forget you're due in muni court in fifteen minutes on the Turner case."

"Right you are," Hal said, gathering up his files and taking one more glance at the great Pacific Ocean, the sight of which always filled him with a sense of well-being.

Ralph W. Winterstein was about to undertake one of the odder jobs he had done recently. He was to meet a Mrs. Duncan, who lived at 7 Valerio Street, and drive with her and a friend to Ventura. And that was when the scheme got really outlandish, for Ralph was then going to commit a felony for the promise of $100. He wasn't sure why he was doing this, but the money would come in handy, little as it was. Besides, it wasn't a high-risk venture, a little playacting, a quick court appearance, and an act of perjury. It was the type of crime Ralph preferred.

Ralph was twenty-six years old when he became involved in this unusual task. He'd been around the block a few times, with a criminal record dating back to September of 1948. In the ten years since his first arrest for auto theft, Ralph had also been charged with being AWOL from the military, disturbing the peace in Santa Maria, California, and transporting a stolen vehicle over state lines. For the last offense, Winterstein had served ten months in the federal penitentiary at Terminal Island, California. He had also been arrested for vagrancy and "hanging bad paper." Probation reports completed on Ralph indicated that his reputation in the Santa Barbara area was poor. He was generally considered to be moody, unreliable, and a man who appreciated his booze a little too much.

Now Ralph was tangled up with this Duncan woman, whom he had met by applying for day labor through the Salvation Army, and he was about to jeopardize his parole status for a measly hundred bucks!

On the morning of August 7, 1958, Ralph met Mrs. Duncan and a woman she introduced as Aunt Anne Bailey, to carry out the plan.

Ralph drove the two-tone '55 Ford Fairlane, while the Duncan woman told him of his part in this affair. She explained that he was to pose as her husband Frank and to testify that he did not oppose the annulment. It boiled down to him keeping quiet and her doing all the talking, something she was obviously good at. Ralph had some misgivings about this plot working, but she was very persuasive. He failed to get money up front.

At 10:30, the trio had reached the Ventura law office of Hal Hammons, Jr. Ralph sat and nodded in agreement while the Duncan woman explained her wish to annul the marriage to Frank. She pointed out to Mr. Hammons that the marriage had never been consummated and that she—Olga Duncan—had married only to hold herself up to the community of Santa Barbara as a married woman.

While this seemed somewhat odd to the lawyer, he'd been in the practice of law long enough not to be surprised over the situations people put themselves in. Hal completed the necessary paperwork and then informed "Olga" that she would have to return with her husband tomorrow because he had a mandatory afternoon meeting with the Downtown Lions Club.

Her response was, "I think this matter is more important than your social meeting, and I have come down here all the way from Santa Barbara. I would consider it a great convenience if we could do this today!"

Like Ralph Winterstein, the attorney found this lady to be very persuasive, if not downright pushy.

"Well, I'm not sure we can get on the court calendar on this short notice," was the curt reply.

"Why don't you try?"

"I'll have my secretary do so. In the meantime, the fee for my service is $175 plus $22 for court costs. Can you pay that now?"

The woman looked offended that Hal could bring up something so mundane as attorney's fees during such an important legal conference. She replied, "I'm a little short at this time. If it's okay with you, I'll give you $100 cash now and you can bill me for the balance. You can send your bill to my home in Santa Barbara, in my maiden name, Olga Kupczyk, 7 Valerio Street, apartment four."

"That'll be satisfactory," Hal said, noting down the information she had provided.

Hal's persistent secretary was able to arrange an afternoon court date and the parties agreed to meet in superior court at 1:30 that afternoon.

The actual court proceedings went smoothly enough. Mr. Duncan testified that he and his spouse had never lived together as man and wife. Mrs. Duncan then took the stand and said that she had never intended to cohabitate with her husband. She further testified that she had married him only to show the community that she was married and now realized what a terrible mistake she had made. Judge E. Perry Churchill granted the annulment (Ventura Superior Court, case number D-47814), based on the testimony of the two Duncans.

Throughout this proceeding, no one was required to show any proof of identification.

Hal Hammons, Jr. later testified during Mrs. Duncan's trial that he had thought two things unusual about this annulment. When Frank signed the annulment decree, he began to write the letter "R" for his first name. He scratched over it, making the "R" into an "F". Hal also wondered what an attractive man in his mid-twenties could possibly see in a woman old enough to be his mother. But Hal had dismissed the questions as further proof of the oddities of people in general.

Lies Upon Lies

She should leave the young people alone to iron out their own problems. If he (Frank) loved the girl he would go with her, and if he didn't they'd eventually come to some type of agreement. Mrs. Duncan didn't like that idea very much. She wanted her son back, period— regardless.

—Ralph Winterstein's testimony, February 25, 1959

Ralph settled into the driver's seat of the Ford and took a long drag on his cigarette. He exhaled fully, watching the smoke curl up against the white headliner.

"Whew, I can't believe they bought that story. It was too easy."

He loosened his tie and removed a comb from his back pocket. Adjusting the rearview mirror so he could see, he combed his wavy, dishwater-blond hair straight back from his forehead. Ralph's blue eyes twinkled when he thought about the successful acting job they'd just carried off. It was always fun to pull a fast one on somebody, especially if that somebody was a man wearing black robes.

"You ought to be on the stage, Mrs. Duncan," Ralph laughed.

"I told you it would work. I've done it many times before and it's always a snap!" Elizabeth said, settling into the passenger seat.

"Well, now I'm convinced." Ralph turned the key and fired up the Ford. He looked into the back to ensure that Emma had closed the door, then pulled the car onto Poli Street, turned in front of the old courthouse, and headed toward the highway.

"So tell me, Mrs. Duncan, why didn't your son come down here to do this?"

"Well, he's just so busy with his own law practice, he couldn't find the time."

"What about the girl, y'know, his wife?"

"To hell with that bitch!" Elizabeth exclaimed, shaking her fist. "She oughta be dead! Besides, she's nothin' but a foreigner and has been trying to get money out of my son. He's an important lawyer in town and his reputation could be hurt if he got the annulment in Santa Barbara. But we can't tell him—"

"Wait a minute," Ralph interjected, "you told me yesterday that he knew all about this and it was okay with him!"

"Well, I was going to tell him when the opportunity arose," the sly woman replied, avoiding his look.

"Uh-oh. This is a horse of a different color. You told me he knew!"

"Just drive the car, Ralph dear. Remember, you're doing this for the money. Let me take care of Frankie."

Ralph's temper boiled to the top. He gripped the steering wheel and thought, *I ought to tell this old broad how the cow eats the cabbage. She'd think twice before she talked to me that way again!* Ralph decided to keep his mouth shut when he remembered that he hadn't gotten paid yet.

"Talking about money," Ralph said, stubbing his cigarette out in the car ashtray, "when do I get paid?"

"I know I promised you a $100, but that chiseling attorney charged me more than I had anticipated. Let me see what I have here."

Elizabeth lifted her purse off the car floor and set it in her lap. She began to dig through it, pushing away various papers and setting a large bottle of pills onto the seat. She opened her wallet and extracted some folded bills.

"I have, let's see . . . ten, twenty, forty, one, two, three. I have $43 here. Will that do until I can get to the bank, sorta act as a down payment?"

Ralph looked at her, realizing his mistake in not getting the money before doing the job, and knowing full well that she never intended to go to the bank, even if she had the money. He quickly snatched the money out of her hand, shoving it into his top shirt pocket. "Sure, that'll do for now," he grunted, accelerating the car to emphasize his displeasure.

They rode quietly for some time, northward on the El Camino Real. Only the squeaking noise of the old woman rolling down the rear window broke the silence. When they approached the Rincon area of Ventura County, where the ocean waves often breach the roadway, Elizabeth finally spoke. "You know, Ralph, you're a nice-lookin' fellow."

"What?" The comment had caught him by surprise.

"Well, you're not married are you?"

"No, I tried that once. It didn't work out too good."

"I have a friend who has a problem. Maybe you could help her out."

"What sort of problem?"

"She's a widow lady, having recently lost her husband to cancer, poor dear. She stands to inherit $250,000 if she remarries within a year. It's part of his will, I guess to keep her from runnin' around after he's dead!"

"Uh-huh," Ralph muttered, looking over at the woman and deciding that her glasses really looked ridiculous with those large wings protruding from the sides. Besides, the way they magnified her eyes gave her an eccentric appearance.

"There'd be good money in it for you," she continued. "My friend would be willing to pay you $50,000 so she could inherit what's due her."

"Really, $50,000?" Ralph whistled, knowing that this was a fantasy story even before he heard the old lady giggle in the back seat.

"Well, what do you think, Ralph? You interested?"

"I don't know, Mrs. Duncan. Like I said before, I sort of had a bad experience with marriage. But let me think on it."

"Sure, Ralph, $50,000 is a lot of money."

"It certainly is," Ralph replied, thinking he'd been around the block a few times too many for this old broad to con him. He turned his full attention back to the roadway.

The day after the annulment, Elizabeth walked to Frank and Olga's apartment on Garden Street. Knowing that no one was home, she knocked on the door of Mrs. Dorthea Barnett, the landlady.

"Hello," Elizabeth said when the landlady answered the door. "I'm Frank Duncan's mother, Elizabeth," she said, introducing herself.

"Yes?"

"I've come to get a suit out of Frank's apartment, but I seem to have lost my key. Would you mind letting me in?"

"Well now, I don't know if I should do that. They've never said it was okay to let anyone else into their apartment. Did Frank say it was all right?"

"Yes, he did. He's got an important case coming up and I've *got* to get his suit to the cleaners."

The landlady thought about it for several seconds. She was aware that Olga had had problems with her mother-in-law, but was not aware of the full force of the clashes.

Mrs. Barnett looked at the older woman and decided that she didn't look too threatening.

"Okay, Mrs. Duncan. I'll let you in this one time, but I'm going to go in with you—just to be on the safe side."

"That'll be fine."

Mrs. Barnett reached over and grabbed a ring of keys off her counter. They walked upstairs and she opened the sliding glass door to apartment eleven. Elizabeth followed her, going directly to the hall closet. She threw open the door and exclaimed, much to the other woman's surprise, "See, this is proof Frank is no longer living here!"

"What?"

"None of Frank's clothes are here," Elizabeth was rummaging through the closet, pushing hangers from one side to the other. She then turned and looked at Mrs. Barnett. "And besides, they're not legally married anyway. They're living in sin. Frank had the marriage annulled. You shouldn't be letting them live in this apartment anyway."

"Mrs. Duncan, I don't think their marital—"

"That woman is bad news! She abandoned a husband and two children in Canada," Elizabeth interrupted. "I tell you, kick her out of here or you'll regret it!"

"Are you threatening me?"

"No, but—"

"I think we'd better go. We shouldn't be in here."

Elizabeth didn't answer, but walked into the bedroom, staring at the bed, her arms tightly crossed while she sized up the scene of the crime.

"She'll never have him. I'll kill her first," Elizabeth whispered, not expecting the landlady to hear her.

"What did you say?"

"Oh, nothing," Elizabeth's hand went to her mouth when she realized she had spoken too loudly.

"It's time we left!" Mrs. Barnett raised her voice.

"Okay, I'm leaving, but you really must listen to me—"

"Out, Mrs. Duncan—please!" The landlady pointed to the door, then reached toward the other woman's arm.

"Don't you touch me! I'm leaving." Elizabeth hurried out the door and rushed down the steps without saying another word.

She left the landlady standing on the balcony, hands upon her hips, trying to understand what the visit had been all about.

Shopping for Killers

Heav'n has no rage like to hatred turn'd,
Nor Hell a fury like a woman scorn'd.
—William Congreve, *The Mourning Bride,* III. viii

"I think your mother is crazy," Barbara Reed was telling Frank, "and she definitely means harm to Olga. You'd better take your wife away before something serious happens."

Frank Duncan sat at a booth in the Blue Onion Cafe on Hollister Street and listened in disbelief to his sister's old friend.

"And then what did she say?" he asked in agitation.

"She said she wanted me to help kidnap Olga. And then she wanted—well there isn't any amount of money in this world that would make me commit murder . . ."

"Hey, Barbara! Are you supposed to be on a break, or what?" the manager shouted at the carhop. "There's a bunch of customers that're gettin' damned tired of waitin'!"

"Okay, I'm comin'!" Barbara shouted in her boss's direction, rising from the booth. "I gotta get back to work. Frank, you better do something about this before someone gets hurt!"

"Well, it sounds pretty preposterous to me, but I'll look into it," Frank said, also getting up from the booth.

A shaken Frank walked out to his car, mulling over what he had just heard. He decided the best course of action would be to question his mother about this allegation.

He later testified in court that he had gone directly home and confronted Elizabeth with Barbara's story. Her response, he said, was, "That girl is lying. I know it sounds crazy, but I was going to kidnap you. I intended to take you to Los Angeles until you came to your senses."

Under questioning from District Attorney Roy Gustafson, Frank continued his tale: "And, quite frankly, I blew my top. I was extremely angry. It seemed such a stupid thing, and I told her she better not be saying anything, doing anything like that again, or even thinking such a thing. It sounded like something a grammar school child might think up."

Barbara Jean Reed, who was an ex-neighbor and old friend of Frank's deceased sister, Patsy, had her day in court. She testified that a few hours prior to her conversation with Frank, Mrs. Duncan had proposed murder.

In a conversation that took place in the older woman's apartment, Elizabeth had offered Barbara $1,000 to help her kill Olga. Barbara was to go with Mrs. Duncan to Olga's apartment, pitch lye in the victim's face, and help throw a chloroformed blanket over the girl. They were then going to drive her into the mountains and toss her over a cliff. Elizabeth pointed out that, once the lye took effect, there would be little possibility of Olga even being identified, thus ensuring that they would not be apprehended.

The astonished Mrs. Reed had said that she would have to think about such a proposition. At her departure, she took with her the encouraging words of Elizabeth, who pointed out that, if her own daughter Patsy were alive, she would gladly have helped her mother with such a worthwhile endeavor.

This conversation, which occurred in the early part of August, proved that Mother Duncan had begun a serious quest for a killer. By the time she succeeded in hiring the assassins, she had approached eight different individuals, none of whom—amazingly enough—ever contacted the police.

Mrs. Duncan's first plan included her old friend Emma Short. Olga was to be lured to Mrs. Short's apartment, where once again it was suggested that Emma hide in the closet. This time, she was to leap out of the closet and garrote the surprised girl. Then with Mrs. Duncan's help, when Olga was strangled, her hair would be cut off and her body hung in Mrs. Short's closet, awaiting transportation to the ocean for disposal the following day.

Emma had balked only at the idea of leaving the victim's body in her closet all night, but for that reason this plot had been shelved in hopes of finding a more workable design.

At this stage, Elizabeth had decided to call upon her co-star in the annulment charade, Ralph Winterstein. Ralph was still working for Elizabeth from time to time, moving and hiding Frank's car. For reasons, unknown, Mrs. Duncan decided that Emma should put the proposal to the shiftless Ralph. So Emma, the dutiful confidante, asked Ralph to "take Olga for a ride and get rid of her."

Unexpectedly, Emma's request met with an outraged response from Ralph, who didn't consider murder to be among his crimes of choice. The indignant man later testified that he felt harm was going to come to Olga, but that he was prevented from going to the police because of his involvement in the annulment. He stated in court, "Normally, sir, a man doesn't go and commit a crime and then go to the police and say, 'Here I am.'"

Frustrated by her early attempts to find a willing assassin, Elizabeth turned to the natural resources created by Frank's work as a criminal defense attorney. While she was frequently in court, applauding her son's efforts and often openly booing the statements of prosecutors, the shopper now began to take a new interest in her son's clients.

In September of 1958, she befriended Diane Romero, the wife of one of Frank's clients, Rudolph Romero. Frank was defending Rudy on a minor narcotics charge.

The attempted recruitment of Diane created yet another bizarre twist in this incredible search for a murderer.

Diane Romero was actually born Diane Johnston. She was also from Canada, and was twenty years old at the time of her involvement with Elizabeth Duncan. Diane was from a lower socioeconomic class and an eager listener when there was an opportunity to earn some quick cash. The wily Mother Duncan had recognized this and started her recruitment with a luncheon date in which she not only bought lunch, but also gave the younger woman some gifts of clothing.

At a subsequent meeting a few days later, Elizabeth gave Diane $5 with which to purchase two cans of Holly brand lye. Without asking why, Diane Romero did the older woman's bidding and bought the lye.

During a third meeting, Mrs. Duncan finally revealed to her young recruit the purpose for the lye. Elizabeth walked Diane to the Garden Street Apartments and pointed out Olga's flat. In court, Mrs. Romero declared, "She said there was a woman called Ollie living there that claimed that she was Mrs. Duncan, but she wasn't; that she was married to Frank Duncan, but she wasn't married to him. Their marriage had been annulled." Elizabeth had continued by telling Diane that Ollie was phoning her and calling her a bitch and blackmailing her son. And finally, while standing in front of the Garden Street Apartments, Mother Duncan posed the murder, suggesting that Diane "look the place over to see if I could get in there, knock Ollie over the head, throw her in the bathtub, and sprinkle lye over her."

Elizabeth then handed Diane a pair of white gloves. The court testimony about the gloves was as follows:

"She told me to wear them when I went up there."

"Did she tell you why you should wear them?"

"So I wouldn't leave my fingerprints around."

"Then was anything else discussed between you and Mrs. Elizabeth Duncan, the defendant, before you walked up to the Garden Street apartment?"

"No, she just left me there and I stood there and she went back to the courthouse."

"What was the purpose in going up to the Garden Street apartment?"

"Well, I was humoring Mrs. Duncan. Her son was my husband's attorney."

While Diane Romero never admitted in court what her intentions were, she did go to the apartment door and knock. She was utterly shocked to learn that she knew the intended victim, Olga Kupczyk, who had cared for her while she was a patient at Vancouver General Hospital.

Diane quickly recovered and pretended that her visit was a social call. After chatting for five minutes, she made her excuses and left.

Olga later told Frank of this unexpected visit, commenting that while she remembered Diane from her hospital stay, they now had nothing in common and she didn't consider Diane a friend. Frank apparently made no connection between Diane and the fact that he was representing her husband.

While Diane never told Olga the real reason for her visit, namely to case her apartment, their past relationship caused the prospective killer to decide against helping the obsessed mother.

Diane Romero returned to the courthouse where Mrs. Duncan was waiting and informed her that, because she was an old friend of the intended victim, she couldn't carry out the plan. Not one to be easily put off, Elizabeth responded, "Good, then you can easily get into her apartment anytime."

When it later became apparent that Diane Romero was not going to cooperate in the murder plot, Mrs. Duncan turned her attention to Diane's husband, Rudy.

Upon the request of Mother Duncan, the Romeros went to Mrs. Short's apartment for a visit. Mrs. Duncan, who was not shy about proposing murder, asked Rudy if he would "do the job," thinking that his wife had already explained what the job entailed. However, the young woman had not briefed her husband about the nature of this meeting, and some awkward moments followed, as Diane's testimony indicated.

"Well, she asked me, 'Did you tell him?' And I looked at Rudy and I looked at her and I said, 'No.' And then Rudy said, 'Tell me what?' And I didn't want to tell him. So she told him."

Her testimony continued, "Then $1,500 was offered. She said it would be easy because I knew Olga and Rudy could take her, seeing that he would be strong enough to."

"And what did Elizabeth Duncan say, if anything, with respect to what Rudy would do with Olga?"

"She said that, seeing he was a Mexican, he could take her somewhere, because he knew the town."

"Well, do you remember what Rudy said to Mrs. Duncan in response to that?"

"Well, he was pretty shocked. I knew he was mad at me."

"Well, what did he say?"

"He hardly said anything at all. He listened and went along with her and then he said that we had to leave, that he had to get home, that he was looking for a job. So we left."

Mrs. Duncan continued the pressure on the Romeros, asking Diane out to lunch at various times. The conversation was always the same, the older woman asking the younger to convince her husband to kill Olga. During one of these meetings, in an attempt to rip off Mrs. Duncan, Diane said she might be able to get her husband to do the job if Elizabeth would make a down payment of at least half the agreed-upon sum. Elizabeth refused the proposal, guessing Diane's real motive. Diane Romero would later admit that her true intention was to take the money, because she knew that Mrs. Duncan couldn't report such a theft to the police.

Elizabeth did give Diane $8 to buy Olga dinner. She hoped to convince Rudy that after dinner, he would be in a perfect position to kidnap Olga and take care of her. Rudy, who waffled back and forth about deciding if he wanted to be involved in this plot, was becoming convinced that there was little chance of the woman coming through with any cash.

The impulsive matron made one final try with Rudy in the first week of November, when she upped the ante to $2,500. But, when she again refused a down payment of $100, Rudy disassociated himself from the plot. Not easily dissuaded, Mrs. Duncan threatened to have him put in jail for the case that Frank was defending. This proved to be an empty threat, since Frank had won Rudy a dismissal on the narcotics charge two weeks prior.

Mrs. Duncan, fearing that the Romeros wouldn't do her bidding, continued her search while still conducting negotiations with the couple. On October 14, she contacted Rebecca Diaz, the ex-landlady of the Romeros. She went to the Diaz residence on the pretext of looking for the Romeros, allegedly because they owed her money. She talked briefly with Mrs. Diaz, getting enough of a feel for her to invite the woman to Mrs. Short's the next day for her now well-rehearsed "dreadful nurse" story.

Upon hearing the tale, a surprised Mrs. Diaz suggested that the harassed woman go to the police with her problems. This well-meaning advice was met with snickers from Mrs. Short. Seeing that she had misjudged Rebecca Diaz, Elizabeth toned down her sales pitch. She asked Rebecca if she perhaps knew someone else who would help her get rid of the pesky nurse. Mrs. Diaz later testified, "I didn't want to get involved, so I left."

The ever-persistent shopper called Rebecca the next day and again asked if she knew of a man who would be interested in doing her job. Mrs. Diaz reiterated that she could not help her.

Rebecca Diaz next heard from Elizabeth about a month later, when she received an unexpected phone call from her. Rebecca testified that Elizabeth said, "Becky, do you remember what we talked about? And I said, 'Yes.' And she said, 'Well, forget about it. I won't need you anymore. It will be today or never.'" To the best of Mrs. Diaz's recollection, this unusual conversation, the more unusual because Rebecca had never agreed to do anything for the obsessed mother, occurred on November 17, the day that Olga was kidnapped.

The hiring of Luis Moya and Augustine Baldonado might never have occurred if Mrs. Duncan's favorite restaurant had been open on Wednesday, November 12, 1958. Unable to drink their morning coffee at the usual stop, Elizabeth and Emma had walked down State Street until coming to the Tropical Cafe. Upon entering the establishment, Mrs. Duncan recognized Esperanza Esquivel as a person that Frank had recently defended in a possession-of-stolen-property case. This chance meeting would provide the fatal combination that Mother Duncan had diligently sought since August of that year.

The Murder

The story out of Ventura, California, was cast by the police in the true mold of classical tragedy in modern dress. A story of the bitterest passion, of murder most foul, of the innocent slain.
—*Newsweek,* January 5, 1969

It was almost midnight on November 17, 1958, when the old car, blacked out, glided to a silent stop in front of 1114 Garden Street. Inside, Gus and Luis were going over final plans for the job they were about to do.

"I'll go up and tell her that Frank is in the car, dead drunk, and I need some help gettin' him to the apartment," Luis explained.

"Okay—and what'll I do?"

"You get down in the back seat while I bring her downstairs. When I open the door, you grab her. I'll push her into the car and you tape her mouth so she can't yell."

"Okay, I got it."

"Maybe I'll have to hit her or somethin', you know, just to knock her out. Then we can use the gun later where nobody can hear."

"Are you gonna take her stuff?" Gus asked. "Like the old broad said? Make it look like she went on a trip?"

"Yeah, after she's in the car I'll go back to the apartment and grab some clothes and her purse. We might even luck out and find some money in it."

"You got to hurry," Gus said. "I don't want to be sitting here with no screaming bitch."

"I know."

Luis looked over at the apartment house and replayed in his mind the words he was going to say.

He took a deep, ragged breath and said, "Let's do it. Get in the back seat." Luis threw open the door, stepped out of the car, and walked around the corner of the apartment complex. He looked up to number eleven, noting that the only entrance to the apartment was a large sliding glass door. The light was on in the living room and he saw a shadow cross briefly in front of a lamp. Diffused through the sheer curtains, the shape looked to him like a hooded figure, large and heavy, perhaps a man. While Luis stood watching the figure, he unscrewed a pint bottle of whiskey and took a long hit on it. He put the bottle back in his pocket and walked toward the door.

Luis rapped lightly on the glass door, stepping back so he could see in more clearly. He quickly checked the gun in his waistband, ensuring that it was well concealed.

The door slid open and an attractive, dark-haired woman poked her head out. "Yes, what is it?"

"Uh, Mrs. Duncan?"

"Yes."

"I have your husband down in the car. He's drunk and said to drive him here. We were out drinking and," Luis pointed towards the street, indicating where the car was parked, "I'll need help bringing him up."

"Okay, then. Let me get a robe. I'll be right down."

Gus crouched in the back seat of the Chevy for what seemed an eternity. "C'mon, Louie," he muttered to himself. He felt around for the bottle of whiskey the two men had been sharing but was unable to locate it in the dark interior of the car. He sure could use a drink to bolster his courage.

Gus wasn't sure why he was doing this. He'd decided to go along with Louie, not wanting to disappoint his friend, when Louie had made up his mind to do this job. Gus didn't really care about the money, and now while his muscles cramped on the floorboard of the old car, he wished he hadn't agreed to help.

Gus was shocked out of his reverie by an unknown face peering into the car at him, *Oh shit,* he thought, *it's time. Was I supposed to open the door, or did Louie say he would?* Gus couldn't remember. Suddenly the door burst open and Olga Kupczyk screamed in anguish as Luis hit her with the pistol, her blood spattering against the side window of the Chevrolet.

"Grab the bitch," Luis yelled. "Get her arm. She's gonna wake up the whole damn neighborhood."

Gus struggled with Olga's left arm while she braced herself against the doorjamb with her right. Olga screamed again and a neighbor's light flicked on.

Luis raised the revolver with his right hand and pistol-whipped Olga again. She slumped forward. Gus dragged her into the back seat, pulling her on top of him.

"Get us the hell out of here!"

Luis ran around the front of the sedan and jumped into the driver's seat. He fired up the car and headed north on Garden Street, making a screeching turn onto Valerio. He traveled for a short distance before turning south on State Street, en route to the El Camino Real.

"Jesus Christ," Luis muttered to himself. "This is really happening, man. We're in deep shit now."

"Hey, Louie, take it easy," urged Gus from behind him. "We don't want the cops to stop us. There's blood everywhere."

Suddenly Olga began to murmur.

"Man, she's not dead," said Gus. "Give me the gun."

"My baby! God, my baby!" the young woman cried out. "Oh God, why are you doing this? My baby . . . "

"Shut her up!" Luis yelled at Gus.

Gus struck Olga, which only caused her to shriek and to thrash around in the back of the car.

"Jesus, Louie, stop the car. I can't handle her. Fuckin' help me, Louie!"

Luis wheeled the car off the highway onto Cabrillo Boulevard, where he ground the car to a stop. He swiveled around in the front seat.

"Give me that damn thing," he shouted in order to be heard over the frenzied commotion in the back seat. "I'm gonna fix this bitch!"

He grabbed the gun from Gus and struck Olga a powerful blow on top of the head, spraying bits of bloody flesh throughout the car and breaking the weapon apart.

"There!" he grunted in satisfaction.

Olga was now face down in a pool of blood.

"What's this baby shit, man?" Luis asked, still looking into the back seat. "The old lady never said nothin' about her having kids."

"Turn on the light," Gus said.

"I can't, someone might see."

"I said turn on the goddamn light!" Gus was feeling around Olga's stomach. "Oh, Holy Mother of God, she's pregnant! I mean she's huge!"

Now Luis snapped on the light. "Shit, man she didn't say nothin' about her being pregnant. This is gonna cost her extra."

"Cost her extra? Are you kidding? We're gonna roast in hell and you're talking about costin' extra. We've killed her baby!"

"Is she dead?"

"I don't know. Let's just drop her here and maybe someone'll take her to the hospital."

"We can't, Gus. If she's not dead, she'll identify us. We gotta finish the job." Luis pulled away from the curb and headed down Cabrillo Boulevard towards the highway.

"Get the tape, Gus, and wrap her hands."

Gus fumbled around in the back seat, trying to locate the roll of white adhesive tape they had brought. He finally pulled it out from under Olga's body and began a halfhearted attempt to bind her hands. He felt something warm drop onto his forehead and looked up towards the ceiling and caught a second drop of Olga's blood in his eye. *Oh God,* he thought, choking back a wave of nausea.

Luis pulled back on the 101 Highway, driving south. The car sputtered and backfired as he accelerated.

"Gus, this car ain't gonna make no Tijuana. It ain't running for shit. Besides, I don't want to drive her that far."

"What are we gonna do?"

"Beats me. You know the area around here. What do you think?"

"I think we're going to hell, Louie. I think God will punish us for this. I think—"

"Shut up, Gus! Now where are we dumping this bitch? C'mon where?"

Gus pulled himself together. "Okay, right up here is the road to Ojai. I've been on it before and it's real deserted, lots of hills. We can find a place along the road."

Luis saw the sign that declared, "Highway 150, Ojai 20 miles," and turned onto the two-lane road. He drove along the dark country lane, the headlights of the car whisking over the California chaparral on the sharp curves.

This time Olga awoke without warning. She howled with her last living strength and thrashed her body around in an effort to get free. Gus grabbed her shoulders and tried to pin her down, but she put her whole body and soul into living, heaving violently against him and kicking out with frenzied force. Gus began to yell, filling the car with bawling curses that penetrated the quiet night, and Luis joined in, trying to gain control, also on the edge of losing it.

"Gus, Gus! Oh, Jesus. Shut her up!"

Olga stilled her body momentarily and began to plead, "I can't die. My baby's ready to be born. You can't kill my little Dorothy. Please, please, I'm begging you."

Her words jolted Luis as he realized what the old lady in the bar had been laughing about. But there was no time to think about it now, because Olga was starting to struggle again.

"Fuckin' help me, Louie! She's so strong. She's fightin' for her baby. Stop the car!"

Luis kept driving, looking desperately for a suitable place to pull over and end this nightmare. He spotted a turnout with a road marker that stated simply B352+75. Swinging the car onto the shoulder, he brought it to a jarring stop, tumbling the thrashing occupants of the rear seat to the floor.

Luis jumped from the car and threw open the back door to help Gus, who was now under Olga on the floorboard. Reaching inside, he grabbed a handful of Olga's hair and jerked her out of the car. She landed on her back with a heavy thud that knocked the breath from her and temporarily silenced her.

"Now hold her!" Luis barked at the panicking Gus.

"I want out of here. Let's just go, for God's sake, just leave her here," Gus whined from the back seat of the car.

Luis grabbed Gus's arm and pulled him out of the Chevy. He pushed Gus toward Olga and snarled, "Just hold her down. We can't leave her here. She's not dead."

Gus sat down on Olga's heaving chest and pushed his forearm into her neck. Olga gasped incoherent words while Luis ran down the embankment to find a place to bury her. He began to dig in the dirt next to a drainpipe with his hands, shoveling the fresh earth through his outstretched legs like a dog digging up a piece of rotted meat.

Olga turned her head slightly sideways and in the moonlit night saw that Luis was digging a grave for her. A look of renewed horror washed over her face and she began to twist her body away from the force of Gus's stranglehold.

"Louie, come help me!" Gus called out.

Luis ran up from the culvert. "You go dig, make it deep, and I'll take care of this witch."

He placed his hands around Olga's neck and began to methodically strangle her, pressing his thumbs deep into her carotid arteries. While he throttled her, Olga's body twisted left and right in a grotesque death dance, her neck pinioned to the ground by Luis's murdering hands. Her legs splayed apart and her heels dug into the soft ground as she finally went limp.

"Die, you fuckin' *puta,*" Luis hissed into her unseeing eyes.

Gus dug like a man possessed, gouging at the dirt with his bare hand and tossing clods of soil in all directions. He soon emerged from the hole, sweating profusely in the chill November air.

"It's ready, Louie," he said. "Is she dead?"

"I don't know. You're the doctor, check her out."

Gus got on his hands and knees and pressed his cheek against Olga's chest. "I can't hear nothin'," he said, "but I don't know for sure. I . . . I mean she could be alive . . . and the baby . . . what about the baby?"

"Let's just dump her," was the cold response.

They rudely dragged the young woman's body down the bank, letting it roll part of the way. Olga's bulk caught on the lip of the shallow hole, as if in protest of this resting place. Luis kicked her into the grave and Gus stepped into the hole and folded her body so it would fit into the space dug out. He and Gus covered the motionless form, using their hands to replace the earth. When Olga was entombed, they tromped down the dirt with their shoes.

"Well, it ain't no proper grave. Just a hole," Luis muttered to himself. Gus looked down at the newly filled area and crossed himself.

"What are you doin'?" Luis asked.

"Nothin'. Let's get outta here."

Olga screamed no more.

Dorothy is Done

. . . When she was halfway across the room there came a great shriek from the wind, and the house shook so hard that she lost her footing and sat down suddenly upon the floor.

. . . It was very dark, and the wind howled horribly around her, but Dorothy found she was riding quite easily. After the first two whirls around, and one other time when the house tipped badly, she felt like she were being rocked gently, like a baby in a cradle.

. . . In spite of the swaying of the house and the wailing of the wind, Dorothy soon closed her eyes and fell fast asleep.

—L. Frank Baum, *The Wizard of Oz*

Gus and Luis drove off of Highway 150 in the Chevy bearing California license plate MUL 024, en route back to Santa Barbara. Gus was driving, smoking a much-needed cigarette.

"God, I can't believe it!" Luis almost shouted. "You know what? It was great! I mean I really got off on doin' that bitch!"

"You're a fuckin' psycho, man," Gus said, inhaling a large drag into his lungs. "Fuckin' sick."

"C'mon Gus, admit it—you dug it. It made you feel real macho, right man?" Luis unscrewed the cap of the whiskey bottle and took a slug off it. He shivered, the booze hitting bottom and adding to the adrenaline rush he was already feeling.

The pair cruised onto the 101 Highway, Gus being cautious so that his driving would not arouse the suspicions of a lurking highway patrolman. He was lost in his own thoughts, reliving the unbelievable nightmare he had just acted out. He didn't have to close his eyes to see her struggling on the ground, her eyes bulging with fear, and her large belly flopping from side to side. It made him shudder to think about it.

Gus's thoughts turned to his own estranged wife, Carmen, whom he hadn't seen for some time. Carmen was carrying twins, Gus's twins, and was probably as large as that woman he had just murdered. Gus knew that God would punish him for this evil.

"Whoopee!" Luis shouted, tilting back his head and taking another hit on the bottle.

"Shut up, Louie!" the other man shot back.

"I feel great, man!" Luis exclaimed. "You know I almost killed a guy once, in a robbery I was doin'. I remember looking in that motherfucker's eyes and seeing all that fuckin' fear. I shoved the gun in that dude's face and cocked the hammer back. I told him, 'S'long, shithead,' and pulled the trigger. I had the power on that guy, kinda like tonight!"

Gus looked at Luis, not really understanding what he was saying, but wanting to know the rest of the story. "Did you shoot him, man?"

Luis looked over at his crime partner and grinned. "See, I knew you'd want to know if I offed the cocksucker." He paused for a moment and then looked out the windshield while he continued his story. "The goddamn gun jammed. The old bastard thought he was shot, I guess, when the hammer clicked. He screamed and pissed him-self and fell over backwards. Man, I just laughed at that old asshole, laying there in his own mess and begging me not to shoot him again. It was a real trip!" Luis looked back at Gus, who had a chokehold on the steering wheel, his eyes fixed on the roadway ahead of him.

"What's the matter, Gus?"

"Nothin'," was the curt response. But there was plenty wrong, and Gus knew it.

"But this was even better!" Luis continued. "Because this time I—we were able to finish it, man. You know, bring it to the final end.

We were the power, man, we had fuckin' control! Do you see what I mean?"

Gus could contain it no longer. He swung the car to the shoulder of the highway, grinding to a stop. Throwing open the door, he leaned out of the car while wave after wave of vomit splattered onto the pavement.

"You fuckin' pussy!" Luis grunted his displeasure.

Gus finally sat up straight and wiped his mouth on the back of his sleeve, which was already marked with bloodstains. Then he just sat looking at his shirt, realizing for the first time that he was soaked in blood. He glanced at Luis, seeing him for the first time since they'd gotten into the car, the moon providing an illuminating backdrop. His partner was covered in a mixture of coagulated blood, dirt, and sweat. His hair was matted, two clumps protruding from the back of his head, lending him a demonic appearance. Gus gawked at this apparition and quickly crossed himself.

"What the hell's wrong with you?" Luis snarled, not understanding the impact this vision was having on his partner. "Let's go, Gus! We gotta get rid of this car."

"Okay, yeah," Gus said, pulling the car back on the highway.

"We'll have to do something about the back seat. Drive to Chelo's house. We'll clean up there." Luis instructed.

Fifteen minutes later, the two men pulled to the curb in front of Esperanza Esquivel's house at 115 Cota Street. It was about 2:30 on the morning of November 18.

Gus tapped lightly on the wooden screen door. Chelo, who had just come home after closing her bar for the night, answered the door and swung it open for the boys to enter.

"Oh my God, you're a mess! Look at you!" she exclaimed when they stepped into the light.

"We done the Duncan job!" Luis exclaimed. "They'll never find the witch. Her body is buried behind a pipe."

Gus, who had composed himself, added, "I had to hit her and she sure screamed."

"Why didn't you shoot her? I thought you boys had a gun!"

"Naw, Louie broke the gun when he hit the bitch. I had to hit her and Louie had to hit her," Gus explained.

"Well, it's done, then," the woman said. "You boys can get cleaned up in the kitchen. Just don't leave anything behind that'll show you been here. And clean the sink when you're done."

"We gotta do something about the seat covers. There's blood everywhere," Luis put in.

"We'll need a heavy knife to cut through that upholstery," Gus said, peeling off his bloodstained shirt.

"There's a roofer's knife on the back porch that the handyman left behind. You can use that," Chelo pointed out, walking down the hall toward her room. She paused in the hallway and looked at the boys. *Jesus, there's a lot of blood. I wonder what they did to her.* She thought about trying to find out more specifics, but then dropped the idea, figuring it was better to know nothing about the details.

"We'll find the knife."

"Good. I'm going to bed now. I have to open up at 5:30." Esperanza ducked into her room.

The men changed clothing and then went down to the car. They took the roofer's knife and some rags and began a halfhearted attempt at cleaning the car. They cut the seat covers on the right side of the seat, exposing the cotton padding underneath. They were forced to cut the back cushion also in an attempt to get rid of the evidence.

"Sarah is gonna shit when we take her car back," Gus said, running the knife through the upholstery.

"We'll tell her that we dropped a cigarette in the back and the seat caught fire."

"Are you gonna call the old lady so we can get our money?"

"Yeah, I'll call her in a couple of hours. Let's go get some sleep. We can finish this when it's light out and we can see better."

"Okay, I got the couch," Gus hurried towards the front door.

Later that same morning, Elizabeth Duncan's phone rang. She answered it, balancing a cup of coffee in one hand and the receiver in the other. She heard Luis Moya's voice simply state, "Dorothy is done."

"What?" she asked, still half asleep.

"I said the job is done."

"Oh, is that you, Louie? Well now, I'm so glad to hear from you, and it sounds like you have some good news. That's wonderful, just wonderful!"

"Yeah, it's done, but it'll cost you extra," Luis continued.

"Oh my, why is that?"

"You know why. Because we killed twice for you! We figured out who Dorothy is—I mean was. That was your grandbaby! You are one cold-hearted bitch!"

"Louie! Watch what you say on the phone. We'll have to discuss this later."

"Yeah, sure, but we want our $3,000 right now!"

"Well, that might present a difficulty."

"Difficulty hell!" Luis interrupted. "We did your dirty work and we want our money, now!"

"Just settle down, Louie. The cops have already talked to Frank and me about Olga's disappearance," she lied. "So I may have to put you off for a couple of days, even though, of course, I don't want to. We can't have some flatfoot making a connection between us, now can we?"

"No way. They've talked to you already?"

"Yes, they have."

"What did you tell them?" he asked, hoping to catch her in this lie.

"I didn't tell them anything. But we'll have to wait until things settle down."

"Well, shit! I guess if we have to, we can wait. But you better not be fuckin' with us."

"Now, Louie, you'll just have to trust me. I'll get you the money when I know it's safe." Forgetting caution in her curiosity, she continued, "Tell me, how did you do it?"

"It's just done and they won't be able to find her," Luis snapped.

"Well, you can tell me all about it when we meet. I'm anxious to hear the details. We can get together on Friday. By then maybe the heat will be off."

"Meet us at the Blue Onion on Hollister Street," Luis instructed. "And bring money! We'll be there at 11:00 A.M."

"I'll see you there," Elizabeth said, hanging up the phone.

"I don't know, Gus," Luis set down the receiver. "I think that bitch might try to rip us off."

"After what we done? Maybe we should have got the money up front."

"Yeah, maybe. Well, let's go finish the car."

They went down to the vehicle to complete the large job they had started the night before. Luis took a can of black lacquer spray paint and sprayed over the areas of metal that were still blood-spotted. Gus took the chunks of seat cover he had previously cut and rolled them up, along with a brown leather slipper that Olga had been wearing. He would later dispose of all these items by burning them. He found the broken handle from the gun and threw it into some bushes on Cota Street.

That evening, Gus returned the car to Sarah Contreras, with the explanation that the seats had been burned with a cigarette. He promised to pay her for the damage, but, of course, he never did.

Part II
THE INVESTIGATION

Where is Olga?

I said, 'Mother, do you know what happened to Olga?' And she said no, she did not. And I believe at that time she said that she felt Olga had probably gone off to scare me, to get me to come over to her place.

—Frank Duncan testimony, March 9, 1959

Adeline Curry hurried to the nurses' station and asked, "Still no word?"

"I just checked with the switchboard and they haven't heard from her," said the nurse at the station.

"Well it's almost 10:00, and this just isn't like Ollie to miss a surgery. There must be something wrong!"

"Maybe we should call her?"

"Yes, I will. Do we have her number?"

The other nurse replied, "Give me a minute and I'll get it from up front. I hope she's alright."

"I'm afraid she may have had complications or a miscarriage. She's been under so much stress lately with Frank and that crazy mother-in-law," Adeline fretted.

While Adeline talked, the other nurse dialed the switchboard. After asking for Olga's home phone number, she waited and then wrote down "Woodland 6-5923" on a slip of paper and handed it to Nurse Curry. Adeline picked up the phone and dialed the number. She let it ring for several minutes, but there was no answer.

"Now, I'm really worried!" Adeline said, her face confirming her stated concern. "I'm going over to her apartment."

"You should take someone with you."

"I'll find Irma; she's done with her surgery. Will you let the floor supervisor know where we are? Tell her . . . well, you know what to say."

"Okay, I'll advise her when I see her."

Irma King and Adeline Curry drove the short route to Olga's apartment. After they arrived, and before climbing the steps to her door, they noticed that the sliding glass door was ajar, the curtains blowing in and out on a soft breeze. Adeline walked up the stairs and stuck her head in the partially opened door. "Ollie," she called out. There was no response. She looked back at Irma, who stood just behind her, shrugged her shoulders, and called again, louder this time. "Olga, are you home? Yoo-hoo, Ollie . . . anyone there?"

"I don't think she's home," came a response from the bottom of the steps.

Adeline jumped at the sound of the unexpected voice. "Oh, you surprised me!" Her hand moved over her heart.

"I'm sorry. I'm Mrs. Barnett, the landlady. I live right below Ollie. I went outside this morning around 7:30 to get the paper and noticed that her door was open. I thought she might have been called in early to work and she forgot to close it."

"No, she hasn't been to work," Irma answered. "Maybe we should have a peek inside?" Irma looked around Adeline, trying to see into the apartment. "What do you think?"

"I think we'd better. She might be sick or injured, and in her condition . . . " The landlady was already hurrying up the steps.

Adeline pushed the glass door, which slid silently on its aluminum track. She stepped quickly into the living room and noticed that the light was on. Since the room was empty, she called out again while the other two women joined her. There was no response to her calls.

Adeline looked back at the others and shrugged her shoulders. She looked at the closed bedroom door and took a deep breath. She was afraid of what she may find behind the door, yet knew that she had to open it. *Well, here goes,* she thought. She involuntarily clinched her right fist and walked to the door. She pushed it open slowly and peered into the room. It, too, had a light on, but was not occupied. Adeline sighed in relief, thankful that she had not found something she didn't want to deal with, but now doubly concerned about the whereabouts of her friend.

Adeline walked back to the other two women after checking the bathroom. "Well, there's nobody here. And the covers are turned back as if she was getting ready to go to bed, but she never slept in it. There's a hot water bottle on the bed and her slippers are next to it. And to top it all off, her purse is on the dresser."

"This is really odd," Irma observed, scratching her head while she looked around.

"I think we should call the police," Mrs. Barnett suggested. "I don't like the looks of this."

"What if she's with Frank and just got confused about her schedule?" Irma pointed out, still scanning the room as if she expected Olga to step out of a closet.

"I doubt that. Ollie is so conscientious," Adeline answered. "Let's call Frank. He works for Mr. Goux in the Howard Canfield Building. Mrs. Barnett, do you have a phone book?"

"Yes, come downstairs and I'll find the number."

The three women left the apartment, being careful not to disturb anything. They went into Mrs. Barnett's apartment and checked the phone directory. The landlady dialed Frank's office number. She was unable to reach the attorney, who coincidentally was in court on the Esquivel case. Mrs. Barnett told Frank's secretary that this was an emergency and she needed to get in touch with him as soon as she could.

At 12:15, the court bailiff approached Frank and relayed the message from his secretary. Frank dialed the landlady's number and

Mrs. Barnett told him that Olga was missing and requested that he come to the apartment immediately. Frank put down the phone and advised the judge that he had an emergency at home and had to leave. The judge, noting it was past lunchtime anyway, granted the recess. Frank went directly to Olga's apartment, arriving fifteen minutes after the phone call.

By the time Frank reached the apartment, two other nurses had shown up out of concern for their missing friend. They were Diane Corriani and Sylvia Butler, who had been with Olga until 11:00 the evening before. The nurses stood around in a clump, talking in hushed tones about the problems that Olga had been experiencing in the last few months.

When they saw Frank walking up the sidewalk, they fell silent, all of them fixing him with their eyes. Frank met them on the walkway, greeted them briefly, and hurried up the steps. Mrs. Barnett looked sideways at the man when he walked by, and then quickly fell in behind him. She had had one bad experience with this man's mother and she didn't want any more problems. Besides, she had never trusted Frank, based on the stories her tenant had told her. She watched him enter the apartment and scan the interior. He quickly walked to a closet, looking inside to see if Olga's traveling bags were still there. Frank did not disturb anything, but hurried out of the apartment, scratching his head while he stood on the balcony. "Well, I guess we should call the police," he said to no one in particular. "I haven't talked to Ollie for some time, but this does seem strange, with her purse here and all."

Frank looked at Mrs. Barnett, who was standing next to him on the landing. He had turned to walk back into the apartment to use the phone when the alert landlady said, "Let's use my phone downstairs. We don't want to disturb anything inside."

The attorney gave her a puzzled look and then began slowly walking down the steps. While he walked, he talked over his shoulder. "Olga's been mad at me. I hope she isn't doing something to get at me . . . you know, to damage my career."

"What?" the surprised woman said to him.

"We haven't talked for some time. I know she's upset with me."

"I don't think Ollie is the type to do all this for the attention."

"Well, I'll call the police, but I hope she's not starting something that'll be hard to get stopped."

Mrs. Barnett just shook her head while she followed the man down the steps. When they walked past the cluster of women, she raised her eyes in an expression of dissatisfaction with Frank's words.

Ten minutes later, Officer Thuren Coony from the Santa Barbara Police Department arrived. He took a look around noting the circumstances and listened to the stories of the two nurses, Diane and Sylvia, who had spent part of the previous evening with Olga. They told him that Olga had said nothing to them about taking a trip of any kind. When he suggested the possibility that Olga might have been contemplating harming herself, they quickly dismissed that, assuring the officer that she had been in an upbeat mood, discussing the upcoming birth of her child and showing them some knitting she had been doing for the baby. Both nurses reinforced that Ollie would never do anything to harm herself or the baby.

After hearing the statements of the nurses, Officer Coony asked to use Mrs. Barnett's telephone. He called the watch commander and advised him that he had a missing person with suspicious circumstances. He requested that detectives respond to do a preliminary investigation into the case. The watch commander told him that he would send a detective from Missing Persons.

A short time later, Detective Brerton arrived at the scene. She, too, talked to the collected witnesses and then initiated Santa Barbara Police Department report number 259404. This report described the circumstances surrounding the disappearance of Olga Duncan. The detective, seeing the many worried faces, reassured the group that in ninety-nine percent of these cases the missing person shows up in good health with a perfectly plausible explanation for their whereabouts. Before leaving, she asked Mrs. Barnett to secure

Olga's apartment and to keep an eye on it until further investigation could be done.

Mrs. Barnett walked up the steps to Olga's apartment to lock the door. When she was away from the others, she called to Detective Brerton, pretending to have a problem with the door. The detective walked up the steps and joined the landlady.

Mrs. Barnett lowered her voice. "You should know that Olga has been having some problems. If she doesn't return, I should make a full statement."

"What sort of problems?"

"I don't want to go into it now, but just keep what I've said in mind if she doesn't come home soon."

"Okay, I'll do that."

Two days passed without any word from the missing woman. The police began to think in terms more serious than a disgruntled missing spouse. They initiated those investigative steps common to all missing persons cases. They generated all points bulletins, distributing them throughout the United States, and sent letters to the chiefs of police in both Vancouver and Benito, Canada, where Olga's parents were currently residing. They also contacted the missing woman's parents, hoping that she had taken an unannounced trip to visit them.

When their initial steps proved fruitless, the detectives began to gear up for a major investigation. They concentrated on learning about the life of Olga Duncan.

Through conversations with her family, the investigators found out that Olga was born on March 19, 1928, to Elias and Eustana Kupczyk in the small town of Turnberry, Manitoba, Canada. She was the middle child of three offspring born into the family of a Ukrainian father and a Ukrainian/Canadian mother.

Olga's father, Elias, who was commonly referred to as Alex, was from the old country. Although he spoke fluent English, he often spoke in the language of his native country. In his capacity as a section foreman for the Canadian National Railroad, Alex had moved his family frequently throughout the provinces of Manitoba and Saskatchewan. There was one common aspect to all these moves: the Kupczyks always landed in a small town.

Olga and her mother, whom everyone knew as Jessie, were especially close.

Jessie gave loving encouragement to her daughter, who began to show artistic talent at a young age. When she grew older, the girl would sit by the hour and play classical music on a piano purchased by her father at considerable financial sacrifice. Her other artistic endeavors included acting and sketching with pad and pencil.

As a young girl, Olga especially enjoyed days in the country with her grandparents, even though these trips required long hours spent traveling on less than ideal roads.

While living in Verigan, Saskatchewan, Olga graduated from Verigan High School in May of 1947. She was one of seven graduates and was remembered by all as a well-mannered and well-liked classmate.

After graduation from high school, Olga attended a technical secretarial school in Regina, Saskatchewan. Upon completion of this course, she returned to Manitoba, where she found employment as a medical transcriber in the town of Dauphin, at the local hospital. It was while working in the hospital environment that she began to form an interest in the profession of nursing.

Her interest was further stimulated when she moved to Vancouver to live in a milder climate. She went to work as a secretary at Vancouver General Hospital, where she made the decision to fulfill her career dream. Although financial considerations caused her some delay, Olga was finally able to enroll in the basic nurse's training at Vancouver General. As the local newspaper stated, "Olga traded her typewriter to become a nurse."

She completed the three-year course and immediately entered into her new occupation. Judging from the comments of her friends and co-workers, Olga had found her niche in life. She was an excellent nurse, admired for her gentle demeanor and for the good care she provided.

Like many other nurses of that era, Olga learned of a nursing shortage in the United States. The lure of a large job market, with its corresponding higher wages, attracted her to nursing in America.

Olga had the added advantage of two very good friends who were living in the Los Angeles area. Steven and Dorothy Woytko, also of Ukrainian descent, had moved from Canada some years previous. The Kupczyk children viewed Dorothy, who had lived with the Kupczyk family at various times during Olga's school years, as a second mother. Olga was thrilled at the possibility of being closer to her surrogate mother.

Santa Barbara detectives found that Olga had entered the United States through Blaine, Washington, with an alien work permit on October 24, 1957.

After visiting her friends in the Los Angeles area, Olga, who was attracted to small-town life, decided to move to a more rural setting. Santa Barbara seemed to offer the best of all worlds. It was large enough to afford ample employment and close enough to Los Angeles to allow her to visit her friends, yet it still had many small-town qualities.

The fully qualified and personally appealing young woman had no trouble finding employment at Santa Barbara's Cottage Hospital starting in the intensive care unit and making $310 a month. This represented a considerable raise from her salary in Canada and was more than sufficient for a single person to live on.

When Olga did not return, the police, in an effort to further their investigation, began to get statements from friends and relatives. They soon learned that the comments had one thread in common: Olga, who seemed a person who shouldn't have an enemy in the world, had a very bitter adversary.

Typewriter Money

She wasn't a beauty, but beauty exuded from her. She was such a nice girl—never yelled. If she couldn't say anything nice about someone, she said nothing at all.
    —Dorothy Woytko, remembering Olga thirty years later

While the police dug in for what appeared to be an extended investigation, Luis and Gus had their own problems. The woman who had convinced them to commit murder on the installment plan was stonewalling them.

In an effort to collect some money, just three days after Olga's disappearance, Luis, Gus, and Esperanza cruised down State Street in Esperanza's car, en route to the Blue Onion Cafe to keep a meeting with their now reluctant "employer." Luis, who had not spoken to Mrs. Duncan since the morning of the murder, was already anticipating problems in convincing the woman to pay up.

"Chelo, she should have money for you, and if she won't give it to you—well—don't take no for an answer."

"What should I tell her—I mean if she don't have it?"

"I'll talk to her personally, sort of jack her up if I have to, but I gotta do it in private. The whole idea of you dealin' with her is to keep me and Gus outta sight in case the cops are around."

They pulled up to the restaurant, dropped the woman off to do their negotiating, and drove off, telling Esperanza that they would circle the block until she came out.

In ten minutes, Esperanza emerged and got into the car. It was obvious from the look on her face that she had not been successful in her efforts.

She relayed a message to the pair that Elizabeth thought the cops were watching her, so she was unable to take any money out of the bank. However, if they would meet her in Woolworth's, she had a check for $200 that she would give them.

This announcement upset Luis, who began to curse and pound his hands on the steering wheel until Esperanza reminded him that it was her car and she didn't want it damaged.

After Luis calmed down, they drove to the Woolworth's store, with Luis explaining in no uncertain terms the plans he had for that woman if she tried to cheat them. While Esperanza waited in the car, Luis and Gus walked into the large department store and met Mrs. Duncan and Emma Short in the record section. Luis was in a foul mood, planning a verbal attack on the woman. He was totally disarmed when the matronly looking woman asked her first question.

"Did the bitch scream when you did it?" She looked intently in Luis's eyes, searching for her answer there. She then cast her head around to be sure they were alone.

"Don't worry about it; she won't bother you anymore," Luis replied, his temper subsiding. "Now, I need my money. I got to go back to Texas to see my folks." He too was looking around with a watchful eye, having caught the woman's uneasiness.

"Hurry up," Gus whispered, thinking there was a good possibility that the cops *were* tailing her.

"I have a check for two hundred dollars that Frank gave me so I could pick up his typewriter. I can sign it over to you."

"Only two bills? You got to be kidding! Besides, we can't take no check; that's a connection the cops would love. Go cash the check and meet us back here," Luis instructed. "We'll take the two hundred for now, but we ain't waiting forever!" he continued, his voice rising until he remembered where he was.

"Okay, I'll meet you across from the bank, in Silverwood's," Elizabeth told him.

Then, in an effort to appease Luis, she added, "I've sent away to San Francisco to get some stocks cashed in. Once they arrive, then I can pay you boys the balance." She winked at Gus. "Please be patient."

Gus winked back at the woman in spite of himself. He later wondered why he had done that.

Ten minutes later, inside the front door of Silverwood's, Elizabeth handed Luis a blue envelope. Luis looked down at the envelope and saw the word "Dorothy" written on it. He blanched upon seeing the name, but before he could say anything the woman had vanished. Luis tore open the envelope and found $150 in cash.

"Shit, Gus, she didn't even give us the full $200," Luis said, handing Gus some money and stuffing the rest in his jeans pocket.

"That bitch is some work of art! Let's go score us some weed," Luis grunted, looking down the sidewalk in an effort to see which way the elusive woman had gone. She was nowhere to be seen.

That evening, after eating dinner in his mother's apartment, Frank asked Elizabeth for a receipt for the check he had given her to get his typewriter repaired. Her response was, "I don't have one and I've got a big problem."

"What kind of problem?"

"I don't know if I can tell you, Frankie. I'm embarrassed about this. But I should tell you, because it involves you also."

"Is this something about Ollie?"

"Why, no. Why do you say that?"

"What, then? Have you spent the money?"

"Sort of."

"Just tell me, Mother, please! Quit playing games!"

"I'm being blackmailed."

"What?" was the incredulous response. "Did you say blackmailed?"

"Yes. I gave the $200 to a Mexican who's blackmailing me."

"I knew it! This does have something to do with Ollie. Now tell me the truth. You're involved, you're guilty! I know you are!" Frank waved his finger at his mother. "What have you done to my wife?" In his agitation, he began to pace up and down in the small living room.

Elizabeth tried to soothe him, lowering her voice and choosing her words carefully.

"This has nothing to do with Ollie. You have to believe me, Frankie dear. It's about the Esquivel case. You know Mr. Esquivel from the Tropical Cafe. The guns that were stolen from the sporting goods store."

"Go on," Frank said, turning on his heel and looking intently at his mother, trying to determine if she was telling the truth.

"Well," she continued, "they wanted their money back because Marciano—that's his name, isn't it?"

"Yes."

"Well, isn't he going to state prison? So they thought you didn't do a good job of defending him."

"Esperanza told you this?" Frank asked in confusion. "Why, I just talked to her. She said nothing about being dissatisfied. Hell, I got the case against her dismissed."

"Of course she didn't say anything to you. Oh, she's a clever bitch, that one." Elizabeth's voice rose shrilly.

"I see." Frank began to back off, walking to the couch and throwing himself down. "Is there more to this story?"

"No."

"Well, there's only one thing to do. I'll call Sergeant Crawford at the police station. He'll know how to handle this. Blackmail is serious business. It's a felony."

His mother sat down next to him on the couch. "Let's think about this, Frankie. Maybe it would be best to just forget it, chalk up the $200, especially with all this Ollie stuff."

"There's no connection, right Mom?" Frank looked directly into her eyes.

Elizabeth reached over and took her son's hand. She fixed him with a poignant look. "Of course not. I'm sure Ollie will show up soon." She looked down, evading his somber stare.

Frank freed his hand from her grasp and jumped up, "Then I'm going to the police. I'm not letting anyone rip me off! Not when I can do something about it! I'll call Sergeant Crawford." Frank walked to the phone and picked up the receiver, then thought better of it. "Maybe I should just go down to that bar and go toe to toe with those people, have this out right now!"

"That's a pretty rough place, Frankie. And those people—they all have friends with knives."

"Yeah, that's true. Hell, I'm always defending them when they cut each other up. I'll swing by the station and talk to Crawford."

Frank grabbed his coat and headed towards the door. He jerked it open and paused, looking over his shoulder. "Mom, you're sure, right?"

"Yes," came the exasperated reply. "I'm telling you . . . "

Sergeant George Crawford sat at his gray metal desk at the back of the detective's bay. His mind wasn't really on the caseload that sat squarely in front of him. He'd already cleared six felony cases, two of them with arrests, so he was sure the lieutenant wouldn't be on his butt, at least for this month. Besides, thoughts of his upcoming vacation were distracting him from the never-ending paper trail of crime that moved across his desk. He was shaken out of his daze by a shout from one of the other detectives. "Hey, George! There's a guy out here says he needs to talk to you."

"Shit," he muttered to himself, then shouted back, "I'm not expecting anyone! Who is it?"

"It's that funny little attorney fella. You know the one. I think his name is Duncan."

"Oh, God," George groaned. He rolled his eyes at the other detectives, who were intrigued at the idea of an attorney, especially a defense attorney, coming to the police station to visit a detective. It was not a common event.

"He probably wants you to be an expert witness, George. Help him get one of his crooks off on a sheriff's office case," a helpful co-worker pointed out.

That brought chuckles and guffaws, while others jumped in to add their interpretations of the meaning of this visit.

"Naw. I did him a favor one time in court, so now he thinks I'm his personal cop."

"What sort of favor?" was shouted across the room.

"It's a long story," George said, pushing himself away from his desk and chuckling to himself. He walked towards the reception area.

"Hell," he said as he left the others, "he's probably here to confess to lying in court. He's an odd duck, y'know."

George made his way to the reception area and, upon spotting the attorney, greeted him with a handshake. The moist palm that George grasped betrayed the other man's nervousness.

Sergeant Crawford had heard that this man's wife had recently left him or had been reported missing. The talk around the station house was that she had probably headed back to Canada after being married to this weasel. George assumed this visit had something to do with her disappearance.

"What can I do for you, Mr. Duncan?" the detective asked.

"Can I speak to you in private?"

"Certainly. Let's go into the lieutenant's office. He's not in today."

Crawford directed his visitor to the office and closed the door behind them. Frank took a seat in a big easy chair and the detective sat on the corner of the large desk.

"Is this about your missing wife?" George asked, studying the owl-eyed lawyer.

"No, actually it isn't. It's an unrelated matter, or so I think. I have a problem with my mother." There was a slight quaver in Frank's voice.

"What's the nature of the problem?"

"Well, she says she's being blackmailed. And she's unable to account for some money I gave her recently. She says it's one of my clients."

"Really now. Why would one of your clients be blackmailing your mother?" George began to hear warning bells going off. What little he knew didn't sound right. He leaned forward to hear the answer to his question.

"She says it's because I didn't put on a proper defense for them."

"Hmmm." George's hand went to his chin and he began to scratch his five o'clock shadow. "Who's them?"

"It's the Esquivels."

"From the Tropical Cafe? Those Esquivels?"

"Yes."

"If it's true, I can't say that I'm surprised. I've worked a couple of cases on those folks during this last year. They're bad news. How much did she give them?"

"Two hundred dollars."

"Well, we'll have to get your mother in here to make a statement before we can proceed with this. When can you bring her in?"

"To tell you the truth, I'm not sure she'll be willing to report this. I'll have to discuss this with her further. Can I call you tomorrow?"

George was surprised by this answer. He always wondered about people who were victims of crime but didn't really want to cooperate with police efforts to help them. It usually meant there was more to the story. He stood up.

"All right then. You call me tomorrow and let me know what she decides. Oh, by the way, what's going on with your wife's case? Has she returned?"

"I haven't heard a thing from her. But it's only been a few days and, quite frankly, I think she might have gone somewhere to be by herself. We haven't been getting along that well lately."

"Y'know how women can be." The detective smiled sympathetically, trying to lighten the moment. "Bring your mother by tomorrow and we'll get working on her case."

Frank rose to leave.

They shook hands and the attorney walked toward the exit. George shoved his hands into his pockets and watched him walk away. *This guy makes an unlikely lawyer. He's just not too connected to the real world,* George thought. He shook his head in wonder and strode back into the detective bay in a more subdued mood. He had a gnawing in the back of his mind, like something didn't read right in the conversation he'd just had. But he knew that Frank Duncan and his mother had a unique reputation in the community, bordering on the bizarre, so he guessed that might be why he was troubled.

George looked across the bay and spotted Charlie Thompson. "Hey, Charlie. Whose got the Duncan-woman case?"

"The lost nurse caper? It's in Missing Persons. I think Brerton's working on it."

Well, hell, George thought to himself, *why am I getting all worked up about this? I have a week's vacation coming up and this lady'll be back before I get home from camping.*

Detective Crawford went back to his desk and sat down. But, before he resumed his vacation daydreaming, he made a mental note to talk to Brerton about the conversation he'd had with Duncan, just to be on the safe side.

The Final Payment

For the love of money is the root of all evil . . .

—I Timothy 6:10

Elizabeth Duncan was obviously uncomfortable in her sur-
roundings. She twisted around, looked at Frank, then returned her
gaze to the officer in the blue uniform. She was upset with herself
for allowing Frank to talk her into reporting the blackmail story to
the police. She could only hope this wouldn't come back to haunt
her later. At least it should get Moya off her back. He was becoming
downright nasty in his efforts to get more money. One thing she was
sure of: police stations were not her favorite place to be.

Sergeant Crawford walked into the interview room and pulled
up a chair next to the patrol officer who was pecking away at the
typewriter.

"You 'bout done?" he asked the officer who was hunched over
the machine.

"Yeah, Sarge. I think we got the high points."

Crawford pulled a pad out of his top pocket and looked over the
shoulder of the officer. He wrote down case number 260142 at the
top of the pad. He noted the date and time reported box indicated
November 22, 1958, at 5:30 P.M. The officer pulled the report from
the typewriter carriage and slid it to Crawford who looked it over
and signed it at the bottom.

"Looks okay, Bud. Thanks for taking the report. You can go. You
probably got calls pending."

"Yep, see ya, Sarge." The officer rose from his chair, nodded at the Duncans, made his way past the Sergeant, and eased himself out the door.

Sergeant Crawford looked more closely at the report, noting the vague descriptions of two male Mexican subjects listed in the suspect column. After reading the descriptions, he decided they fit about eighty percent of the male Hispanic population in Santa Barbara. He continued scanning the report and saw that Esperanza Esquivel's name was included on the report as a possible suspect in the crime of extortion. He briefly went over the narrative, formulating some questions in his mind while he read.

When he had finished his perusal, Crawford looked up at Frank and his mother.

"Mrs. Duncan, it says here that you gave these two fellas $200 yesterday. Is that correct?"

"Yes, it is."

"And this occurred in front of Silverwood's?"

"Inside the store."

"Oh, I see, you were actually in the store. Did anyone see this exchange?"

"Yes, my friend, Emma Short. She was with me."

The detective looked down at the report, seeing that Emma was listed as a witness.

"Oh, yes I see here. Do you know if anyone else saw you? Like a store clerk, someone of that nature?"

"I just don't know. We were there only a moment. And I was so frightened—I just wanted to get out of there before they hurt me." Elizabeth reached over and slid her hand under Frank's arm, grasping his forearm. He patted the top of her hand to comfort her.

"Naturally, that's certainly understandable," Crawford said. "Now, if I've got this right, and please correct me if I'm wrong, this is all about a case your son defended Mrs. Esquivel on?"

"Yes, that's correct. That's why they're blackmailing me—I mean, really us." Elizabeth nodded towards her son, squeezing his forearm while she spoke. "Mr. Esquivel is going to state prison instead of being deported back to Mexico. They had some guns that were taken in a burglary. So the Esquivel woman said I must return the $500 they paid Frank to defend him or the two boys will hurt my son."

"Then this really relates to Mr. Esquivel's case and not Chelo," the slightly confused detective queried.

"Like I told you before, Sergeant, I got the charges against Esperanza dismissed," Frank reminded Crawford.

"Oh, yes. You did mention that yesterday." The detective looked down at the report again, trying to determine if the patrol officer had caught the differences that were just explained to him.

"This is all because Frank was not able to get Marciano deported," Elizabeth reiterated, her voice rising with frustration at the detective's inability to quickly comprehend what she felt was a simple set of circumstances.

"Now I think I understand." Sergeant Crawford looked into the magnified eyes of the bespectacled woman. *There is something missing here,* the detective thought to himself while he studied the woman's eyes.

"'What're the chances of catching these guys?" Frank broke the momentary silence.

"With the Esquivel connection, I would say real good. That's where I'll start, with her."

Elizabeth removed her hand from her son's arm and sat forward in her seat, straining to look at the report. "Does it say that she works at the Tropical Cafe?"

"No, but I know where to find her."

"Good!" the woman sat back and crossed her arms. "I bet you've had lots of problems with that one!"

"I'll put together some mug shots of the locals who hang out at the Tropical and get them to you. Hopefully, you can pick these characters out of the mugs. I'd also like to install a tape recorder on your telephone so we can record a conversation. You indicated in the report that they've been calling you frequently."

"Yes.

"That sounds like a good idea," Frank put in. His mother shot Frank a "mind your own business" look, which was not missed by Sergeant Crawford

"Perhaps we can mark some money for the next payment," Frank continued.

"That might be a possibility, but we don't have funds for that, so you'd have to front the money. I can show you how it's done."

"That shouldn't be too much of a problem," Frank said, looking at his mother for some type of agreement. She now sat mute, her arms folded over her chest.

"Well, I think I have all I need to get started." The detective rose.

Frank and Elizabeth also stood up. The two men shook hands, but Elizabeth did not offer hers. The officer walked to the station door to show the Duncans out.

"I'll give you a call when I get those mug shots together," Crawford said at the door.

"Thank you." Frank waved while he and his mother descended the steps in front of the police station.

Crawford walked back into the detective bay with the report in his hand. He looked down at his watch, noted the time, and threw the report on his desk. *One more day 'til vacation,* he thought to himself as he pulled on his coat and headed for the door.

The next morning, Sergeant Crawford was surprised to see his boss, Lieutenant Leonard Peck sitting on the corner of his desk when he arrived at work. "What's up, Lieutenant?" he inquired.

"Let's go in my office."

"Okay, let me grab a quick cup." George made his way to the coffeepot and poured a cup of the black stuff into his mug. He took a quick sip, so he wouldn't spill, then hurried to the lieutenant's office. Lieutenant Peck was sitting behind his desk and motioned for George to take a seat in an easy chair.

"George," Peck said, "I'm moving the Duncan case out of Missing Persons and giving it to you."

"Say what?" the surprised detective responded. "But boss, I've got the Sanchez homicide, a search warrant to do on that attempted murder on Bath Street, and—most of all—a vacation starting tomorrow!"

"I know, but that other stuff may have to go on the back burner."

"Even the vacation?"

"Well, probably not. We can have Bouma carry the ball until you return. How long you gonna be gone?"

"One week, incommunicado!"

"We can survive a week without you. Anyway, this missing nurse is starting to create a stir in the community. The press has picked it up and Chief Cooley has been getting calls. There's talk the FBI may be entering the case because the woman's a foreign national. Besides, it has all the signs of a murder, from what Brerton tells me. So, I told the chief I'd move it to Homicide and give it to our best man, and you're elected." The lieutenant grinned at his ace investigator.

"Thanks for the compliment . . . I think." George took a sip of his coffee, considering this new addition to his growing caseload. He finally piped up, "FBI, huh? We haven't had a big enough case for those boys in awhile."

"Yeah, lucky us. Check with Brerton on her progress. She's already interviewed some of the neighbors, friends, and family. I think her husband."

"You know I took an extortion report involving the Duncans yesterday."

"Really, I didn't know! I'd say that's real interesting. Where is the report?"

"It's still on my desk. The Duncans came in late yesterday afternoon. Mrs. Duncan claims she's being blackmailed by a disgruntled client of her son's. The whole thing stinks! Maybe it's just a coincidence, all this stuff happening to this family, but somehow I doubt it."

"Yeah, maybe. I haven't had a chance to talk to Brerton lately, but apparently this nurse had a problem with her mother-in-law. That's the lady you talked to yesterday, right? Want to bet there's some connection between the two reports?"

"No takers here. The old lady hardly looks the murdering sort, kind of a grandmother type, but you never know these days. She gave me a real uneasy feeling yesterday when I was talking to her. Just cop's intuition, I suppose. It'll be a place to start after I get back."

The lieutenant's phone began to ring, so George took that opportunity to step out of the office and return to his desk. He had hoped to tie up a few loose ends on the Sanchez case before he left, but he could see that this one was going to be a priority. He picked up the report he had left on his desk the night before, separated the carbon copies, and placed the original in his out basket for the records clerk to file. He reached into his desk, pulled out a manila folder, and wrote "Duncan" in bold black ink on the tab. He placed a carbon copy of the extortion report in the folder before getting up to go talk to Detective Brerton in Missing Persons. On his way to her office, he swung by the coffeepot and poured another cup, then stopped by the lieutenant's office and laid a copy of the report on his desk.

Luis Moya picked up the telephone and dialed a phone number that he had committed to memory. He felt totally frustrated after having made numerous calls in the past several hours to the Duncan woman, trying to set up another meeting. When he was finally able to reach her, she put him off with her "the police are watching me" line and refused to meet with him. Luis had had to become openly threatening in his efforts to collect.

On November 24, Frank stopped by the police department and picked up a group of mug shots. Among the many pictures were likenesses of both of the murderers. The officers had included them, as Luis would later proudly speculate in court, because "everything that went on in Santa Barbara we had something to do with."

While George Crawford was vacationing, his partner, Sergeant Tom Bouma, and another detective, Charles Thompson, took over his caseload. Thompson, who was a young hard charger, known for his brash approach to life, had just returned from a disciplinary "vacation" of two weeks. He'd gotten into a shouting match with his lieutenant and made the critical error of cursing at him. This act, commonly referred to as insubordination in police rules and regulations, was the reason for the unscheduled days off.

The two detectives paid a visit to Mrs. Duncan's apartment where they installed a tape recording device on the woman's telephone in hopes of improving their case against the so far unidentified blackmailers. It was while they were at the apartment that they met Emma Short, who was very curious about the workings of the recording device. Thompson, in particular, seemed to hit it off with the elderly woman, showing a rare degree of patience in explaining how the device worked. The conversation, he would later realize, was closely monitored by a concerned Elizabeth, who hovered over his shoulder while he talked to Emma. Of course, Elizabeth could not have cared less about the phone hook-up, but she was very concerned about Emma talking to the cops—any cops!

Unfortunately, try as she might, Mrs. Duncan was never successful in recording the many phone calls she received from the blackmailers. The district attorney, who was unable to understand what was so difficult about pushing one button to turn on a tape recorder at the proper moment, later brought up this issue in court. When Roy Gustafson provided a phone and the same tape recorder in court so Elizabeth could demonstrate the problems she'd had in operating the machine, the obstinate witness refused to cooperate, stating that the phone was different from the one she had at home.

The district attorney didn't press the issue, guessing that her refusal had made its point with the jury.

On November 25, Luis was finally able to convince Elizabeth to meet Esperanza at Jordano's Food Store, which was within walking distance of Mrs. Duncan's apartment.

While Luis waited outside, Esperanza went into the store to meet the woman in yet another attempt to collect the money. However, instead of bringing cash, Elizabeth brought the two mug shots of the killers that had come to her by way of the police department. She showed them to Esperanza and then told the surprised woman that the police had contacted her about the two men and had said that they were responsible for numerous crimes in the Santa Barbara area. After realizing that she was not getting anywhere, a confused Esperanza left and told Luis about the strange encounter she'd had with Mrs. Duncan. Luis put it down as an attempt to scare him into discontinuing his efforts to collect the payment. He felt confident that Elizabeth had not talked to the police, for in doing so she would have implicated herself.

After this meeting, Elizabeth told her son that she thought she recognized the pictures of Luis and Gus as the blackmailers. He later relayed this information to Sergeant Crawford, who felt this was a solid lead in the extortion case.

Three days after the meeting at Jordano's, Luis received the last payment the killers would get for doing "the Duncan job." Elizabeth had agreed to put what money she had into an envelope and leave it at the Blue Onion for later pickup by Luis. Emma Short delivered the envelope, which was marked "Dorothy" on the outside. At about 5:30 that afternoon, Luis went to the restaurant and asked the manager, Frank Haywood, if anything had been left for his Aunt Dorothy. Frank, who was busy counting the day's receipts, had his assistant manager give Luis the envelope. Mr. Haywood was later able, in court, to clearly recall this occurrence, because he rehired Luis that day, tentatively to start work the next week.

Luis walked away from the cash register and expectantly tore open the envelope, but to his dismay found only one crisp ten dollar bill inside. He looked hard at the bill, as if he believed it might be counterfeit, snapped it quickly between his fingers, and then wadded it into a tight ball. In his anger, he thought briefly of tossing the money into a nearby trash can, but decided not to when he recalled what he had done to earn this paltry sum. He stormed out of the store, vowing to crank up the heat on the old bitch.

Narrowing the Field

I asked her (Olga) why Frank didn't have his mother committed to an institution. She said he refused to consider this because it would ruin his law practice.

—Statement of Adeline Curry,
as reported in the *Santa Barbara News Press,* December 17, 1958

Lieutenant Peck reached to the top of the blackboard and wrote the name DUNCAN in bright yellow chalk. He pressed hard, causing a fine yellow dust to slide down the board, powdering the black surface as it drifted to the floor.

The lieutenant looked at the faces of the detectives who sat around the conference table. In front of the officers were a wide variety of files and papers in general disarray on the table. Paperclipped to each officer's file was a picture of Olga Duncan. Dressed in a white nurse's uniform, she smiled up at the assembled officers from numerous locations.

Lieutenant Peck kicked off the meeting. "Okay, folks, what've we got?"

No one spoke and only the rustling sounds of paper broke the silence. None of the officers wanted to be the first to dive in.

At that moment, the door burst open and Detective Charles Thompson hustled into the room.

"Sorry I'm late, boss, but it was worth it!" the investigator waved a piece of paper he carried in his hand.

"Glad you could make it, Charlie," the lieutenant said dryly. "What ya got there?"

The detective took a seat, holding the paper in front of him. He referred to it briefly, puffed himself up, and then made an announcement. "I have found out that our mother-in-law, who's everyone's idea of the perfect mother, right?" he glanced around the room, waiting for a response. Getting none, he continued, "She's not so unblemished. The old lady has a rap sheet!"

"No way," exclaimed one of the detectives.

"Yep, hot off the wire. Busted twice in San Diego for bogus checks back in '32, and once here for what looks like a city ordinance violation, in 1933. Anyone know what section 2.722 was?"

"Are you kidding? That was twenty-five years ago."

"Anyway, no other criminal charges. She was an applicant twice, one in '47 with the State Board of Equalization and again in '53 with San Francisco P.D."

"Well, that's interesting," Sergeant Bouma said, "but that hardly makes her a murderess—two arrests for bad checks and a city ordinance violation."

"Yeah, but it is a start," Thompson pointed out. "I'll do some more checking, see if I can find out what the city code arrest is. I'll also give Frisco a call and check on the application."

"Okay, that's good, Thompson. Brerton, you got anything?" Lieutenant Peck asked, taking control of the meeting.

"Yes, Lieutenant. I interviewed Mrs. Barnett, Olga's landlady. She said that Olga told her many times that she'd been having problems with her mother-in-law. According to Barnett, this woman came to Olga's apartment one day and conned her way inside. The landlady said that she heard the woman threaten to kill Olga. I guess Duncan was talking to herself when this occurred and Barnett was standing next to her. I also talked to a bunch of the nursing staff at both St. Francis and Cottage Hospitals. There's plenty of evidence that the victim was receiving threatening phone calls from an older woman, probably her mother-in-law. It was common knowledge around St. Francis."

Lieutenant Peck picked up the chalk and wrote the word SUSPECT at the top left-hand margin of the blackboard. Under that word he began to write MOTHER-IN-LAW, then erased it. "What's her full name, anyway?"

"It's Elizabeth Ann, but many of her friends call her Betty," Sergeant Bouma informed him.

"I also have some information about an annulment that I haven't been able to run down yet," Brerton added while Peck wrote ELIZABETH/BETTY in the suspect column.

"What's the story on that?" Detective Thompson asked.

"It seems that Elizabeth may have gotten her son's marriage annulled. That's according to Mrs. Barnett," the detective further informed the group, scanning her notes while she spoke. "But this seems so far-fetched and I haven't been able to find any record of it in this county. Barnett is vague about the details and it appears to be just a rumor so far."

Lieutenant Peck wrote MISCELLANEOUS in the middle of the board and then wrote ANNULMENT under the heading. He drew a line from ANNULMENT to ELIZABETH/BETTY. "That's certainly a new twist, getting your son's marriage annulled, if it happened. Anything else?"

"No."

"Well, what about Frank Duncan? What's his part in this?" the lieutenant threw out to the group.

"I talked to Crawford about Frank before he left for vacation," Sergeant Bouma said. "George doesn't think he's involved, doesn't see him as the killer type. But he hasn't been interviewed in depth, so he should probably make the suspect list. We also ran him out of Olga's apartment a couple of days after the disappearance. He said he was in there cleaning up. I guess we should have changed the lock on the door. He recently made a press release, claiming that one of Olga's traveling bags was gone. But I don't know if that's true or not."

"Is there anyway we can confirm that?" Peck asked.

"We're trying to contact Olga's friends in Los Angeles to determine if they know what type of luggage she had."

"Good." Peck wrote FRANK DUNCAN?? in the SUSPECT column. He then went to the right-hand top edge of the board, wrote TO DO, and underlined the words. Under TO DO he wrote INTERVIEW FRANK.

Now the lieutenant directed a question to Bouma. "While we're talking about the apartment, have we done any lab work in there?"

"Not as yet. The apartment is sealed now, so there's no rush. I can have the lab boys go out ASAP. But there isn't much of a crime scene. Nothing looks out of the ordinary."

Peck wrote LAB under the TO DO column and then said, "Let's get them out there to throw some dust around and take a few pictures. We may get lucky."

Bouma continued along another vein. "I've been in contact with the missing girl's family. They're sending me some letters that Olga wrote in which she said that Elizabeth had threatened her, came to her apartment and banged on her door, that kind of thing. They should be here any time."

Peck underlined the words ELIZABETH/BETTY. "It's certainly getting stronger all of the time. Were there any other men in Olga's life?"

"I was working on a lead with one of her coworkers. The guy's a lab tech by the name of Bradley. But he looks squeaky clean, no record, that sort. Apparently he gave her rides to work on occasion, but never saw her socially," Thompson told the group.

"Should I list him as a suspect?" the lieutenant asked.

"I don't think so. She also dated a fellow named Roy, but I haven't been able to run him down. I don't have a last name and she apparently hasn't seen him since she got married."

Peck wrote the name ROY under the SUSPECT column, then moved across the board and wrote ID ROY in the TO DO column. "Anything else?" Peck asked.

"Yeah," Thompson said. "I talked to Dr. John Manning; he's an OB/Gyn. He saw Olga on the afternoon of November 17. Manning told me she was very "weepy" when he saw her; he called her very depressed. The doc said it wasn't beyond the realm of possibility that Olga may have done herself. He indicated that he thought she had some type of psychiatric background, but I can't confirm that."

"I really doubt that's the case," Brerton responded. "Everyone I talked to said this lady wouldn't do anything to harm her baby, herself, or anyone else for that matter. Just a real nice person, real gentle." There was a momentary silence in the room while the others digested the words of the investigator.

"I agree with Brerton," Bouma said, adding to the assessment.

"Me too," the lieutenant added. "But I'd better indicate that suicide is a possibility, even if it's a remote one, since at least one professional has raised the issue." Peck wrote POSS. SUICIDE/PER DR. MANNING at the bottom of the blackboard.

"Is that it?" Peck asked, wiping the chalk residue off his hands.

Detective Thompson checked his notes before speaking. "No. I talked to neighbors of Elizabeth's who saw a man with a flashlight at 0400 hours on November 16. He apparently went to her door and was allowed in. I don't know who he was or what he was doing at that hour. But it seems suspicious."

"Sure does." Peck wrote down ID VISITOR/NOV. 16 under the TO DO column. He moved across the board and underlined Elizabeth's name again.

"What else?" Peck looked at the group as they checked their notes. There was no response, so the lieutenant issued directives as he wrote once more on the board.

"Okay. Bouma, you and Crawford, when he gets back, can interview Frank Duncan. You can also talk to Elizabeth, but put that off for a couple of days until a few of these other things develop." The lieutenant wrote INTERVIEW ELIZABETH on the board. "We've also got to clear up this extortion case that the Duncan woman is reporting, figure out the significance of that in the scheme of things. I'll leave that with Crawford, since he's already into it." The lieutenant made further notations on the blackboard.

"Have we heard if Elizabeth has recorded any conversations?" Sergeant Bouma threw out.

"No, she hasn't gotten back to us, but she may be waiting until Crawford comes back. The Duncans seem to trust him, for some unknown reason."

"That brings to mind the Short woman. We should interview her," Detective Thompson suggested. "But she'll be hard to get to because she's constantly with Elizabeth."

"Okay, I'll leave that for you to figure out, Charlie. You can probably charm your way into her apartment somehow." The lieutenant grinned at the detective, then turned to continue writing the various assignments.

"What about motive?" Peck threw out to the group. "It looks like old lady Duncan is number one on our list, but why would she do this? After all, Olga was going to have her grandbaby." The lieutenant looked at the silent group.

Charles Thompson fiddled with his pencil, doodling on the front of his case file.

Finally he spoke up. "There doesn't seem to be any financial gain from this. We haven't had a chance to check insurance yet, but I doubt Olga would leave money to her mother-in-law, unless of course, her husband was somehow involved."

"That strengthens Frank as a suspect, if there is insurance," Bouma pointed out.

Peck wrote CHECK INSURANCE under the TO DO column as the detectives continued to discuss the case.

"Maybe it's some type of obsession—the mother for the son," Bouma said. "George told me that he's seen Frank and his mother come into court hand in hand, kind of like husband and wife instead of mother and son."

Lieutenant Peck whistled. "You mean an Oedipus thing? I don't like the sound of that!"

"Oedipus?" Charlie Thompson said. "I remember that story from my college days. Real kinky stuff."

"Well, it certainly could be an inducement to murder," Peck said, moving back to the backboard and writing MOTIVE/OEDIPUS under the MISCELLANEOUS row. There was silence in the room while the detectives considered the implications of the motive they were discussing.

While the meeting grew longer, Lieutenant Peck wrote note after note until the blackboard was a mass of yellow. It soon became apparent to the investigators that they had their work cut out for them, as the TO DO list grew longer and longer. Just before the meeting adjourned, Sergeant Bouma pointed out, "I can't wait till Crawford comes back. He's gonna be working day and night for the next few months trying to solve this baby." They all chuckled over his comment, knowing full well that he meant they'd *all* be working long hours before they put this case to bed.

The meeting broke up, the detectives heading to their phones to look for that particular clue that would give them the edge up.

What the investigators didn't know was that they were already in possession of a major piece of evidence because of the efforts of two very alert patrol officers.

At 1:00 A.M. on November 28, Officers Cruickshank and Bagley, working beat car 196, stopped a 1948 Chevy sedan for running a red light. The driver, James (Chico) Rojo, the same man who had lent the gun to Moya and Baldonado, was arrested for driving without a driver's license, a bookable offense at the time. The car, which bore California license plate MUL 024, was returned to the owner, Sarah Contreras.

The very next night, at 12:15 A.M., Cruickshank and Bagley noticed the car again.

This time it was parked at the corner of Chapala and Figueroa Streets, blacked out, with a lone occupant behind the wheel. Because of the late hour, as well as the events of the night before, the officers in beat car 196 became suspicious. They drove slowly by the Chevy and noted that the license plate on the vehicle had been changed. They made a U-turn, pulled up behind the car, and lit it up with their red light and spotlight. Officer Bagley noted that the license plate appeared to be wired on with a piece of baling wire. He wrote down the license, JLY 228, while his partner approached the driver. While at the scene, they were backed up by Officer Pierce in car 83.

Officer Cruickshank found the man in the car to be Carlos Montoya, the brother of Sarah Contreras. Montoya stated that he'd borrowed the car from his sister to attend a football game and had no knowledge of what plates should be on the car. He had no plausible reason for sitting where he was two hours after the end of the game.

The officers issued Montoya, who was a juvenile, a citation for violations of section 238, California Vehicle Code, entitled No Evidence of Registration, and section 158 (a), California Vehicle Code, entitled Vehicle Bearing Plates Not Issued to It.

Officer Pierce drove Montoya home while Bagley and Cruickshank did an inventory search of the vehicle in order to tow it. They noted that the right-hand side of the back seat was badly torn, with the cotton batting showing. They found nothing else unusual about the car before Woods Garage towed it to be stored for future investigation. The officers subsequently learned that the license plate JLY 228 belonged to a 1941 Chevy owned by Paul Rodarte.

Neither Bagley nor Cruickshank discussed the towing of this vehicle with detectives, nor had they reason to do so at that time.

Following Up the Leads

Mrs. Duncan displayed an uncanny ability to get other persons to do her bidding. Not personally attractive, she nevertheless held an uncanny sway over many men.

—Bob Holt, "Update,"
Ventura Star Free Press, November 17, 1968

George Crawford pored over yet another report, his typewriter clicking slowly while he hunted and pecked his way around the keyboard. He looked briefly at his notebook before throwing the carriage and continuing the laborious process.

"Geez," he muttered to himself, "I should have stayed on vacation. The paperwork in this case is enough to sink a ship."

Sergeant Tom Bouma walked in, his coat draped over his arm. "You ready to go?" Bouma asked Crawford.

"Yeah, in a minute. I just want to finish up this report."

Bouma walked over to the coffeepot. He poured himself a cup and walked with it to his desk. He took a few sips, then sat down, pushing some papers to an unused corner before propping his feet up and leaning back in his chair. He pushed his hat forward, covering his eyes, obviously thinking about grabbing a few winks.

"Wake me when you're ready."

Thirty minutes later, the two detectives were driving to the Howard Canfield Building to interview Frank Duncan about the whereabouts of his wife. Their boss had left them with a clear message: "Find out if that guy did it!"

They were ushered into Frank's office by his very curious secretary, who lingered longer than normal at the door. The two men looked around the room, noting the well-furnished office. They took seats in the two high-backed chairs across from Frank. The secretary finally eased her way out, silently closing the door behind her.

Bouma started the conversation. "Thanks for seeing us on such short notice, Mr. Duncan."

"No problem," Frank replied, pushing some papers aside so he could give the two men his undivided attention. "I thought it was only a matter of time until we had this conversation," the attorney continued.

"You're right about that," Crawford put in. "Of course, you realize it's mostly a formality, just to clear a few things up."

"What does that mean? Am I a suspect?"

"To tell you honestly, Frank—may I call you Frank?" Crawford interjected.

"Certainly."

"Everyone is a suspect at this point, at least until either Olga returns or we figure out what happened to her."

"That's understandable. And I want you to make note that I do agree to talk to you about Olga's disappearance, for the record."

"Okay, then, can you tell us about your relationship with the Esquivels?" Bouma asked.

"Yes, at least I think I can without violating the attorney-client privilege. What is it you want to know?"

"When did they hire you?"

Frank reached into a desk drawer and pulled out a manila folder. He flipped it open and began to read down the page. While he was doing so, Sergeant Crawford reached into his coat pocket and removed a notebook. He began to take notes, writing the time and date on the first fresh sheet he found. Below that he noted "Frank Duncan Interview," then made a notation that the attorney had agreed to discuss the case, and wrote the date and time. He then paused while he waited for Frank to speak.

"Let's see . . . they hired me on September 24, a couple of days after the arrest. Mrs. Esquivel made a payment of $500 on September 26. Marciano—that's Mr. Esquivel—was charged with three counts of receiving and Esperanza was charged with one count. The case revolved around some guns taken from a sporting goods store."

"Yes, we know, the All American Sporting Goods Store," Crawford interrupted.

"By the way, you guys ever figure out who did that burglary?" Frank asked.

"Well, not as far as I know. Property Crimes worked the case, so we didn't have anything to do with it," Bouma replied, looking at Crawford, who just shrugged his shoulders. "Why do you ask?"

"Oh, I don't know. Just curious."

Bouma pursued his line of questioning. "What was the outcome of the Esquivel case?"

Frank closed the folder and looked directly at the detective. "Marciano pleaded guilty to one count and the case against Esperanza was dismissed."

"Did either of the Esquivels ask for their money back?"

"No, not to me. I thought they were happy with the outcome. Marciano knew all along that he had a chance of going to jail if he pleaded guilty. It was part of the deal we worked out."

"Were you surprised when your mother told you about the extortion?" Crawford asked.

"I certainly was. That's why I came to see you—to try to get to the bottom of this."

There was a long pause and Sergeant Crawford noticed the squeaking sound of a fan overhead. He looked up at the wooden fan, its blades moving slowly, the motor rocking gently from the long brass conduit that secured it to the high ceiling. Crawford thought about further questions, but then looked over at his partner, who seemed to have hit a dead end. George decided to pop the all-important question, in order to gauge the response. "Frank, what were you doing on the night of November 17?"

The attorney looked startled. Though he had been anticipating this question, the fact that it had now been asked brought this conversation to a different level. Being a criminal lawyer, Frank was well aware of the importance of his response. He took a deep breath before answering, "I was home watching television."

"By home, you mean your mother's apartment, correct?"

"Yes."

"Anyone with you?"

"Yes, my mother. We were together. We watched television until about 11:00 and then I went to bed."

"I see," Crawford said. "Did she also go to bed at that time?"

"Yes, I think so, but I can't remember for certain."

"Was anyone else there?"

"No."

"Did you leave the apartment anytime that night?"

"No."

"How about your mother, did she leave during the night that you're aware of?"

"Not that I am aware of."

Crawford sat back in his chair, considering this alibi while he again watched the fan blades spin slowly above his head. *Sounds sort of airtight,* he thought to himself.

"Do you remember what you watched?" Bouma took up the slack.

"Well, not for sure, but it seems like *Gunsmoke* was on—or is that on Saturday nights? I can't be positive on that one. Nothing really stands out in my mind."

"When's the last time you saw your wife?"

"I haven't seen her since November 7. We just weren't getting along that well."

"How so?"

"It was my mother. She didn't care for Ollie and there was a considerable amount of conflict. Mother constantly interfered in our lives."

"Did you ever hear your mother threaten Olga?"

"No, I didn't." Frank quickly dropped his eyes to his desk. *Uh-oh, that sounded like a lie,* Crawford thought to himself.

"Never?" Crawford asked, not able to mask the disbelief.

"No, never."

"Mr. Duncan, we have a statement from one of Olga's landladies that your mother did threaten your wife in your presence. Let me see . . . " Crawford began to thumb through his notebook, looking for the correct entry. "It was during an argument while you were living on Bath Street, about a week after you were married," he read from his notes.

"We did have a fight about that time, but I don't believe my mother threatened Olga. She was mainly concerned about getting me to come home with her. It was a very emotional scene, everyone yelling, you know."

"Oh, I see, but no threats that you recall?" a disbelieving Crawford responded, jotting something down in his notebook,

"None."

"Has it ever crossed your mind that your mother might be responsible for the fact that your wife is missing?"

There was a pause while Frank considered the question. "Quite frankly, it has. In fact, I even asked her, but she said that Ollie was just trying to frighten me and that she'll turn up soon. And she was with me on the 17th," Frank now looked up calmly, fixing first one detective and then the other with his gaze.

Crawford continued his line of questioning. "Do you know if there's a connection between your wife's disappearance and the extortion?"

"That thought has occurred to me also, but I don't know what the connection could be, if any. And my mother assures me that the blackmailing has nothing to do with Olga."

There was a pause while Crawford made further notes in his book. He waited for his partner to ask another question. When none was forthcoming, Crawford looked at Frank and asked, "Do you or Olga have life insurance?"

"Yes, I have a policy. It's for around $29,000 and Ollie is the beneficiary. As far as I know, she has no life insurance, but we never really talked about it, so it's possible she may have an old policy."

"Who's your insurance agent?"

"Valentine Ponomaroff."

"Can you spell that?"

"P-o-n-o-m-a-r-o-f-f. He's in the phone book."

"Okay, got it."

Sergeant Bouma looked at his partner. "Do you have any other questions?"

"Just one." Crawford leveled his gaze at the attorney on the other side of the desk. "Is there anything you know about your wife's disappearance that you haven't told us? Anything at all?"

"No, not a thing. I love my wife and I just want her to return." Frank lisped when he answered the question, betraying his nervousness.

"Would you take a lie detector test?"

"I'd have to think about that. It's not that I have anything to hide; it's just that I don't trust those contraptions. There is a reason they're not allowed as evidence in court, y'know. And that's because they're not reliable."

"Does that mean you won't take one?"

"Like I said, I'll have to think about it."

"Well, then that's all for now. I would appreciate it if you would keep our conversation confidential." Crawford stood and reached across the desk to shake the lawyer's hand.

The attorney rose and shook hands with the detective. "Now, that wasn't too bad," Crawford said, grasping Frank's slightly moist palm.

"No, not too bad. I hope you understand about the polygraph . . ."

"We'll discuss that at a later date, if need be. Thanks for you cooperation. We'll find our way out." They left the office and walked out to the street. Both men paused to light a cigarette before sliding into the car.

"What do you think?" Bouma asked his partner when Crawford had settled into the passenger's seat.

"I don't know. He told at least one lie—the part about his mother threatening Olga. I thought that was pretty obvious. I don't think the guy's very good at lying, in spite of the fact that he's an attorney."

"Yeah, I picked up on that too," Bouma reached down and turned the ignition. He looked over his shoulder before he pulled out into traffic. "Personally, I wouldn't trust that guy as far as I could throw him. But then, I feel that way about most of these ambulance chasers. Let's go by the station and see if anyone else has anything goin'."

When the detectives arrived at the station, they went to the chalkboard in the conference room to determine if there were any new notes on it. Not seeing any, Crawford put a big yellow check mark next to INTERVIEW FRANK and wiped the chalk off his hands.

They next went into the detective bay and saw Charlie Thompson. Charlie obviously had some news. He was on the phone, but upon seeing them, picked up a piece of paper and waved it in their direction. Bouma snatched the paper out of Thompson's hand as he waved it back and forth. The paper was a Teletype from the San Francisco Police Department indicating that Elizabeth Duncan, with numerous aliases listed, had been convicted for keeping a house of prostitution.

"So, a little more wood on the fire," Thompson said, hanging up the phone.

"Yeah, how did you come up with this? It wasn't on her rap sheet," Crawford asked.

"The license request from San Francisco P.D was to open a massage parlor. One thing led to another. I mean, who ever heard of a legit massage parlor, especially in San Francisco? I talked to a records clerk up there and they said it didn't get on her sheet because they failed to report the arrest to the state."

"Now this is what I call good detective work," Crawford said, taking the paper from Bouma and confirming the information. "Has Peck seen this yet?"

"No, he's out, but you can bet he'll be real interested. Did you notice all the names that woman has used? She's either got something to hide or she's been married a bunch."

"Using different names is consistent with the prostitution thing," Bouma pointed out.

"And besides, it'll give you more to run down on her." Crawford threw the paper back on Thompson's desk. "You seem to be having fun, so far."

"Yeah, I am. This old gal is sorta interesting," Thompson replied, grabbing his ringing telephone.

That afternoon, Sergeant Crawford received a brief phone call from Frank Duncan.

Frank advised him of the booking numbers of the two men his mother had identified as the blackmailers from the mug shots she had. Crawford cross-referenced the numbers and came up with the names of Gus Baldonado and a fellow known to most of the local officers as Moya Junior.

"Well, look who we have here," Crawford shouted across to Bouma after he learned the identities.

"Who? And for what?"

"Old Lady Duncan says that Moya Junior and another guy named Gus Baldonado are the blackmailers."

"T'lene? I know him real well," Charlie spoke up.

"What did you call him?"

"He goes by T'lene; it's a nickname. He and Moya will be easy to find. They're always around; they hang at the Tropical."

Crawford glanced up at the clock hanging on the wall. "We can scoop them up tomorrow. Right now, it's quitting time and I could use a cold one. I'll buy the first round," Crawford announced, his chair scraping across the linoleum as he slid away from his desk.

"Sounds good," echoed through the detective bay. There was a general exodus toward the door while the officers headed for their favorite watering hole.

Lineup

Truth telling, I have found, is the key to responsible citizenship. The thousands of criminals I have seen in 40 years in law enforcement have had one thing in common: every single one was a liar.
—J. Edgar Hoover, *Family Weekly*, July 14, 1963

Luis Moya reported for work on time on the afternoon of December 4. When he got to the Blue Onion, his employer, Frank Haywood, informed him that two of Santa Barbara's finest had been to the restaurant looking for him. Luis, figuring the best defense was a good offense, feigned surprise that the local cops should be asking for him. He told Frank that he realized this was his first night back to work, but felt he should go down to the station to straighten out whatever is was they wanted. Haywood consented, asking him to hurry back that evening. Surprisingly enough, Luis actually went to the police station and asked for the officer who had left his card at the Blue Onion.

George Crawford walked to the reception area of the detective office and recognized the young man who was sitting rather uneasily in a straight-back gray metal chair. George was surprised at how much Luis looked like his mug shot, figuring it must have been a recent picture.

"How's it goin', Moya?" George called to the young man, approaching him and offering his hand.

Luis looked up briefly, but did not look into the detective's eyes.

George noticed that Moya was staring at the middle of his chest when he offered his hand. "Hello, Mr. Crawford."

"Well, I see you got my message. I hope my stopping by didn't create any problems with your new job?"

"No, it didn't. My boss said you wanted to talk to me. But I don't know what for. I've been working and—"

"Why don't you come back here and I'll tell you all about it." The detective escorted Luis through the detective bay, directing him to an interview room, a small, boxy place with a table and three chairs squeezed into it.

"Have a seat. I'll be right back." Crawford walked out and shut the door. Luis noticed that he didn't lock the door, so he thought he must be free to leave. For a moment he considered doing so, then thought better of it. But this place did feel like a jail cell and an uneasiness crawled up his spine.

Sergeant Crawford walked into the detective bay to talk with Tom Bouma. He had Bouma call Elizabeth and request that she come to the station to view a lineup. While Bouma did this, Crawford returned to begin interrogating Luis.

Crawford returned to the room and threw the case folder on the table in front of him before taking a seat across from Luis. In his usual style, he talked softly to the apprehensive Moya, trying to gain his confidence before getting into the meat of the conversation.

"So, how ya been doing lately, Moya? I haven't seen you around for awhile."

"That's because I've been stayin' cool."

"Yeah, I guess you have."

"Hey, Crawford, I know you didn't ask me down here to pass the time of day. What's goin' on?"

"You mean to tell me you don't know why I wanted to talk to you?"

"Honestly, I have no idea," Luis said with a shrug.

"Do you know a woman named Elizabeth Duncan?"

Luis felt an early warning of fear, a tugging at his stomach. "No," he said, looking away from the detective.

"Really," came the disbelieving response. "Well, she sure knows you!" The detective leaned closer to the man.

Luis looked at the detective, trying to gauge him, wondering what he really knew, and hoping to manipulate the conversation, sort of turn the tables on the cop.

"So who is this woman?"

"Just a lady who says you've been giving her a real hard time." The detective flipped open the case file in front of him and began to make notes.

Luis craned his neck in an effort to see what the detective was writing. Finally, unable to contain his curiosity, the younger man asked, "What ya writing in the folder?"

"I'm just noting down when you lie to me, you know, the time and such."

"Now wait a minute—"

"Can it!" the investigator said, leveling Luis with a knowing look. "This lady says you've been blackmailing her and that she's given you a couple hundred bucks. You hang out at the Tropical Cafe, don't you?"

"Sometimes, but I ain't blackmailin' nobody. Why would I be doing that to some dumb bitch?"

"She's explained the reason. You know as well as I do. It isn't a secret." Crawford began to sort through the case file folder in front of him. "Yes, here it is," he muttered to himself, loud enough for Luis to hear. He began to read the report, looking up knowingly at the nervous man on the other side of the table. Luis glanced away, feeling a sudden overpowering need to leave this place. The walls were beginning to move in on him.

"She describes you to a T," Crawford continued. "All except the hair, and it looks to me like you just got a haircut."

"Well, like I already said, I ain't blackmailin' nobody," Luis insisted. He reached into his front shirt pocket and pulled out a pack of cigarettes. He searched through his pockets, looking unsuccessfully for matches. When it became apparent that he had none, Crawford leaned over and lit the cigarette with his lighter.

"Thanks."

"Sure, Moya. Why don't you level with me, help me get this thing cleared up?"

"No way, man. I'm on parole and I'm damn sure not goin' back to the joint on some bogus beef like this. Especially since I'm innocent, man!"

"Moya, you and I know you haven't been innocent for a few years now. Your name comes up around town all the time. You're always up to something."

"You guys just got it in for me! I know you been watching me lately, trying to make a big bust. Hey, am I under arrest or what? If I ain't, I gotta get back to work. My boss'll be ticked if I ain't back soon."

Crawford sat back and watched the man inhale the cigarette. "You're not under arrest, at this point. We're just having a friendly conversation, you know, trying to tie up a few loose ends. But I know how to clear up this whole thing," the detective continued.

"How?"

"Well, this Duncan lady is coming in and I want to put you in a lineup. Shouldn't be any problem, especially for an innocent man like yourself." The detective gazed into the uneasy eyes of the young man.

Luis thought for a moment, looking away from the other man. Finally, he tried changing the subject, a ploy meant to sidetrack the detective.

"Hey, man, is this room bugged?" he asked, a curl of smoke wafting about his head. He stared at a suspicious-looking light fixture.

"No. What d'you say? We can get this whole thing over with now! You have nothing to hide, right? If she doesn't pick you out, you're out of here."

"You've never even told me why I'm suppose to be blackmailing this woman," Luis leaned forward and stubbed the cigarette out in an ashtray. "Hell, I don't even know why I'm here!"

"Okay, I'll tell you. Mrs. Duncan said you're working for the Esquivels trying to collect money from her because her son is a rotten attorney and Chelo's old man is going to prison instead of being deported like her attorney promised."

"You got to be shittin' me? That doesn't make any sense. I know Chelo and I've helped her around the Tropical, but like I said before, I'm not getting money from this Duncan woman."

"If you're innocent, then do the lineup, man!" Crawford leaned forward again, raising his voice.

While Luis was considering his options, Sergeant Bouma stuck his head into the room and spoke to Crawford. "Can I see you out here, George?"

"I'll be right back, Moya. You think about what I said." The detective stood up and left the interview room, stopping in the hallway.

"The Duncans are here. Do you want me to set up the lineup room?"

"Yeah. I haven't convinced him yet, but he'll come around. Do you have enough guys to put on a halfway decent lineup?"

"I'll round up a couple of guys from patrol. It's shift change, so there should be someone in the locker room."

"Okay. Put the Duncans in the viewing room. I'll have Moya Junior ready to go in about fifteen minutes."

Crawford walked back into the blue smoke of the interview room. Luis was on his third cigarette, judging from the butts in the ashtray.

"Have you thought about what I said?" the detective asked, grasping the back of the chair with his hands and not bothering to sit down.

"Sort of."

"Let's just do it so we won't be coming around to your work

in a couple of days. You're here now; may as well clean this up right now."

"Okay, fine. Let's just get this done so I can get outta here. This is a real bullshit story and I ain't done nothin'. Like you said, Mr. Crawford, I don't have anything to worry about."

Luis stood up and threw the cigarette butt on the floor, grinding it into the linoleum with his foot.

"Fine. I have to set it up, so just sit down and relax. I'll be right back."

The detective loosed his grip on the back of the chair and scooped up his case file. He walked quickly out of the room, heading for the lineup area. He didn't lock the door behind him, but asked one of the guys to keep an eye on it.

Luis Moya was placed in the number six position and put into the lineup with five cops. He was wearing a tan suit and hung his head very low in an effort to keep from being clearly seen by the witnesses. Since he couldn't see them, he wasn't sure that Mrs. Duncan was on the other side of the one-way glass. He'd learned through the years not to trust what the cops said. They'd lied to him so many times in hopes of tripping him up.

He was finally led off the stage and stood around in an anteroom for a couple of minutes before going back under the glare of the lineup lights. He stood on the same number, still trying to keep his head bowed.

Once again he was led off the stage. This time, he was returned to the interview room to await the outcome of the lineup.

In the meantime, Elizabeth had refused to identity Moya, much to the concern of her son. Frank had easily picked Luis out, since he closely resembled the mug shots that the officers had given him. The frustrated Frank, sitting with Elizabeth in the detective bay, was hissing at his mother, trying to get her to cooperate, when Sergeant Bouma suggested that they bring Moya into the room to discuss the situation. Although this was a somewhat unusual tactic, George

Crawford agreed to it, especially since he now felt the case wasn't going anywhere because it was obvious that his witness was unwilling to identify the crook.

Luis would later testify to this encounter in court: "About thirty minutes later, I was brought into a room with Mrs. Duncan. When I walked in, she said, 'No, this isn't the man that I thought it was, that I picked out of the mugs. The other was much taller and had shorter hair.' Well, she just refused to identify me."

"And you didn't acknowledge that you knew her?" the district attorney asked.

"That is true."

"So were any words or glances or looks passed between you at that time?"

"Well, I recall myself telling Mrs. Duncan that I was very glad she had corrected this mistake that she had made because I wasn't blackmailing anybody. Of course, it was merely an act for the police officers."

Mrs. Duncan also testified in court to the events of that day. In her testimony, she indicated that she finally did identify Luis Moya after being threatened by her son.

The exchange, with the district attorney asking the questions, went as follows.

"At any time that evening did you tell Sergeant Crawford that you recognized Moya?" Roy Gustafson asked.

"Yes."

"How long was it, approximately, before you told Sergeant Crawford that Moya was one of these men?"

"My son told me . . . "

"What?"

"My son said to me, he said, 'You know you recognize one of these men. If you don't tell right now, I'll leave home tonight!'" The witness continued, "And then they brought—I don't know if it was Sergeant Crawford or my son that insisted on Moya being brought into the room where we were at. I saw him and I am not for putting people in jail. I can't help it. I am not! But I said, 'Sergeant Crawford, that is the man!'"

Later in his testimony, Moya stated that he was sitting out in the hallway when Mrs. Duncan passed him. She looked down at him and hesitated a moment. He whispered, "I think everything is going to be okay."

Those were the last words Luis Moya would say to Ma Duncan as a free man.

George Crawford explained to the Duncans that Elizabeth's reluctance to identify Moya Junior made this case all but impossible to prosecute. While this did not sit well with Frank, his mother was more than happy to wash her hands of this part of the affair.

Luis was released that night after a stern warning by Sergeant Crawford to keep his nose clean. Crawford walked with Luis to the front door of the police station. While they walked, Moya guaranteed the concerned officer that he wouldn't be a problem, having learned his lesson from the last time he was in jail. He walked out the front door of the police department and was halfway down the steps when Crawford shouted to him.

"Hey, Moya, you know a woman named Olga?"

The stunned man whirled and looked up at the detective. He quickly recovered, guessing that if this guy really knew anything he obviously wouldn't be walking down these stairs. *It's a fishing trip,* Luis decided.

"Hell no!" Luis shouted over his shoulder, turning and hurrying down the remaining few steps.

Luis now felt that enough was enough and after the encounter at the police department he made no further efforts to collect the money owed to him and Gus.

Arrests are Made

I cannot and will not discuss evidence. But the investigation will
not cease until we arrive at a conclusion in the matter.
—Vern Thomas, District Attorney of Santa Barbara County,
Santa Barbara News Press, December 16, 1958

After the release of Luis Moya on the extortion case, the investigators interviewed both Esperanza Esquivel and Emma Short about
their knowledge of the blackmailing case. While they had discount-
ed a successful prosecution, the investigators were hoping to uncov-
er a link between the players in the extortion and the murder of
Olga Duncan. Emma Short gave a well-rehearsed version of events,
and Esperanza flatly denied any knowledge of the supposed blackmail plot.

Leaving no stone unturned, they learned that the mysterious visitor Elizabeth had in the early morning hours of November 16, the
night before Olga's disappearance, was her doctor, who treated her
for a gall bladder attack.

While the investigators hoped to interview Gus, they had not
been successful in finding him. Gus was in Ventura County, visiting
his wife and twin sons she had just given birth to. His visit to Ventura
County General Hospital had not gone as Gus had hoped. His wife,
Carmen, was hardly glad to see the missing father. In fact, she
reminded him that he was behind on his child support payments and
she intended on contacting the district attorney's office upon her
release from the hospital. Carmen didn't have to point out to Gus

that he was now responsible for two additional dependents, though they were no longer legally married. When he tried to cast doubt on the parentage of the babies, she gave him a knowing look, pointed to the two children who closely resembled their father, and informed him that these certainly were his sons. Gus, hoping to avoid the inevitable warrant for his arrest, tried to convince Carmen that he would be more dependable in the future.

While Gus was having his problems down south, Chief R. W. Cooley of the Santa Barbara Police Department was experiencing his own aggravations. He had just received a phone call from the chief agent of the Los Angeles office of the Federal Bureau of Investigation. Agent B. K. Brown advised Chief Cooley that his office was entering the case. This was not welcome news and the chief was quick to question why the feds thought they had jurisdiction. Brown responded that their interest was based on the fact that Olga was a foreign national. While the chief had never known the FBI to use this excuse to enter an investigation, he had no recourse but to accept their help.

That week, Lieutenant Peck reconvened his staff in the detective conference room. The well-used chalkboard dominated the place, its yellow words running together on the ends of chalky lines.

"The chief is pissed," Peck declared, kicking off the meeting. "He doesn't want the feds in town, nosing around. And he sure as hell doesn't want them solving this case before we do! He told me in no uncertain terms that he wants something to happen real soon!"

"Hell, we ain't miracle workers," Tom Bouma pointed out.

"Where did all the heat come from?" Sergeant Crawford asked.

"I'm not sure, but I think it might have been from Olga's friends down in the L.A. area who contacted the FBI. What was their name?"

"Woytko."

"Yeah, those folks. I heard they told the feds we weren't putting enough manpower into the case, and—"

"Oh, bullshit!" Charlie Thompson interrupted his boss.

The lieutenant swiveled his chair and glared at Thompson, then continued, "At any rate, I want to brainstorm this thing with you guys before the agents show up. So let's have some new ideas!"

"Don't you think if we had any new thoughts on this case we'd have done it. I mean, I haven't been sleeping nights thinking about this goddamned murder."

"You're right, Charlie, and I know it. We've all been bustin' our balls trying to come up with something. But it's time we did a round robin here to clear the air and think this thing through."

Thompson threw his hands up in the air and leaned back in the chair, sighing loudly. He began to add something, but remembered his recent days off without pay and thought better of it.

There was a long silence, the detectives squirming around in their chairs under the scrutiny of their boss.

Crawford scratched his chin and then spoke up. "We've got to crack the connection between Old Lady Duncan and that black-mailing business. That's got to be the key to this case. Maybe we could try following her for awhile."

"We discussed tailing her before," Charlie jumped in, "but she doesn't drive, so we'd have to follow her on foot. That would present some real problems, considering where she lives. But I do have another idea."

"Well, let's have it," Peck instructed.

Thompson got up and walked to the blackboard. He picked up the yellow chalk and circled the name EMMA SHORT, which was written near the bottom of the board. "This person is the key," Charlie continued. He tapped the board with the chalk to empha-size his point. "She can tell us what happened. We need to get her in here away from Duncan and take a serious run at her." He set the chalk down and returned to his seat.

"I already talked to her once. She just parrots what Duncan tells her to say," Bouma pointed out.

"I'd like to try her. We hit it off pretty good the day I put the wire in Duncan's apartment. Besides, you guys were talking to her about the extortion. Maybe she hasn't been thoroughly briefed on murder."

"Anyone see a reason why not?" Peck asked the group. His question met with silence. "I guess that means we'll try talking to her again," the lieutenant continued. "We'll leave it to you, Charlie, to figure out how to get her in here. I understand the Duncan woman keeps a real close eye on her."

"In the meantime, you guys can expect the Fan Belt Inspectors to show up sometime soon and start nosin' around. I told the chief that we'd cooperate with them fully. But you know how they are. The local cops will do the legwork and the feds'll do the press releases."

After that meeting, Charlie Thompson made several covert attempts to talk to Emma, but he soon confirmed that she was seldom without her close friend. The detective, knowing that it was crucial that Mrs. Duncan didn't find out that he wanted to talk to Emma, only approached the apartment with a well thought out reason for being there. One of the excuses he employed was to pick up the tape recording device that Elizabeth had failed to use. He took that opportunity to reintroduce himself to the old woman, but was unable to talk to her alone.

A few days after the brainstorming session, Lieutenant Peck was briefing Chief Agent Brown and his six special agents about the progress they had made to date. The investigators, fresh in from the Los Angeles office, immediately realized that there was little legwork they could do that hadn't already been accomplished. However, the presence of the FBI did act as a catalyst to get the investigation "unstuck." The case became an even higher priority in the eyes of the Santa Barbara Police Department, as they intensified their efforts to solve the crime before the Federal Bureau of Investigation did.

On December 12, Detective Thompson's patience had finally worn out. Shortly after noon, he enlisted the aid of Sergeant Bouma to act as a diversion. Bouma went to the Duncan apartment with the intention of keeping Mrs. Duncan busy for half an hour so Thompson could have some time alone with Emma. After Bouma walked upstairs, Thompson approached the door of Emma's apartment and rapped lightly. He kept a nervous watch upstairs for what seemed an eternity and then breathed a sigh of relief when Mrs. Short finally opened the door. The gray-haired woman was dressed in a housecoat, with fuzzy purple slippers on her feet.

The detective spoke softly, hoping not to frighten her, afraid of blowing this one chance to learn the truth. "Mrs. Short, do you remember me?"

"Why certainly, you're that nice young man from the police, aren't you?"

"Yes. May I come in and talk to you for a moment? I won't take much of your time."

Mrs. Short nodded her head and stepped back. Thompson shot a quick glance upstairs, then swung open the door and walked into the room.

"You know," Emma began, padding into the small living room, "I knew you would want to talk to me sometime."

"Oh? Why is that?" came the hopeful reply.

"All this to-do about that Olga woman. Won't you sit down?" she said, pointing to the well-worn davenport against the wall.

Detective Thompson sat and, out of habit, began to pull a notebook out of his jacket pocket. He then thought better of it, deciding to trust the first part of this conversation to memory.

"Since you were expecting me anyway, can we talk about what you know?"

"I'm afraid of her!"

"Who?"

"Betty."

"You mean Elizabeth—Mrs. Duncan?"

"Yes, Betty—that's how I know her."

"Why are you afraid of her?"

"She knows things, does things."

"What things?"

"Terrible things!" The old woman buried her head in her hands and pushed herself back in the chair. She sat for several seconds in this position, lost in her thoughts. She finally spoke, "Y'know I'm just an old woman. I don't want no trouble."

Thompson began to fear he was losing her, so he tried to put her at ease. "We have ways of helping people, protecting them so no harm will come to them. I'm sure I can help you if you will talk to me."

"Oh, I don't know . . . " Emma wrung her hands in distress.

"Surely she can't be that bad."

"Oh, yes she can."

The woman looked up at him and he could see the bona fide dread in her eyes. *Perhaps she can be "that bad,"* he thought to himself.

"How so?" The detective gazed at her with a sympathetic expression, sensing that he was on the verge of learning something very important. Her countenance told the detective that she had much built-up torment that begged to spill forth. He looked down at his watch, seeing that the moments had ticked away, leaving him little time before the agreed upon half-hour would be up.

"Perhaps we should go to the station, continue the conversation there. Would that be all right?" he asked.

"Yes, perhaps we should. Wait just a moment, I'll get dressed."

That afternoon, at the Santa Barbara Police Department, Emma Short would tell for the first time the unbelievable tale of Elizabeth Duncan's murderous obsession. The story did not flow, but was coaxed from her by the patient yet insistent prodding of the young detective. By the end of two hours, he had learned of the annulment episode and that two "Mexican boys" had taken Olga "south of the border."

While Charles Thompson questioned Emma, the rest of the investigators, including agents from the FBI, sat around the detective bay in silence. The decision had been made to let Charlie go it alone, at least initially. He had built a rapport with the old woman that another interviewer might have inhibited.

After the detective had achieved a breakthrough, which he proudly announced to his waiting co-workers by walking into the bay and yelling "Yes!" at the top of his voice, it was decided that the remainder of the questioning would be conducted with the help of the district attorney.

Emma was whisked off to the DA's office, where the interview was continued.

District Attorney Vernon Thomas, like everyone else in Santa Barbara law enforcement, had been closely monitoring the case from its beginning. With the help of his investigator and of Detective Thompson, the questioning of Emma Short went into even more detail.

After confirming the annulment and learning its location, the detectives called the Ventura County Sheriff's Office and verified that the Duncan marriage had been annulled on August 7 of that year. That confirmation encouraged the investigators, lending credibility to the tale that Emma was telling.

In the meantime, detectives acting upon information provided by Mrs. Short went to Esperanza Esquivel's house and picked her up for questioning. Esperanza, seeing that there was no hope in feigning ignorance, corroborated many of Emma's statements. She also provided the names of the two killers, names Emma was unable to remember, in the hopes this cooperation would mitigate the case the police were now building against her.

Vern Thomas decided that, without Olga's body, there was insufficient cause to arrest the principals for murder. However, with the confirmation of the annulment, it was clear that Elizabeth had falsified a document and bribed a witness, both felony charges. In addition, they had enough information to conclude that the two suspected killers had kidnapped Olga Duncan, so there was sufficient reason to arrest them on that charge. They also confirmed that any involvement by Luis Moya in criminal conduct put him in violation of his parole.

On the evening of December 12, detectives drove Emma to the offices of the Los Angeles Police Department to administer a lie detector test. The results of the two-hour test proved that Emma was being truthful in her allegations. She was then returned to a Santa Barbara hotel, where she was hidden away under armed guard for this night and many more to come.

With the statements of the two witnesses in hand, an army of officers from the Santa Barbara Police, the Santa Barbara District Attorney's Office, the Ventura County Sheriff's Office, and the Ventura County District Attorney's Office, along with agents from the FBI, went in search of the three suspected killers, hoping to arrest them on a variety of charges.

Luis Moya was the easiest to find. Sergeant Bouma scooped him up from the Blue Onion Restaurant at noon on December 13. Luis was taken into an interview room, but steadfastly denied any knowledge of Olga or her disappearance. He was held on the violation-of-parole charge.

The next day, Chief Investigator Clarence Henderson and Investigator Tom Osborne of the Ventura DA's Office took Elizabeth into custody at her apartment. She was arrested on the felony charges stemming from the annulment and transported back to Ventura for questioning. Elizabeth readily admitted to the annulment. However, when detectives from the Santa Barbara Police Department talked with her about the murder, she flatly denied any involvement.

Gus Baldonado, who had just returned from Camarillo and a visit to his family, was also arrested in Santa Barbara on December 14. He maintained his innocence and was kept in the Santa Barbara Jail for two days. It soon became apparent that without a confession there was insufficient evidence to file a kidnapping case against Gus.

Investigators from the Ventura District Attorney's Office contacted Gus's wife and had little trouble persuading her to swear out a complaint for nonsupport. The warrant was served and Gus was transported to the Ventura County Jail, where he was booked on the failure-to-provide warrant. Investigators felt that the nonsupport charge would keep the man in custody until they could further develop the case of murder.

Softening Them Up

It's easy to make a man confess the lies he tells himself; it's far harder to make him confess the truth.
—Geoffrey Household, author

With the primary suspects in custody, an army of officers began working to close the loopholes.

By teaming up local officers with agents from the FBI, the jurisdictions were able to find a mutual ground that they could work within. This also gave the federal agents the advantage of not having to reinvent the wheel and retrace the steps of the local detectives.

After the arrests, the main emphasis was on locating the body. The district attorney was hesitant in pursuing prosecution without establishing the *corpus delicti* of the crime. In this case, he was missing a key element: Olga's remains.

Therefore, officers from several departments began an intensive search for the body of the missing nurse. They began by ordering the excavation of two hundred feet of Garden Street directly in front of Olga's apartment building after they learned that the public works department had laid some pipe at the time of her disappearance. While crews had backfilled the project with loose dirt on the afternoon of November 17th, they had not completed the project by compacting and paving over the area until the next day.

Other officers, working on tips from the public, went to the Miguelito Canyon area of Santa Barbara County to reconnoiter a ranch where both men may have been employed.

They also contacted the owner of the Missile City Rock Company, who operated a quarry in the Montecito area. The foreman was unable to positively identify either arrestee as being former employees at the quarry. This was actually good news, since the quarry had blasted 10,000 tons of rock during the time period that Olga was reported missing. The officers realized that finding a body at that location would be an impossible task.

It soon became apparent that without more concrete information, the task force of police was not going to find Olga. The emphasis was changed from following up leads provided by a very concerned and helpful public, toward obtaining the information from the principals in the case. A variety of officers began to interview the three arrestees, who were in custody with bails set large enough to keep them in jail.

True to form, Elizabeth proved to be the most obstinate of the three. She continued to deny any involvement, calling the accusations against her "filthy lies." In an attempt to weaken her resolve, she was confronted with her now ex-best friend, Emma Short. When Emma began to recount her tale, the amazed Elizabeth blew up at her friend, screaming at the top of her lungs, "That's a lie, that's a lie! Emma don't say that, that's a lie!"

When Elizabeth was read statements of some of those she had solicited to commit murder, she shook her head and called the whole bunch a pack of liars.

Seeing that Elizabeth would be a tough nut to crack, if not impossible, the detectives turned their attention to her two cohorts. Luis proved almost as recalcitrant as the woman who had hired him, though he was more congenial in his denial. He gave the impression that his alleged involvement was merely a matter of mistaken identity which he was confident would be straightened out at any moment. Emma also confronted him. The only comment he made after hearing her allegations was, "No, ma'am, you are making a terrible mistake."

Realizing that Elizabeth and Moya Junior had summoned the strength to resist their efforts, the detective next tackled what they hoped would be the weak link of the trio: Gus Baldonado. They proceeded slowly with Gus, spending hour after hour, rehashing and poking holes in his story. They pointed out to the man that he did not have an alibi for his whereabouts on the night of November 17. They convinced him that a steady stream of people was coming forward, pointing their fingers at Gus and Gus alone. This tactic psychologically isolated the man, causing him to think that he alone was going to take the fall for Olga's murder once her body was located.

Finally, during an interrogation conducted by Lieutenant Peck and Agent John Canny, Gus allowed a crack in his armor. He made the statement that he "had no intention of going through with the job." This statement, used against the man in dozens of different ways, led to further incriminating utterances. Lieutenant Peck then asked Gus to direct them to the body. Gus, who had been psychologically overwhelmed by the constant barrage of questions, told Peck that he couldn't take them to Olga. "It's not that I won't, it's just that I can't. I don't have the strength." With these statements in hand, the investigating officers knew that it was just a matter of time before they would find the deciding piece of the puzzle.

It was during the search for Olga's body that detectives learned that a critical piece of evidence was already in their possession: the 1948 Chevrolet sedan used to transport Olga to the hills above Lake Casitas. This fact came to light during an interview with James Rojo, who was initially considered a suspect in the crime. Rojo had been arrested in the vehicle on November 28 for driving without a license. He was still in jail on the charge and cooperated fully with the police. He informed the delighted investigators that the car was still in impound at Woods Garage. Technicians were sent to the garage to process the car.

After taking numerous photos, the local officers requested help from the Los Angeles Police Department. The LAPD sent chief criminalist, Ray Pinker, who was the foremost expert in his field in Southern California, to continue to process the car. He was able to lift four latent fingerprints. Despite the spray paint and the damage done to the upholstery, Pinker also took blood samples from the upholstery, the back window, and the passenger windowsill. Pinker recovered dirt from the tire treads and fender wells of the old Chevy for later spectroscopic comparison analysis with dirt found at the crime scene. The blood samples recovered from the car proved to be insufficient for comparison to Olga's type B blood. However, Pinker was able to conclusively show that the blood was human. Pinker was unable to locate any fiber or hair evidence that would strengthen the case against the killers.

Detectives compared the three arrestees' prints with those found in the car. When none of these matched, they began pulling in other involved parties to roll comparison prints. These included Frank Duncan, who had no objection to the process. A match was never made on the prints.

At the same time, investigators also impounded a 1955 Ford Fairlane that belonged to Esperanza Esquivel. They were told that the vehicle had a large amount of dried blood in the trunk. Esperanza insisted that the blood residue was from a hog that her husband had slaughtered and transported in the trunk. Subsequent tests confirmed that the blood was not human.

On December 17, Frank Duncan made his first public announcement since the disappearance of his wife. He told reporters that he was "still very much in love with Olga" and hoped that she would return. He also maintained that a simulated alligator-skin hatbox and matching train box had been missing shortly after her disappearance. Frank stated that those items had mysteriously returned to Olga's apartment, but offered no explanation for this puzzle. Frank also told the press that "the police have been very careful not to mention one important statement I made to them. This statement was that my wife had threatened me with unpleasant publicity." When he was asked to elaborate on that statement, he refused to do so. He wrapped up the press conference by characterizing reports of the many threats that witnesses claimed his mother had made towards Olga as "not accurate."

The afternoon of December 17, Frank represented his mother in her arraignment before Judge Richard Heaton in the Ventura County Municipal Court on the annulment charges. During this court proceeding, Frank was able to convince Judge Heaton that her $50,000 bail was excessive for the falsification of documents and the bribery charges.

Frank successfully argued that there was no proof of a connection between his mother and his missing wife. He further pointed out that it did not appear that the Santa Barbara authorities were going to charge his mother with anything and that it was time for them to "put up or shut up." He persuaded Judge Heaton to lower the bail to $5,000, which was still too high for the Duncans to make. Mrs. Duncan remained in custody, with her preliminary hearing scheduled for the end of December.

Apparently Frank's "put up or shut up" line motivated Vern Thomas in Santa Barbara. Two days after the arraignment, the district attorney filed a multi-count complaint against all three defendants. The affidavit, sworn to by Detective Charles Thompson, requested the issuance of arrest warrants for violation of California PC section 182, conspiracy to kidnap and murder Olga Duncan.

In the meantime, the search for the body had shifted to the Ventura County area of the Ojai Valley, near the recently completed Lake Casitas. Though officers followed up every lead, which included the finding of women's garments in various locations, they all knew that they would need more specific information. As one frustrated federal agent stated, "When we find a logical place to hunt, we'll start digging."

The link to finding Olga's body was Gus and detectives continued to soften him up, hoping it was only a matter of time before the man would break down and reveal the location of Olga's grave.

Confession

Ask me no questions, and I'll tell you no fibs.
—Oliver Goldsmith, *She Stoops to Conquer,* III. i.

Ray Higgins was a "cop's cop," according to those who knew him at the time he became involved in the Olga Duncan murder case.

The lanky, sharp-featured detective had a reputation for getting to the point, often at the expense of others. This bluntness would cause him problems later in his career, but worked to enhance his investigative skills when he found himself working on a once-in-a-lifetime case.

Ray, who had just passed his fortieth birthday, was employed by the Ventura County Sheriff's Office as an investigator. After many years with the department, he had just proven to himself that he was a good street cop by failing a civil service promotional test. Passing this test was considered to be the first step in moving out of police work into an administrative position. In a sense, failing the test had been a type of victory for him, confirming that his strength was on the streets. He could live with that!

Lieutenant William Woodard called Ray into his office in the marble-facade jail building at 501 Poli Street, on the west side of Ventura.

The lieutenant was sitting in a high-back chair, talking on the telephone. He motioned for his subordinate to take a seat while he continued his conversation.

"Okay, Clarence. I understand your problem. And you say he's close to revealing the location? Yeah, right, sure sounds like it. Say, Clary, Ray has just walked in, so let me talk to him and I'll call you back. Okay. Goodbye." He hung up the phone and looked at Ray. "I bet you can guess what that conversation was about."

"It's got to be the Duncan case. I mean, the whole rest of the world is working on it. Isn't it still a Santa Barbara case?"

"You guessed it. But we've started our own inquiry to support Santa Barbara's efforts."

"And now I'm going to get my shot at being involved, right?" Ray interrupted his boss.

"You're so astute, Ray. That's what I like about you, always thinking," Woodard grinned at Higgins. "Haven't you worked a case involving this character, Baldonado, before?"

"T'lene? Sure, I know him. He and I go way back. I busted him for a couple of burglaries in Camarillo. Sent him to the hall when he was a kid."

"I just got off the phone with Henderson at the DA's office. Baldonado has made some incriminating statements and the feeling is he is real close to leading someone to the body. Do you think he'd talk to you about this Duncan thing?"

"Oh, I'm sure he would. What's the charge now?"

"He's being held for non-support. The DA got a warrant just to hold him until someone—God knows who—can convince him to show us the location of the body. The Santa Barbara DA is also seeking a warrant for conspiracy, but last word I got, the judge hadn't issued it yet. Anyway, you seemed like a logical choice to talk to the man since you've had prior experience with him."

"Can't say that I'm surprised he's in a jam. He grew up in less than ideal conditions. Hell of a mess! Well, what's the game plan?"

"Get in touch with Clarence Henderson. He can bring you up to speed. When you're ready, pull Baldonado down from the jail and see what you can get out of him."

"Sure, lieutenant. T'lene shouldn't be too tough. He's not all that bright."

"Sounds good, but he hasn't copped out so far and quite a few others have had a shot at him," the lieutenant pointed out.

"Hey, he'll be putty in my hands," Higgins stood up. "Is that it?"

"Yep, go get 'em and bring me back some good news," Woodard dismissed the detective.

In the late afternoon of December 20, Ray Higgins began working on Gus. He went into the jail and pulled Baldonado out of the tanks, clapping him on the back when the two were out of sight of the other inmates. He reminded Gus how far back they went, joking about the many other interrogations that they had suffered through together. He made them sound like the good ol' days, almost like this upcoming conversation was going to be about a day at the beach, not murder. He worked slowly with the man, laying the groundwork for what he hoped would be a far more productive session the next day.

At a little after 6:00 in the evening, Higgins finally returned Gus to the lockup. He was careful to ensure that Gus got the evening meal he had missed and that the prisoner knew Higgins had arranged it.

The next morning at 8:00, the persistent detective started again with the suspected murderer. Without the necessity of having to advise the man of his rights, and with few limitations on the number of hours he could spend interrogating his quarry, Ray was prepared to expend the whole day talking with Gus. But by 11:00 that morning, Higgins could tell that he was getting close as his continual game of psychological manipulation began to pay off. He had just brought Gus to a hopeful moment, telling the man that perhaps Olga wasn't dead at all; maybe she had just run away and the others had lied about him being a murderer.

Gus took a deep breath and began to relax.

Then the detective lowered the boom on the overmatched man. "Well, y'know, you guys are really just fucking baby killers!" Higgins snarled, causing Gus to recoil back in his chair as if he'd been struck with a bullwhip. This had been the detective's ace in the hole, to throw the man's inhumanity in his face, deflate him totally. This technique had to be carefully played, attacking him when he was the most vulnerable. The wrong timing could cause the man to clam up or explode, ending the interview.

"And when that word gets around the tanks upstairs, your life ain't gonna be worth a plug nickel. In case you don't know, the boys upstairs don't like baby killers!"

Gus knew full well and the detective need not have reminded him of one of the unwritten rules of the jailhouse. Anyone who victimized children was persona non grata, lucky to stay alive day to day.

"You gotta know, T'lene, I'm not beyond ensuring that word does get out since you insist on shining me on." Higgins looked hard at the man. He pointed up towards the tanks and said, "Besides, I'm nothin' to worry about compared to the assholes up there."

Gus suddenly jumped to his feet, ran his hands through the widow's peak of his hair, and exclaimed, "All right, I'll tell you! I'll do it for my kids, my family!"

Detective Higgins nodded his head and said, "That's good, Gus. It's a good reason to come clean." He then sat back in his chair, crossed his arms, and prepared to listen.

And Gus did tell all. It flowed from him like a fast-moving river crashing down a steep gorge. At times he rambled, at other times he shouted, waving his hands in exaggerated motions, while he recounted and relived the murder of Olga Duncan. When he was finished, he sat down, a look of relief spread over his face, the weight of his deed visibly lifted from his body.

Ray Higgins tore a piece of paper from a yellow legal pad and slid it to Gus. "Now, it's time to write out what you just told me," Higgins instructed.

Gus looked at the paper, picked up the pencil that Higgins provided, and in his own cramped handwriting explained in detail the murder of Olga Duncan: " . . . So we started driving out of Santa Barbara. When we got to a good place alongside the road we stopped. She was alive. We got her out of the car and took her down a gully. I was holding her by the neck and Louie was digging a hole. I told Louie I couldn't hold her so I dug and Louie took over holding her in a strangling position, and Louie said I guess she must be dead by now and Louie released her. Then we both dug. She presumed to look dead so we put her in a hole and covered her up."

There were subsequent interviews with Gus, conducted by Detective Higgins and Chief Investigator Clarence Henderson. The evening of December 22, Higgins and Henderson tried to clear up various points that the admitted murderer had talked about previously. During this interview, Gus tried to mitigate his initial involvement, stating, "I put her (Mrs. Duncan) off as long as I could. I put it off as long as I could. I had the car and she came and she was determined to make it before the weekend. Look, it was supposed to be done during the week and I kept putting it off and I kept wanting to go to the show and killing time—and I wasn't—and believe me if I had known that this lady was pregnant—Jesus, I would have backed out so fast it wouldn't have been funny. I was still—I was still against it when we were parked there."

Later, during questioning by Investigator Henderson, Gus demonstrated how he had strangled the helpless girl.

Henderson asked, "How did you put the stranglehold? Did you strangle her with your arm like this? Or with your hands, like this, when you were holding her?"

"No, I was holding her like this."

"Show me how you . . . "

"Like this, with my hands," Gus instructed, as he held his two hands straight out from his body, slanted towards the floor.

"Like her head was in here?" Henderson asked.

"No, down here, right here." Gus now lowered his hands towards the floor.

"Uh-huh, on the ground . . . "

"And you had her on your forearm, pressing down on her neck?"

"Uh-huh."

"I see, and you held her that way and she was still fighting, was she?"

"Uh-huh."

"And then what happened."

"Then I said I couldn't hold her and I started digging and Louie held her."

Later Gus described burying the victim. Henderson asked, "And did you ask him if she was dead?"

"No, I put my ear to her heartbeat and I couldn't feel it."

"You listened to the heartbeat of Olga Duncan and you could hear nothing. And did he also listen for her heartbeat?"

"I don't know."

"You don't know?"

"I don't remember—it was all just—"

"You drug her into the hole you dug and doubled her body up."

"Yeah."

"So it could fit in the hole. And then you put the dirt in on top of her. Did you stomp, tromp the dirt down with your foot then?"

"Uh-huh."

"And you stomped it down with your foot?"

"That's it."

Perhaps that was it. While this matter-of-fact account explained the heinous crime that had been committed, it did little to fully illustrate the truly brutal nature of the act.

Olga is Found

My day begins when your day ends.
—Homicide investigator's slogan

Homicide detectives, being the cynical bunch that they are, generally believe that a majority of murder victims have it coming. This attitude becomes a hazard of the job, as detectives plow through case after case of unsavory characters who are either slower on the draw or who finally meet their match in some street brawl. The end result is often called a "two-fer." That is to say, a crook gets murdered, eliminated forever, and another gets banished to jail for a long period of time. Thus the cops are able to cash in on the "two-for-one" action, in effect harvesting benefits of the ills from society.

While Detective Ray Higgins bought off on this theory, he also understood that there is occasionally, in the world of murder and mayhem, that victim who didn't deserve his or her untimely end, a truly innocent victim of crime. Ray was convinced that the woman described in Ventura Sheriff's Department case number 540–48, Olga Kupczyk Duncan, was such a victim, which made the solving of her case all that more satisfying.

Although Ray was doing an exemplary job of not showing it, he was absolutely jubilant on the morning of December 21. Gus had just finished his handwritten confession and had requested another piece of paper so he could draw the detectives a map of Olga's burial site.

"My pleasure," Ray said and then winked at his partner Clarence Henderson when he was sure Gus wouldn't see him. He pulled a fresh sheet off the yellow legal tablet and slid it across the table to Baldonado.

Gus looked at the paper for a second and then turned it slightly sideways. He began to draw two lines running parallel, starting at the bottom of the paper. While he drew, he explained, "This is the Casitas Pass Road, where it comes in from the 101 Highway. We traveled up this way towards Ojai for five or six miles before we stopped."

"Is there a turnout or wide spot in the road where you pulled in?" Henderson asked the man who continued to draw.

"Not really. I think we just parked on the highway. There wasn't no traffic at that time. Least I don't remember seeing any cars. But I was sorta busy."

"I guess you were," Henderson smirked.

"Is there some kind of landmark? Something we can use to identify the spot?" Ray asked.

"Well, there's this bridge over a culvert and a sharp curve to the right," Gus pointed to the paper, matching his description with the drawing.

"That whole road is one curve after another, Gus," Ray said, looking at the map. "And there's all kinds of culverts that feed Lake Casitas, each with a bridge over it."

Gus looked up at the detective, setting the pencil on top of his drawing. "Well, I guess I can always take you to the spot, if I really have to," he reluctantly offered. "But, I swear, I've never wanted to go back there, never ever wanted . . . " His voice trailed off.

Clarence looked at the young man and for the first time felt a slight pang of sympathy for him. He could understand that feeling, having to relive a nightmare. But the moment of sympathy passed quickly.

"I've got to ask you to take us out there," Clarence began. "For the sake of the family, we've got to recover the girl's body so she can have a decent burial. You know, put this thing to rest."

Gus looked at the man and nodded his head.

"Yeah, you're right, man. She—I mean they—deserve a proper resting place. I'll do it.

Shortly before 1:00 P.M. on that cool December day, Gus Baldonado climbed into a police car with Ray Higgins, Clarence Henderson, and Tom Osborne and began the drive to locate the victim's body. They traveled north from Ventura on the 33 Highway, towards Ojai. When they reached the area known as Mira Monte, they turned left onto Highway 150, the Casitas Pass. Once on the country road, they drove slowly, with Gus craning his neck and looking out the side window to try to locate the gravesite. He stopped them twice on dry runs, apologizing afterwards that he was so unsure of the location.

Finally, after an hour, Gus looked hard at a spot on the right side of the road, where a road marker informed them that they were 6.95 miles from the Santa Barbara County Line. When Gus saw the marker, he let out a cry, "This is it. This is the place. I'm sure!"

His head swiveled around and he looked out the back window while the sedan drove past the spot before coming to a complete stop. Ray backed up and pulled off the highway. He brought the car to a dust-swirling stop. There was complete silence in the vehicle, the occupants staring out the side window, deep in their own bittersweet thoughts, preparing themselves for what they hoped to unearth.

Tom Osborne was the first one out of the vehicle. "Well, let's get down to business," he said, throwing open a car door and stepping out.

He helped the handcuffed Gus out of the vehicle and the two walked to the front of the police car and peered over the side.

Looking down a twenty-foot embankment, they saw the culvert and a concrete drainage pipe protruding from the ground. When Ray walked up next to Gus, the killer said, "This is it. I'm positive. This is the place. If you dig right next to the end of the pipe, you'll find her." Gus pointed down the embankment. "Mr. Higgins, can I go back and sit in the car? I can't handle this."

Ray looked at the younger man, who had a childishly pleading look in his brown eyes. "Sure, T'lene. Go sit down."

While Gus was returning to the police car, Osborne made his way down the side of the embankment, rocks and dirt following him down the steep slope. He stopped where the ground leveled out in a roughly triangular pit formed by the road embankment and the sides of a ravine, in front of the concrete pipe. He shouted up at Ray, who was looking down at him, "You got a shovel?"

"Naw, I didn't bring one."

"How the hell am I supposed to dig?" came the exasperated response.

"The way they buried her: use your hands," Clarence instructed.

Tom muttered to himself, then kicked at the dirt, which was loose and sandy from the water that ran through the pipe. *It's a perfect place to bury a person,* he thought to himself, the sandy soil sticking to the toe of his shoe when he made indentations in it. He took off his jacket and removed his necktie, laying them gently across the protruding pipe, then bent over and began to scoop away dirt in the spot Gus had indicated. Going to his knees, he gingerly pushed the surface layer aside, considering the possibility of disturbing the evidence.

Shortly after the dirt began to feel moist and to turn a dark brown color, the investigator uncovered a patch of cloth. He worked slowly, moving handful after handful of the earth until he had uncovered an identifiable piece of clothing. He looked closely at it before he determined that it matched the description of the nightgown Olga had been seen wearing on the night of her disappearance.

"Hey, guys, I've got her. She's here!" Osborne shouted up to the two investigators still standing on the side of the road. While their real interest was with Tom, they had stayed by the car to keep a watchful eye on Gus.

"Okay! I'll call for the coroner and let the watch commander know. I imagine they'll want the press out here, too," Ray responded.

"Yeah. I'm not gonna do any more digging until the crime lab and coroner get here. They'll want to take pictures and start collecting the evidence."

Ray walked over to the police car and looked into the back seat. Gus was sitting with his head bowed, not looking up.

"We found her, Gus," Ray murmured to the man through the open window.

"Yeah, I heard him shout. I knew she was here. Oh Jesus, Mr. Higgins, I told Louie we'd pay for this. Now it's gonna happen, isn't it? Maybe I should see a priest?"

Ray looked at the pathetic man, whose face was screwed into a pleading mask.

"Sure, Gus. I'll take you soon as I can get things worked out here."

By 3:00 P.M., the three investigators had more help then they could use, including the brass from numerous departments. Such higher-ups are notorious among the foot soldiers for showing up at major crime scenes and interfering in the collection of evidence, and these were no exception. They milled everywhere, giving an assortment of releases to an ever-growing press corps.

At the direction of Coroner Virgil Payton, the detectives manned the shovels and carefully exhumed the decomposed body of the victim. A black, zippered plastic bag was lowered to the site and the remains were rolled onto it. Olga's body, which had been curled in a fetal position, was manipulated to fit inside. When the coroner pulled Olga's left arm away from her chest, he saw a bright sparkle on her hand. Payton brushed away some dirt and exposed the simple gold wedding band that had been the symbol of the undying love of her husband.

The remains were zipped into the bag, and a rope was attached to the ankles. The body was pulled up the steep embankment, to be transported to the morgue for autopsy.

Gus was returned to the jailhouse, where he would await his upcoming trial. No one bothered to find him a priest that day.

Luis Tells All

Ye that do truly and earnestly repent you of your sins, and are in love and charity with your neighbors . . . Draw near with faith, and take this Holy Sacrament to your comfort, and make your humble confession to Almighty God, meekly kneeling upon your knees.
—Prayer Book, 1662

Luis Moya sat before a group of reporters on the day after Gus Baldonado had led officers to the grave. He was freshly scrubbed, sitting behind a table, the gray bars of the Santa Barbara Jail providing a backdrop. Handcuffs joined his hands at the wrists, which he self-consciously kept hidden from view in his lap.

While the flashbulbs popped, Moya attempted to keep a smile on his face, looking younger than his years.

Finally, the questions started, and the smile faded.

No, he had not harmed anyone.

No, he had no idea why Baldonado would implicate him in a murder.

Sure, he had known Gus for some months.

No, he had never heard of Olga or Elizabeth Duncan.

Yes, he had an alibi for the night of November 17, but he would tell it to his attorney only.

Finally, the hands emerged, sweating and trembling, while he ran them through his hair. They dived into his front pocket and pulled out a pack of cigarettes. Luis quickly lit the smoke, his dexterity not hindered by the metal bracelets. The smoke curled around his dark hair and the questions slowed down. The trembling of his hands would not.

The smile returned, bringing with it a fresh young image. Not the appearance of a killer.

A photographer shouted from the back of the room, "Hey, Luis, can I get a close up?"

"Sure," the young man shot back, smoothing his hair in preparation for the picture.

He stubbed out the cigarette, again dropping his hands below the level of the table. He smiled for the cameraman, who had made his way to the front of the room. Luis waited patiently, but nothing happened. There was an awkward silence and then the photographer spoke.

"Uh, Luis, I wanted a shot of your hands."

"What?"

"Your hands, a picture of your hands."

"What for?" the puzzled young man asked, not producing the sought-after extremities.

There was a long pause. Some reporters shifted uncomfortably in their chairs, the photographer not certain how to tell him that he wanted a picture of the hands accused of such brutality. Finally, Sheriff John Ross, who had been standing behind Luis, walked forward. He pointed to two wine goblets sitting on the table. Luis, while killing time in his solitary cell, had fashioned them from the tinfoil used in cigarette packages.

"Moya, he wants to take a picture of the hands that crafted these fine goblets," the sheriff said, smiling at the young man. Sheriff Ross reached into his hip pocket and produced a set of keys. He selected the handcuff key and slid it easily into the cuffs, releasing first one and then the other. They made a ratcheting sound when he pushed them into a leather holder he had on his belt. "That should make you more comfortable."

Luis smiled uneasily while the photographer zeroed in on his hands. The flashbulb popped and the sheriff took that opportunity to conclude the press conference.

Moya Junior was led back to his cell to await the next turn of events.

He didn't have to wait long. That afternoon, Detective Ray Higgins and Investigator Clarence Henderson drove to Santa Barbara to transport Luis back to Ventura County to answer to the charge of murder. While Luis tried to rally support from Sheriff Ross to keep from going one county south, there was little hope of Ross not releasing him.

Like all Santa Barbara law enforcement officers, Sheriff Ross had breathed a sigh of relief when he learned Olga's body had been found more than six miles over the Ventura County line. He was even happier when the word got out that Gus had confirmed that Olga was actually murdered inside the neighboring county. While she was kidnapped in Santa Barbara, the more serious charge of murder had happened in another jurisdiction. That meant that he would not have to bear the brunt of what was bound to be a very long and costly trial.

While Luis was being led from the Santa Barbara Jail, the sheriff simply clapped him on the back and said, "Be seein' ya, Junior."

After Luis got settled into his new home at 501 Poli Street, Ray Higgins went to work on him in earnest. The persistent detective spent many hours talking to Moya, trying to convince him that the best course of action was to confess. It was during one of these sessions that Luis inadvertently gave Higgins an opening. Luis professed a newfound interest in religion, telling the detective that he was relying on his strengthening beliefs to get him through the torturous times he was now experiencing.

On Christmas night, in yet another interrogation, Higgins decided to use Luis's disclosure of his religious beliefs to get to the truth.

To further that end, the detective called a friend of his, the Reverend Floyd Gressett, to talk to the reluctant man.

Gressett, who was pastor of the Avenue Community Church in Ventura, was a long-time resident of the city. He was a well-respected member of the clergy and had always been a friend to law enforcement. The Reverend Gressett had been called on before to talk to criminals who needed spiritual guidance in order to confess their various sins.

Upon his arrival at the sheriff's station, Detective Higgins briefed Gressett. He then went into the interview room with Luis, silently closing the door behind him.

He stretched out his hand and introduced himself.

Luis shook the pastor's hand, presenting both of his since he was handcuffed.

"Ray Higgins asked me to talk to you."

"I appreciate your coming."

"Ray says you have something to get off your chest, something that's haunting you."

"I don't know. I'm scared, Reverend. I'm so scared!"

"When I feel that way, I find that prayer helps. Shall we pray?"

Luis bowed his head before the man, while Gressett began a prayer. "Dear Lord, help this young man to overcome his fear of the truth. Lord, lead him to the path of righteousness, so that he may walk down it and find peace within himself."

While the minister continued his prayer, he heard Luis crying, his breath coming in spurts as he gulped air between sobs.

When Gressett had concluded his prayer, he asked Luis gently, "Are you now ready to tell the truth?"

Luis wiped the tears away, not able to speak. He finally shrugged his shoulders, showing his uncertainty.

"Come sit with me." The pastor moved his chair directly in front of Moya's location. They sat knee to knee, the Reverend Gressett grasping Moya's hands in his. Luis bowed his head, reluctant to look into the eyes of the other man.

"You know, Moya, some time and some place you'll wish to be forgiven for your sins. And I think you are living with a great misdeed now."

Luis looked up, the tears streaming down his cheeks and rolling off the bottom of his chin. He nodded his head in agreement.

"You must be strong now. And it will take great strength, but you must confess your wrongdoing."

"I will, I will," Luis sobbed. "Please forgive me?"

"I cannot forgive you. Only God can do that. And he won't forgive you if you lie. If you lie to man you will lie to God."

"No, never, I wouldn't . . . "

"You must come clean on this. Hell is awaiting you!" Gressett's voice boomed while he squeezed Luis's hands.

"Oh, Jesus, what can I do? Please forgive me." Luis threw himself to his knees on the floor. He began to beat his pinioned hands on the cold concrete crying out in his anguish. "I want to tell God the truth! I want to get this over!"

The Reverend Gressett knelt down next to Luis and whispered to him, "My young man, if you are truthful, God will forgive you." He squeezed him with an arm draped over Luis's back, then rose to leave the room. He looked down at Luis, hunched in a miserable ball in the center of the room, his body racked with his cries. Gressett opened the door and exited the room. He walked up to Detective Higgins, who had been waiting for nearly an hour in the hallway, and said, "He's ready, but you best give him a couple of minutes to compose himself "

And ready Luis was, spilling forth, unassisted by questions, the story of the brutal murder that the three conspirators had arranged.

Luis rambled through his confession, starting at day one and not finishing until he had explained every detail. He stated, "The reason she gave to us for getting rid of her daughter-in-law, as she put it, was for . . . was because she was blackmailing her son. She showed us various checks that was stamped . . . and that, she said, was the reason for wanting to get rid of her."

"On the night of the 17th of November, me and Augustine Baldonado, we went to Olga Duncan's apartment . . . and we had it planned that I was to go up and tell her that her husband was downstairs, that he was drunk, and that he had asked me to bring him home and this was the address that he gave me, but I needed some help, help bringing him upstairs to her apartment. After I . . . afterwards she went downstairs with me to the car—Sarah Contreras's car. Augustine Baldonado was in the back seat waiting for her. As she opened the door, presumably to take her husband out, I hit her over the head with this .22 pistol that I borrowed from Rojo, and apparently I didn't hit her hard enough because she started screaming. Baldonado grabbed her and put her in the car."

Luis described the route they took out of town and continued his story when Olga regained consciousness. "I turned off the main highway and took the Cabrillo Highway, which is down by the beach in Santa Barbara, and stopped. All this time, Baldonado had hit her a couple of times with the pistol, but apparently he didn't knock her out, so I stopped the car and I took possession of the pistol and I hit her once, a hard blow, because with that blow the pistol broke. She passed out and I drove away."

Luis reacted to a question from Detective Higgins, who showed him a picture of the location they had chosen to bury Olga. "Yes, sir, there is the culvert marker: B352+75. That's on the Ojai highway. There we dragged her out of the car, but the lady wasn't dead yet. There's only one thing that I'd like to express at this moment, is that we didn't know that she was pregnant. Honest to God, we didn't, and that is the honest-to-God truth. I want you people to know . . . that if we would have known that she was pregnant we would have probably repented right there and then. I love kids and so does Gus. Well, afterwards, we took her down to the culvert and—we—I held her down while Baldonado dug a grave for her and afterwards he held her while I dug. The lady was still struggling. We thought she was struggling for her life. If we would have known she was struggling for her baby's life, I wouldn't have done it. But it's done and I am

196

confessing that I took part in it. We, as he said, we strangled her till we thought she was dead. By that time, I had dug a hole—no grave—a hole for her and her child and we put her in there and buried her."

Luis then went on to describe the drive back to Santa Barbara and the many subsequent attempts to collect money from Mrs. Duncan.

While both men maintained to their death that they didn't know Olga was pregnant, others involved in the case doubted that they could not have known. The Reverent Gressett stated it clearly: "They lied about that. They knew, they had to have known."

Now armed with the two confessions, with a host of witnesses, and with a considerable amount of incriminating evidence, detectives and prosecutors began to prepare for the next phases: indictments and trials.

Part III
THE TRIAL

A Nickname

The place of justice is a hallowed place.

—Francis Bacon, *Of Judicature*

Bob Holt shouldered his way through a crowd of fellow reporters. Like the others, he had just spotted Frank Duncan in the hallway leading to the grand jury hearing room. The voices clamored out, "Hey, Frank! Frank, over here!" The newsmen jostled each other in an effort to catch up to the attorney.

The pursued man finally stopped and turned around, looking warily at the group as it closed in.

"Is your mother innocent?" one reporter shouted.

"Yes. I think she is. She would have to be insane . . . no sane person would ever have done such a thing."

"Have you seen your mother since the discovery of the body?"

"No, I haven't, and I don't intend to until the grand jury has ruled."

"We heard the district attorney was unable to find you to serve a subpoena. Where have you been?" Bob Holt called out to Frank.

"After I heard Olga had been found, I went to Hollywood. I wanted to be alone."

Frank pulled out a handkerchief, daubing at tears that began to roll down his cheeks. A hush fell over the crowd of newsmen, who watched the man wipe his eyes.

"That's . . . that's all I can say for now." The crying man turned on his heels and made his way down the hallway, leaving behind the crowd of newsmen.

Bob looked over at another reporter who was finishing up some notes in journalist shorthand. "He's really taking this hard."

"Understandable though. Losing your wife and now his mother is gonna be on trial."

"Not a spot I'd want to be in. Hey, who's that?" The newsman pointed towards a woman being escorted by two plainclothes deputies. The group began hurrying in her direction.

Such was the scene outside the grand jury hearing room as the most spectacular case in Ventura County history began to unfold. On the day after Christmas, 1958, District Attorney Roy Gustafson brought fifteen witnesses before the grand jury. Following nine hours of testimony and a scant fifteen minutes of deliberation, the panel returned indictments against Mrs. Elizabeth Duncan and her two cohorts. Besides the murder indictment, Elizabeth was also indicted for offering a bribe, for soliciting perjury, for preparing a false document, and for forgery in the annulment scam.

An intensive search to find her co-actor in the annulment proved fruitless. A $50,000 warrant was issued for Ralph Winterstein, who had fled the state.

The December 30 edition of the *Ventura County Star Free Press,* authored by police and courts reporter Bob Holt, bore the headline: "LURID MURDER PLOT BARED IN TRANSCRIPT; SECRET TESTIMONY TELLS OF HIRING."

The story lead read: "Witnesses and the two men who claim they were hired to kill Olga Duncan told the Ventura County grand jury last week a grisly, macabre, almost unbelievable story of the events leading up to the murder of the thirty-year-old Santa Barbara nurse. Their testimony was revealed in a transcript of the proceedings of last Friday's all-day grand jury session, during which fifteen witnesses, including the two confessed killers, testified. Witnesses are quoted in the transcript as being offered money to poison Olga, to dump her in a bathtub and cover her with lye, to hurl acid on her, to club her, and to carry her body off to Mexico. These were among the plans attributed to Elizabeth Duncan by grand jury witnesses to get rid of a daughter-in-law she believed had stolen the love of her son, Frank. The transcript contains testimony that Elizabeth Duncan and her attorney son lived as 'man and wife,' not mother and son. It tells of secret meetings, intrigue, plans for killing, plans for payoffs, and offers of pay for 'getting rid' of Olga."

In writing this article, Bob Holt had used his considerable talent and had called in a couple of favors to breach the normally secret testimony of the grand jury. He produced a story many pages long, which went into graphic details of the murder, quoting Luis Moya and Gus Baldonado, in addition to other principals in the case. This story, and the many others that followed, inflamed the ire of the citizens of Ventura and Santa Barbara Counties, fueling a feeling of intense hatred for the murderers.

The round-cheeked man charged with the prosecution of Elizabeth and her two thugs was an attorney equal to the challenge. Roy A. Gustafson, District Attorney of Ventura County, was well respected among his peers as an able and effective criminal prosecutor.

Like many others living in Ventura County, he came to the balmy Southern California community by way of service in the United States Navy, which maintained two major bases on the Ventura County coast. Originally from Duluth, Minnesota, Gustafson rose to the rank of lieutenant commander while serving as a navy lawyer during World War II. After release from the military, he returned to the West Coast, where he hung out his shingle in Oxnard. He did so by starting a law firm with another Minnesotan, H. F. Rosenmund.

After three years in the practice of civilian law, the relatively unknown attorney challenged and beat the incumbent district attorney in a close election, assuming his new responsibilities in 1950.

By the time the Duncan case came to his office, Gustafson was a well-known and experienced prosecutor, having been reelected to three terms.

The feisty lawyer was continually embroiled in controversy, as his strong pro-victim advocacy frequently found him at odds with defense attorneys and judges alike. However, this forty-year-old, slightly balding man, who always wore suspenders to court, was not one to take on a problem and then drop it for lack of action. In 1955, he lost a death penalty conviction in the Earl Compton Green murder case, after the jury received what Gustafson considered insufficient evidence of the defendant's prior criminal record during the trial.

Miffed by the identified weakness in the trying of California capital cases, Gustafson wrote and shepherded legislation to establish a new three-phase trial system, which replaced the previously used two-phase procedure.

The Gustafson method, which became California court procedural law, was used by its author for the first time during the Duncan case. This law split the hearing into three distinct stages: guilt, penalty, and sanity. By separating the guilt and penalty phases, all evidence—both favorable and unfavorable—could be brought up in the latter without prejudicing the jury as to guilt. This allowed the prosecution to introduce, at the penalty phase, a defendant's past record, so the jury could better determine appropriate punishment.

At the time of the Duncan trial, Gustafson had eight attorneys and four investigators working for him. However, there was never any doubt that he would personally try the notorious case. He had successfully tried two other capital cases, sending one man to his death in the gas chamber at San Quentin.

The Superior Court of Ventura County sat on the second floor of an impressive building located at the base of the foothills north of the city. Spread below its Roman Doric construction was a commanding view of the City of San Buenaventura and the sparkling Pacific Ocean. The building itself, with its marble facade, was finished in 1913 and declared the finest government building west of the Mississippi River.

The courtroom rang of traditional American jurisprudence, with a high judge's bench, rich wood paneling and railings, and a large gallery for the audience. The woods were ornately carved and exuded an odor consistent with the highly polished condition in which they were kept.

It was into Superior Court Division One, the courtroom of Judge Charles F. Blackstock, that the people of the State of California brought their case against Elizabeth A. Duncan et al.

On December 30, 1958, at 9:30 A.M., the trio was arraigned before Judge Blackstock. The cameras whirred and Mrs. Duncan, who was quickly becoming accustomed to her newfound fame, agreed to do a photo shoot for the news photographers. She removed her glasses, patted her well-coifed hair, and grinned and preened in front of the cameras. She balked only at having her photo taken with her crime partners, causing Gus to ask her, "What's the matter, you ashamed of what you done?" She shot a cold look at her co-defendant, and then turned her attention back to the cameras.

While Elizabeth appeared calm and passive in court, after hours was a different story. She was often physically aggressive, requiring deputies to forcefully subdue her.

Deputy Mary Forgey, who was assigned the unheralded task of providing security for the infamous defendant, found herself in more than one scuffle with the woman, who was definitely not a submissive inmate. Mary's subsequent experiences with the defendant would run a wide and interesting gamut from out-and-out fighting her in the early days, to being invited to play cards with Elizabeth while the jury was deliberating her fate.

Mary's close contact with Mrs. Duncan eventually helped her to understand the woman and Deputy Forgey would become the only sheriff's staff member who could easily handle the defendant.

Elizabeth's cooperation level improved after Mary agreed to allow Frank to put a diamond heart locket on his mother every morning before court. Mary would stand by and watch while Frank lovingly put the trinket around his mother's neck. The deputy would remove the locket after the day's proceedings and return it to Frank.

After Mrs. Duncan received a defense-ordered electroencephalogram at Camarillo State Hospital, her mood seemed to improve even more. Though Elizabeth never acquiesced to the wishes of the other jailers, she would normally do what Mary asked of her. This often caused the staff members to call the deputy at home. Mary would drive to the jail at all hours to retrieve items out of Mrs. Duncan's cell or to convince her to stop threatening the matrons or other inmates.

While the drama of various court appearances continued, Olga's father and brother traveled from Canada to take care of the arrangements for the victim's funeral. Although Olga's mother had been scheduled to make the trip with them, she was unable to because of the way she learned of her daughter's death. Mrs. Kupczyk had received a phone call from an insensitive journalist who wanted to be the first to get her reaction to the news, news she hadn't yet received. The announcement over the telephone had caused the surprised mother to faint, the phone receiver dropping to the kitchen floor. She was rushed to the hospital and was still there on the day that other family members began the trip to the States.

While the trio of murderers was being arraigned across town, Olga's funeral was in progress. The service not only was attended by family and friends, but also attracted more than a few of the curious. The funeral attendees held up well until Olga's distraught father threw himself on the closed casket of his daughter. His voice reverberated through the Ted Mayer Funeral Home, crying out in distress, "Oh, what did they do to you, my baby? What did they do to you?" The grieving man then went limp and slumped to the floor, his hands sliding down the side of his daughter's coffin. He had to be carried from the funeral home.

Olga's sealed casket sat below a large white flower cascade with "Love Lasts Forever" inscribed across the center in a bold yellow banner. Frank, who had purchased this token of his love, apparently later felt that love lasts somewhat short of forever, since he subsequently failed to pay for his wife's funeral.

After the arraignment and the appointing of attorneys for Luis Moya and Augustine Baldonado, all three of the accused were returned to their cells to await their next court date.

Frank Duncan, who had originally represented his mother following her arrest, had now hired the noted Los Angeles criminal attorney, S. Ward Sullivan.

On the morning of January 7, 1959, Bob Holt had cornered a front-row seat in Superior One in anticipation of Mrs. Duncan's presence to enter a plea. Holt, who had just moved from the sports desk to the police and courts beat, was determined to get the whole story, a report he was sure would be hard to match in the years to come.

Outside, in the hallway, Elizabeth, with the aid of bailiffs and her attorney, shouldered her way through a crowd of two hundred and fifty spectators and press, trying to get into Superior One. The throng, which had earlier been cheerful and lighthearted, almost to the point of being in a carnival mood, turned ugly when Mrs. Duncan appeared in the hallway. One of the first of the congregation to see her, a woman with a large white purse alerted the rest of the mob with a shrill cry, "Look! There she is now! There's Ma Duncan!"

The large gathering, now fully aware of the defendant's presence, began calling out curses and threats to the woman, many of them using this new nickname. As Elizabeth pushed herself through the swinging doors that led into the courtroom, the lady with the purse shook it at her and yelled, "Where's the mama's boy, Frankie?" Ma's only response was an icy look that quelled any further jeers from the woman.

At the pleading, Elizabeth entered pleas of not guilty and not guilty by reason of insanity. A grumble was heard throughout the courtroom when the defendant declared herself innocent.

The usual courtroom procedures were followed. Judge Blackstock appointed two psychiatrists to examine her and ordered up a panel of two hundred and fifty prospective jurors, instead of the standard thirty-five. The judge later reduced this number to one hundred and fifty.

The defendant's attorney submitted an affidavit stating that he felt his client would not receive a fair trial in Ventura County and requested consideration of a change of venue. He cited the disturbance that had just occurred in the hallway as further proof of the bias of the local citizens. He later withdrew this request when the district attorney objected that he was not provided a copy of the motion in order to argue against it. Judge Blackstock stated that he would hear such a motion at a later date.

Deputy Forgey escorted Ma Duncan from the courtroom. After they had cleared the crowded hall, Elizabeth and Mary passed Deputy Ruben Zavala in the hallway.

Mrs. Duncan looked the attractive man up and down and whispered to Mary, "He could put his shoes under my bed anytime." Mary only smiled, wondering at the complex nature of this woman who had just pled not guilty to the most atrocious crime in recent memory.

Ma Duncan's trial was set for February 16, 1959, to commence at 9:30 A.M.

Bob Holt had his story for that day. He hurried down California Street, at the base of the courthouse, en route to the offices of the *Star Free Press* to file his report with the editor. Just before entering the building, he looked back at the courthouse.

In front of the impressive structure, Father Junipero Serra's statue stood sentry to the halls of justice. Holt stood for a moment, looking at the impressive figure, wondering what the devout Father of the California Missions would think of such an unchristian crime. Since he had no answer, Holt quickly ducked into his office.

An Impartial Panel

The hungry judges soon the sentence sign,
And wretches hang that jurymen may dine.
　　　　　　　　—Alexander Pope, *The Rape of the Lock*

The man in black robes who sat behind the bench in Superior Courtroom One was Judge Charles F. Blackstock, age eighty-three at the start of the Ma Duncan murder trial.

Judge Blackstock, who was born on December 30, 1875, in a house that was later destroyed to make way for the new courthouse, now sat a mere fifty feet from his birthplace.

He was the only male graduate of Ventura High School's class of 1895 and had married one of his classmates, Grace Woods.

He attended the University of California and became a schoolteacher, working in both Los Angeles and Simi Valley before taking a principal's position in the Hueneme School District.

Following in his father's footsteps, Charles Blackstock then entered the practice of law. Like many attorneys of that era, he had no formal schooling in jurisprudence, but developed his expertise by "reading law" in his father's office.

The younger Blackstock was admitted to the bar in 1903 and soon became a recognized expert in the area of law relating to water rights. He traveled throughout California representing litigants in their never-ending fights over that scarce Southern California commodity.

He became the first president of the Ventura County Bar Association and was a noted public speaker, often peppering his comments with quotations from Shakespeare and from other literary classics. Blackstock maintained a law office in Oxnard from 1910 to 1946, when Governor Earl Warren appointed him to the newly expanded Superior Court.

By the time that he sat on the Duncan murder trial, Judge Blackstock had begun to show physical deterioration and required a cane to get around. But his mind, a vast storehouse of legal knowledge, remained unaffected by age.

The quick-witted but admittedly often sharp-tongued judge had made several important judicial decisions in this case prior to the first day of jury selection. He had ensured the custody of the accused by refusing to lower their bails to a manageable amount and had combed the list of local attorneys, appointing two capable advocates to represent Baldonado and Moya.

While Judge Blackstock prepared himself for the most important case of his career, controversy swirled around the out-of-court antics of the attorneys and principals alike.

Roy Gustafson gave an extensive press release on December 22, 1958, in support of the death sentence. He was quoted as saying, "The brutal, calculated, revolting killing-for-hire of Olga Duncan is one of a number of horrible crimes which have recently been committed in California. I simply cannot understand how some of our leaders, in the face of these events, can seriously contend that the death penalty is not appropriate punishment for the perpetrators of such crimes." He went on to say, "Retaliation is a basic instinct of the human race. From biblical times, a life for a life has been recognized as just and fair."

This press release, as well as subsequent ones, raised an uproar from the three attorneys representing the accused. The most strident response came from Burt Henson, appointed to represent Luis Moya, and himself a former deputy district attorney. In a rebuttal press release of January 2, Henson lambasted Gustafson: "The district attorney has seen fit to try this case in the newspapers and in the court of public opinion. In the court of public opinion, he appears to have assumed the combined roll of judge, jury, and lord high executioner. The impact on the minds of prospective jurors is the same as though he had sent out invitations to a hanging. I hope that he will stop thinking about his personal death row batting average and start thinking about fundamental basic justice."

Henson further commented on the fallacy of Gustafson's argument of society's need for retribution: "I cannot believe that anyone will adopt the barbaric theory of retaliation killing as expounded by the district attorney. I cannot believe that any useful purpose would be served by a retaliation killing of a young man of the age of twenty."

The great degree of publicity generated by the district attorney would later become the primary focus of requests for changes of venue by all three defense attorneys.

On January 13, 1959, the attorneys for Augustine Baldonado and Luis Moya entered pleas of not guilty and not guilty by reason of insanity before Judge Blackstock.

Burt Henson also submitted affidavits supporting a change of venue. Included in the request were statements from nine persons that the trio could not receive a fair trial in Ventura County. Other submitted statements included quoted opinions that the defendants were guilty, that they should be hanged, and that the lynch law should be invoked. And, to further prove the extreme prejudice of the citizens, Henson pointed out that even his eleven-year-old daughter had told him it was a "bum case" and wondered why he had taken it. John Danch, the attorney for Baldonado, concurred in the affidavits submitted.

The district attorney countered these legal arguments by stating that he and other officials had "the right to release information to the press" and that the newspapers had "the right to publish it." He further argued that the publication of news, and the fact that persons form opinions based on reading the news, are not sufficient reasons to rule that a prospective juror cannot fairly judge testimony and arrive at a just verdict.

The matter was taken under submission by the judge, who issued the denial of the request along with this statement: "If I had the slightest doubt in the world about the ability of the defendants to receive a fair trial in Ventura County, I would without the slightest hesitation grant the motion for a change of venue. But, since I have no such doubt, motions are denied without prejudice to a renewal thereof after *voir dire*." Although speaking of Moya and Baldonado in this instance, Judge Blackstock would later make a similar ruling in regard to Elizabeth's subsequent request for a change of venue.

Finding suitable accommodations for a growing press corps began to create problems for a courthouse not accustomed to such sensational events. Correspondents from the *London Mirror* and *Vita* magazine, an Italian publication, were but a few of the hundreds of reporters competing for releases as the trial date drew near. The local reporters, who were able to provide background and substance to the many out-of-towners, became almost as newsworthy as the persons charged in the case. Bob Holt, who had ten years' experience reporting the events of the county, was a highly sought-after commodity. He soon became the lead reporter on the case and even acted as a sort of wire service after some of the out-of-state press had departed. They would call him daily, asking for updates and his impressions about how the case was going.

In the meantime, bowing to the demands of the press, the county clerk had to give up part of his office to establish a press room, complete with banks of black telephones for those all-important phone calls to impatient editors.

Although under pressure to rule otherwise, Judge Blackstock denied live radio or television coverage in the courtroom.

Sixteen days after pleading not guilty to the murder, Luis Moya unexpectedly went to court and changed his plea to guilty. He maintained his defense of insanity, and a trial of the issues of sanity and penalty was scheduled for April 20, 1959. At the time of the plea change, Burt Henson issued a press release. It said in part, "This decision on the part of Luis Moya was made only after prayerful consideration of whether or not this was the right thing to do. He believes that this way is the way God would want him to go."

Henson concluded his statement by again criticizing the district attorney, this time faulting him for failing to file murder charges against many of the others who had stood by and allowed the crime to occur. He stated, "There is apparently no law which makes it a criminal offense for one to sit idly by and see another person murdered. It appears from the testimony taken before the grand jury that Frank Duncan, Diane Romero, and Rudy Romero all had knowledge of the attempts by Mrs. Elizabeth Duncan to have Olga Duncan killed. It appears from the testimony before the grand jury that Esperanza Esquivel and Emma Short had knowledge that would lead a reasonable person to be practically certain that Olga Duncan was about to die. It appears from reading of the grand jury transcripts that these people did little or nothing to prevent the tragic death of Olga Duncan. It would seem that they should bear some legal responsibility for her death. It is clear that they bear some moral responsibility for the tragedy."

While Gustafson never responded to these criticisms, one of his investigators would later state the obvious: the others, with the exception of Frank, were not prosecuted so their testimony could be used against the three primary defendants.

Frank, who remained loyal to his mother and was a primary defense witness, was not prosecutable under the law because there was no provable criminal case against him.

On February 10, Augustine Baldonado took the same route as his crime partner and withdrew his plea of not guilty. He was somewhat reluctant to admit to murder in the first degree, but did so after an animated conversation with his attorney. The pleadings of the two defendants delighted Mrs. Duncan's attorney who knew that a combined trial with all three defendants would be very damaging to his client.

At 9:45 A.M. on February 16, Elizabeth Duncan, dressed in a plain black dress as if in mourning, sat in Superior One next to her son Frank. At the request of photographers, she straightened her son's tie and smiled for the camera. Jury selection had begun and would continue for the next five days. During the course of selection, ninety prospective jurors were closely questioned by both attorneys before twelve jurors and two alternates were selected.

S. Ward Sullivan's questions to prospective jurors followed a pattern similar to that of all criminal cases. He asked about occupations, prior jury service, relations to police officers, and if a policeman's testimony would carry more weight than that of any other witness. Sullivan also tried to determine the amount of pre-trial publicity each juror had heard and if the fact that Olga was pregnant when killed weighed heavily on the individual. He also asked if the prospective juror had been an assault victim in the past. His final question was, "Would you want your wife (or yourself), accused as is Mrs. Duncan, tried by a jury made up of men and women in the frame of mind in which you now find yourself?"

Roy Gustafson's major concern in selecting a jury was determining each one's view of the death penalty. He eventually removed twenty-six prospective jurors who said they did not support the ultimate penalty. In an effort to counter Sullivan's frame-of-mind question, Gustafson asked prospective jurors, "Could you not put aside any preconceptions gained from newspaper accounts or conversation with friends and try the case solely on the evidence presented in court?"

By day four of jury selection, S. Ward Sullivan had only six peremptory challenges left out of the original twenty allowed by law. The use of the peremptory challenge allows either attorney to remove a prospective juror from the panel without having to state and justify a specific cause for doing so. In an atmosphere considered to be biased, these peremptory challenges are crucial to the proper defense of the accused. In this case, after using all of his challenges, Sullivan was forced to accept what his client called a biased jury. The issue of the fairness of the jury would later be appealed to the United States Supreme Court.

Judge Blackstock had taken a conservative approach to the removal of jurors for cause. On day four of the selection process, Sullivan was able to remove only one prospective juror who stated that he would not be able to overcome his prejudice towards Mrs. Duncan and give her a fair trial. Any juror who wavered on this issue was generally found fit to be impaneled by the judge. Blackstock evidently bought Gustafson's argument that the law did not require that a prospective juror have an unprejudiced mind, but only that they be willing to decide the case solely on the evidence produced in court and on the rules of law propounded by the judge.

On day five, having used all of his peremptory challenges, and not being able to remove the seated jurors for cause, the defense attorney reluctantly accepted the jury.

Among the panel were three individuals who admitted that they had opinions adverse to Mrs. Duncan from publicity that they had seen or heard, but all three indicated that they could put these feelings aside and judge her fairly.

Ma Duncan stared at the panel while it was being sworn in and blurted out in open court, "There are so many against me!"

An Overwhelming Array

We have reason to believe you have committed an offense.
—Heading for London police ticket for overdue parking

While initially very closemouthed about the number of subpoenas he had issued, District Attorney Gustafson would later estimate that around one hundred witnesses would be called in his bid to send Ma Duncan to the gas chamber.

Testimony in the case began on February 24, 1959, after the prosecutor made his opening statement. In his comments, Gustafson told the jury he would provide them with a verbal picture sufficient to allow them to follow the evidence in the case. He discussed a motive for the murder, which he claimed was the extreme jealousy that Elizabeth Duncan felt towards Olga. And, regarding her effort to dissolve the marriage, Gustafson provided the jury with a theory of the defendant's progressive use of violence to accomplish her aim. According to the prosecutor, this chain of events started with threatening phone calls, moved to in-person threats of violence, graduated to the annulment plot, and ultimately ended with the murder of the victim.

Of Olga, Gustafson said, "She was a very lovely, wonderful, pretty, likable, calm girl who deserved to live a long and happy life."

In an altered approach to a standard murder trial, Gustafson then came out shooting by calling his primary witnesses prior to establishing the actual death of the victim. By the second day, he had presented testimony of Rebecca Diaz, Diane and Rudy Romero, and Barbara Reed, all of whom said they were approached by Elizabeth to kill Olga.

Mrs. Duncan, who was now an old hand at playacting for the press, displayed a variety of moods during the first phase of the trial. It became notable news when she broke down in tears during the testimony of Barbara Reed, who was asked questions about her girlhood friend, the deceased Patsy Duncan. Earlier, the defendant had been clutching a rosary, and she stated during one of her recess press conferences that Frank had given it to her nine years ago and that she was now praying regularly for a favorable outcome to the trial. Mrs. Duncan's reliance on religion appeared to be only for the press. Behind the scenes, she refused to accept a bible that was mailed to her from a well-meaning citizen who hoped that, through its passages, she could find salvation. The sheriff returned the item with an accompanying letter thanking the Good Samaritan for her kind thoughts.

Day three saw a controlled Luis Moya on the stand, driving a weeping Frank Duncan from the courtroom with his emotionless description of Olga's murder. His testimony, which varied little from the original version to the grand jury, was virtually unattackable by the defense.

Ralph Winterstein also took the stand. He had recently been extradited from New Orleans after being tracked down and arrested by agents from the Federal Bureau of Investigation. Winterstein, who had already pled guilty to charges of perjury in connection with the phony annulment when testifying about the scam, stated that Mrs. Duncan had told him that Frank had found out about the annulment the day after it was granted. This statement disturbed Frank Duncan, who immediately told reporters that he hadn't known about the annulment for many weeks after it was granted. Frank would maintain this fact throughout the trial, though other witnesses besides Winterstein disputed it in court.

Hal Hammons, the Ventura attorney who had obtained the annulment, was called to the stand next. His statements supported those of Ralph Winterstein.

On February 27, the district attorney finally got around to proving the death of the victim. Olga's identity was established through testimony of the medical examiner and the introduction of dental records. Her body was otherwise unidentifiable.

Dr. D. Gordon Johnson, the autopsy surgeon, was hesitant to fix the exact cause of death due to the decomposition of the body. He noted that most organs of the body had undergone liquefaction and that there was no blood fluid available on which to run standard tests. When asked to identify the cause of death, Dr. Johnson stated, "The mechanism of death, I believe, was one of three things: strangulation, suffocation, or brain damage due to trauma." Gustafson then tried to clarify Dr. Johnson's statements.

"In other words, it could have been either the blows on the head with the pistol . . . "

"Yes, sir."

" . . . or the actual strangulation or suffocation?"

"Strangulation or suffocation. Being placed in an environment with no oxygen, such as being buried."

Dr. Johnson, using generic terms, also confirmed the death of Olga's baby, which he described as "a female fetus, 43 centimeters in length from crown to heel, found in the uterus."

The district attorney then shocked the jury when he unbagged the fluid-soaked clothing of the victim and presented it as evidence. There was an audible groan from the jury members as the pungent odor of death spread throughout the courtroom. While this act was horrifying enough, it was quickly followed by an exhibit of autopsy pictures of the remains, with the fetus clearly visible within the victim's womb. This sent two jurors reeling from the courtroom, causing Judge Blackstock to call a hasty recess.

This day also saw very damaging testimony by Esperanza Esquivel and a now reluctant Augustine Baldonado, who had apparently lost his nerve to testify. However, through Gus's halting statements, Gustafson was able to support the assertions of Luis Moya, who, in contrast, had seemed proud of his involvement.

Gustafson's star witness turned out to be the former friend of the defendant, Emma Short. The lanky, gray-haired woman testified for two days, at times displaying a faulty memory, though at other times reciting event after event during the period of time Mrs. Duncan had searched for the killers. At one point, the frustrated Elizabeth spat, "You liar!" while Mrs. Short told her tale. The elderly woman, who avoided making eye contact with her previously close friend, would not even walk past the defense table out of fear of being attacked by the defendant.

The last witnesses called by the prosecution added a new dimension previously little known. Julia Ellen Price, Gladys Kline, and Barbara Edwards were all cellmates of Ma Duncan's in the county jail. Kline and Price testified to the hatching of an escape plot by Mrs. Duncan. Mrs. Kline stated that Elizabeth had offered her $2,000 to help her kill the jail matron, after which the accused had said they could escape to Hollywood and have their appearances and fingerprints changed by a doctor friend.

Julia Price lent more details to the plotted escape, which had been set for January 10 after midnight. Mrs. Duncan was to lure Matron Mildred Wolfe into the cellblock by requesting some medications. They would kill the matron, take her keys, and escape. Mrs. Price, who had no stomach for murdering an officer, had tipped off authorities.

When information about the jailbreak plot had originally surfaced, Frank had formed his own opinion about the reasons behind the story. He accused the sheriff of looking for a way to inhibit himself and his mother's attorney from visiting the defendant in an effort to hinder her defense.

However, many years later, Deputy Mary Forgey would remember the jailbreak plot. There was no doubt in her mind that the threat was real. Mary said, "She (Elizabeth) once told me that if she could get a key she would be gone. Personally, I think she would have killed to get out."

After the discovery of the escape plot, Elizabeth was kept in a segregated cell. This was done not only to prevent her escape, but because the other female inmates didn't want to be housed with her out of a genuine fear of the woman.

The prosecution also managed to raise the eyebrows of the courtroom spectators when Mrs. Kline testified to some jailhouse banter she attributed to Elizabeth.

"Did she ever refer to her (Olga's) nationality?"

"Yes."

"What did she say?"

"She said she (Olga) wasn't really from Canada. That she was from someplace else. She was a Russian spy . . . "

Roy Gustafson, always willing to attack either of the Duncans, then moved into another area with Mrs. Kline.

"Now, did Mrs. Duncan ever say anything to you with respect to statements that had been made about Mrs. Duncan's relationship with her son Frank?"

"Well, naturally that she loved him very dearly and that more or less he was her whole life and all she had was his best interest at heart. The only other thing that she ever said was—we all sat around, naturally, and discussed our families and there was one of the girls mentioned the fact about her . . . about her son sleeping with her. She said, 'Well, I don't see anything wrong with that because on cold mornings I've still gotten in bed with Frank. There's nothing wrong with that!'"

The defense attempted to soften this view by getting Mrs. Kline to admit that all Frank was really doing was "consoling" his mother on nights that she could not sleep. Mrs. Kline was hesitant to accept that theory, but the next witness did testify to that fact.

Barbara Edwards was the last prosecution witness called to the stand. In discussing the death of Olga, Mrs. Edwards stated that Elizabeth had told her that Moya and Baldonado "beat her and beat her and beat her, but the bitch wouldn't die. Isn't that just like a mean old Russian?"

The prosecution rested its case on the afternoon of March 3. During six full days of testimony, the district attorney, who fell well short of his original estimate, presented twenty-seven witnesses to prove Ma Duncan guilty of murder in the first degree.

Speaking of the prosecution's case, Frank admitted to the press that he could not deny that, taken as a whole, the case had a certain cumulative effect.

Throughout the six days of testimony, it was hinted by the defense that Mrs. Duncan would take the stand in her own behalf. The next morning, in anticipation of this occurrence, more than twice as many curious onlookers arrived than the courtroom would hold. At the opening of the doors to Superior One, the mob rushed to their seats, eager to view the drama that was about to unfold.

The Defendant's Word

She was mean.
—Deputy Mary Forgey on Ma Duncan

Judge Blackstock, who was trying to get an upper hand on what often proved an unruly gathering in the gallery, looked sternly at the packed courthouse, pounding his gavel on its wooden block.

"I'm warning you folks. Any outburst today and I will clear this courtroom. And that is final!"

"Mr. Sullivan, you may call your first witness."

"Thank you, Your Honor. I call Mrs. Elizabeth Ann Duncan."

Bob Holt whipped out his old leather-covered notebook and opened it to the first clean page. He noted that in spite of the warning the judge had just issued, a murmur spilled from the crowd when Mrs. Duncan, dressed in a black and white cotton print dress, got up and faced the clerk to be sworn in. After being sworn, the woman made her way to the stand. Looking briefly at the jury, a slight smile curved on her lips as she took her seat. To Holt, her walk to the stand reminded him of a princess carrying herself to her throne. He made a note of that thought for later use in a story.

Thus began, on March 4, 1959, the long-awaited testimony of the woman who'd come to be known as Ma Duncan.

The defense attorney tried to lead the woman gently through her early life, but at the mention of her deceased daughter, the witness broke down and cried, peeking at the jury from around a handkerchief balled up in her trembling hands. While she spoke, Roy

Gustafson filled page after page of a legal pad, writing feverishly and flipping through the pad, attempting to keep up with her testimony.

Elizabeth readily agreed that she had had no use for her daughter-in-law because she considered her to be of "low moral character." She had come to this opinion because Olga had obviously been intimate with her son Frank prior to their marriage. In spite of her own questionable relationships, when it came to her son, she did not hesitate to apply a double standard.

After the preliminary questions, S. Ward Sullivan got to the meat of the defense, namely that his client was the victim of a blackmail plot concocted by Mrs. Esquivel and enforced by the two thugs, Luis and Gus.

In front of a now hushed crowd, bent on absorbing her every word, Elizabeth testified that her problems had started on November 12, 1958, when she and Emma happened to be passing by the Tropical Cafe while going apartment hunting. At that time, Mrs. Esquivel, who was out sweeping the sidewalk, had recognized Elizabeth as the mother of her husband's attorney. Mrs. Esquivel had invited the two women in for coffee and they had chatted amicably over their steaming cups. After the coffee, Elizabeth and Emma had departed, feeling like they had made a new friend. However, on the next day, while again passing by the cafe, Luis Moya had rudely forced Mrs. Duncan into the establishment. At this point, Esperanza had demanded a refund of the $500 that she had given Frank to defend her husband. The reason she had wanted the money refunded, according to the defendant, was that she had learned from Frank just that day that her husband, Marciano, was going to be sentenced to state prison instead of being deported to Mexico as she had hoped. According to Elizabeth, Mrs. Esquivel was highly disappointed by this turn of events and felt that Frank had not defended her husband adequately. In fully describing the event, Elizabeth spoke directly to the jury, "Well, I was frightened, and Moya said, 'Give me your purse!' He jerked my purse open, and he said, 'How much money do you have?'"

"What did you reply?" Sullivan asked.

"I said $10 or $15."

Then, according to the defendant, Moya, who had noticed her jewelry, had suggested that Mrs. Duncan pawn her wedding ring. And, in order to terrorize her further, Moya had told the frightened woman that he'd been in the pen before and that one more stretch wouldn't hurt him. He'd go away for life anyway, so killing her wouldn't make any difference to him.

A terrified Mrs. Duncan (she said) had then left the Tropical Cafe and walked down the street, being tailed by Gus to ensure that she actually went to get the money and had pawned her rings for $175. She had returned to the cafe and had met Moya in the kitchen, where she had given him the money.

This transaction, she thought, had occurred on November 13. However, she was unsure of that date or unwilling to confirm it even though a pawn slip supporting that fact had been previously entered into evidence by the prosecution. During cross-examination, she was hard-pressed to dispute the written record on the pawn slip.

According to the defendant, all subsequent meetings with Esquivel, Moya or Baldonado were for the purpose of making additional payments to keep the hoodlums from hurting either her or Frank until she had repaid the $500.

It was the payment of the "typewriter" money, she said, that finally alerted Frank that something was amiss. Mrs. Duncan testified that she had been compelled to give Luis Moya the $200 intended to pay for a broken typewriter. After he had refused to accept this check, she had cashed it, eventually giving him only $150 in an envelope marked "Dorothy." It was when Frank had asked for a receipt that Elizabeth had finally told him that she was being blackmailed, causing Frank to go to the police.

While Bob Holt sat listening and jotting down notes outlining the woman's story, he had to admit there was a certain air of credibility to her account. But Bob recognized that this person was very adept at conning others, and therefore reserved final judgment until he heard the cross-examination, which was sure to be filled with fireworks.

And fireworks there were as the district attorney attempted to breach her defenses, often during heated clashes with the recalcitrant witness.

In one damaging exchange, Gustafson coaxed the defendant into admitting that she had lied when she had attempted to smear Olga's character. He also managed to involve Frank, who jumped from his seat and began yelling at the prosecutor. Frank, when he had settled down enough to listen, was then ordered by the court to be quiet or face eviction from the courtroom. The court recorder captured the exchange as follows:

"So then, because you were mad at Frankie, you said that his wife had had two children before?"

"That's right."

"But that was a lie, wasn't it?"

"Yes, it was."

"And didn't you say that the baby Olga was carrying wasn't Frankie's child?"

At this point Frank Duncan leaped to his feet in the gallery and shouted, "Mr. Gustafson, just one moment. My name is Frank. It is not Frankie. When you refer to me—"

"Will you please sit down! Your Honor, I will ask that this man be ejected."

Judge Blackstock responded to Frank, "Don't make any moves like that again."

Elizabeth piped in, "Well, his name is Frank, your honor."

And, from the defense attorney: "Will the court request Mr. Gustafson, when he speaks of Frank to call him Frank or Mr. Duncan?"

After further argument over the use of Frank's name, the court finally established that Gustafson could use the term "Frankie," which additionally irritated the witness. With arms folded in defiance, she informed the court that she would not answer questions put to her in which the district attorney used the term "Frankie" when referring to her son. And, true to her word, she didn't, much to the consternation of the court and her own defense attorney.

Roy Gustafson did further damage to the defendant's credibility when he was able to cast doubt on whether or not Mrs. Esquivel could have known on November 13, the day that Elizabeth had pawned her wedding rings, that her husband was going to state prison.

Gustafson stated, "Well, now, as a matter of fact you know that that is a complete falsehood."

"It is not."

"And you yourself, made this story up and then it dawned on you—"

Elizabeth's chin jutted out at the prosecutor, her voice shrilled, "Don't you *dare* say that to me!"

Gustafson was ultimately successful in casting doubt on whether Elizabeth could have had the information about Marciano's sentence when she said she did. He accomplished this in spite of the fact that Frank testified that he had learned on November 11 or 12 from Mr. Esquivel's probation officer that Marciano was going to jail and had relayed that information to Mrs. Esquivel on one of those days.

Besides constantly twisting the defendant's responses, Roy Gustafson was not above using courtroom theatrics to his advantage. During one such exchange, while asking why Elizabeth had cut up a wallet given to Frank by Olga, Gustafson was told by Mrs. Duncan to get away from her. He hustled away from the defendant, scooting behind the prosecutor's table and asked the defendant if he was safe at that location. She replied, "That's the best place for you, right up there!"

In still another dramatic exchange, when Gustafson was hammering Elizabeth about her constant interference in her son's marriage, the district attorney scored points.

"Maybe this will help you understand, Mrs. Duncan. The fact is that you testified here yesterday that after you abandoned the idea of tying Frank up and kidnapping him, you said at that point, 'Well, I am going to let Frankie work things out for himself.'"

"That's right."

"Now, a very few weeks elapsed between that time and the time that you did interfere, all by yourself. You went about getting an annulment."

"Maybe I changed my mind."

"Well, I think that is exactly it. And maybe that is what we want to find out. You not only interfered by getting an annulment, but you later interfered by hiring two men to kill Olga Duncan, isn't that true?"

"That's a lie! That is a lie! That is an absolute lie!" Elizabeth spat at the prosecutor.

"Maybe you had another change of mind?" Gustafson asked, smiling knowingly at the jury.

Elizabeth lowered her head, looking at her lap. "I didn't have any change of mind on such a thing," she answered in a low voice.

The damage was done.

On Mom's Behalf

I am ashamed of those members of my own profession, some judges and some lawyers, who knew about the fraudulent annulment and did not tell the authorities, at a time when Olga's life might perhaps have been saved. They did so out of a false sense of protection for one of their fellow lawyers, Frank Duncan.

—Roy Gustafson, reported in the *Star Free Press,*
March 14, 1959

On the evening of March 6, Bob Holt worked late typing up the story that would appear in the next day's edition of the *Ventura County Star Free Press.* Bob had sat in court all day, listening to Frank Duncan bolster the story that his mother had told the jury a few days previously.

Unlike his mother, the attorney had talked in controlled and well-modulated tones. He had not been flamboyant, but slow and steady.

Frank, answering questions under direct examination, started with his law-school days and explained the life that he led with his mother. He covered the suicide attempt and how he had met Olga as a result of that act. He confirmed that he had begun to "keep company" with Olga in the early part of February. He stated that by April he was seeing her exclusively, but did not tell his mother of the relationship. When Sullivan asked him why, he explained, "My mother has always been petrified of being alone. It is a great fear that she has always had. She at many times stated to me how she couldn't stand to be alone like some elderly lady that she knew and, well, I was always there . . . "

Frank admitted that many of the disturbances that Elizabeth was said to have caused in their married life had actually happened. He characterized the night that he left with his mother while Olga lived on Bath Street as a "donnybrook."

The defense attorney then asked Frank, "Were you in love with your wife, Olga?"

"I was, sir."

"What was the reason that you resided at home with your mother at this time?"

"My mother was, of course, opposed to me getting married. She indicated that she had no particular liking for my wife. I love my mother and I love her still, and I loved my wife also. I felt that I could keep some type of peace with my mother and my wife, that when the baby was born—by this time, Olga was pregnant—that, well, my mother would see the baby, and, well, she would come around and it would be a happy affair. And I felt I could accomplish this. I tried my best."

After covering other areas, Sullivan finally questioned Frank about the all-important date that his mother's defense hinged upon. Frank testified that he was aware of the probation officer's recommendation that Mr. Esquivel go to state prison "no earlier than the 10th of November and no later than the 14th of November. My only recollection is that I found out the recommendation of the probation officer on the 11th."

When Sullivan realized that November 11 was a holiday, he tried to straighten out the date with the witness.

"The 11th?"

"That is correct. The report as I recollect—"

"Wasn't the 11th a holiday?"

"That is correct. It was the day after the 11th."

"On the 12th?"

"On the 12th, that is right. I know there is a holiday in that period and, as I recall it, it was the day following the holiday, which was on a Monday."

Frank then went on to testify that he told Mrs. Esquivel of the probation officer's recommendation on that same day.

Gustafson, upon hearing the testimony about the dates, turned to his investigator and whispered to him. His assistant arose and hurriedly exited the courtroom.

Sullivan then moved to another line of questioning, bringing up the testimony of Barbara Reed.

Frank admitted that he had met with Barbara at the Blue Onion Cafe. He stated that Barbara had told him that his mother had approached her and asked her to kidnap Olga.

His response to her was, "Well, it sounds pretty preposterous to me." After talking to Barbara, Frank went immediately to his mother's apartment and confronted her with Reed's story. Elizabeth's response was, "That girl is lying. I know it sounds crazy, but I was going to kidnap *you*. I was just going to tie you up. I was going to take you to L.A. and I thought you would come to your senses."

When asked by Sullivan for his reaction to this, Frank stated, "Quite frankly, I blew my top. I was extremely angry and it seemed such a stupid thing. I told her she better not be saying anything, doing anything like that again, or even thinking such a thing. And that ended it!"

Frank vehemently denied that he had ever slept with the elder Mrs. Duncan, but did say that he was "proud" to call Elizabeth Duncan his mother. And finally, in concluding the direct examination, the witness stated that he had never heard or seen anything that would lead him to believe that Elizabeth contemplated harming his wife.

The fact that Elizabeth was a good liar was not lost on the district attorney. He knew that there was always the possibility, no matter how compelling the state's case, that Mrs. Duncan and her son could convince one or more jurors that they were telling the truth.

Knowing this, Gustafson went for the throat in cross-examining Frank, in an effort to discredit the son as much as he had the mother. He would give neither of them quarter.

Gustafson was particularly bothered by Frank's continued protestations of love for his bride. These assertions always brought a response from the district attorney, as the court reporter's transcripts indicate.

"Going back, then, to the time (on December 5th) when you left Santa Barbara."

"I went to San Francisco," Frank answered.

"And you were still quite concerned about Olga's disappearance?"

"I was."

"You still loved her?"

"I was—I did."

"And you were hoping she would still be found well and alive?"

"Of course."

"You would have gone back to her as her husband had she been found?"

"I certainly would have."

"Then why, Mr. Duncan, did you, on December 10, 1958, in San Francisco, have a date with Catherine Covington and not tell her you were married?"

There were numerous objections by the defense, but Frank was obliged to answer the rephrased question. He stated, "I did take her out." He also admitted that he didn't tell the young woman that he had a wife or that she was missing, even though Catherine specifically asked him if he was married.

Gustafson then asked, "And isn't it a fact that you didn't tell Catherine Covington on the date you had with her that you were married because you knew in your mind that you weren't married, because you knew your wife had—your mother had already had your wife killed?"

Frank answered the loaded question in a flat, emotionless tone. "That is not correct."

The prosecutor also proposed his own theory about why Frank had not seen his wife for the ten days prior to her disappearance. The prosecutor stated, "Isn't it true, Mr. Duncan, that the entire reason why you never saw Olga after November 7 is that by that time her physical condition by reason of the pregnancy was such that you could no longer have sexual intercourse with her, so that you didn't care to see her anymore?"

Frank, finally losing control, grasped the railing in front of him, his knuckles turning white, and shouted at the district attorney, "That is a lie! The answer is no, positively no!"

Gustafson then proposed to Frank that he had never wanted to marry Olga in the first place. The prosecutor stated, "As a matter of fact, even before your marriage to Olga in June '58, you did not want to marry Olga, did you?"

"That is not true."

"You did not love Olga."

"That is not true."

"And your feeling was you would like to pawn her off on somebody else."

"That is not true."

"Isn't it true that you had a conversation with Mr. Val Ponomoroff approximately June 1, that you were in too deep with Olga and you would like to pawn her off on somebody else?"

"That is not true."

"Isn't it a fact that the only reason you married her was because you had her pregnant and you felt you necessarily had to marry her?"

"I would have married Olga whether she was pregnant or not."

Gustafson touched briefly on Frank's knowledge of the annulment his mother had obtained. Frank denied that he had known of it days after it occurred and also denied that he had told Santa Barbara attorney, Charles Lynch, who brought it to the attention of a judge, that he could have covered it up if Lynch hadn't interfered.

The prosecutor wrapped up his questioning of Frank and the attorney stepped off the stand, glaring at Gustafson as he briskly walked past him.

The next day, the district attorney presented rebuttal witnesses in rapid-fire succession in hopes of completely discrediting the tale of the two Duncans. He started with Charles Lynch, the attorney from Santa Barbara. Lynch's testimony centered on how he had come to find out the annulment Elizabeth had obtained was fraudulent. He stated that he was informed of the annulment by Mrs. Duncan, who had come to his office to ask him to convince Frank to provide his mother with more money. She further explained that the money Frank used to spend on her was now going to Olga.

Lynch was quick to point out that, although he was her attorney, he didn't feel comfortable asking Frank for money under these circumstances. At that point, Elizabeth explained that Frank was no longer legally married to Olga because she had gotten an annulment through the Ventura attorney Lynch had previously recommended. The shocked attorney, who had indeed recommended an attorney for Mrs. Duncan in Ventura, though he had not known the nature of her business, now sat and listened in disbelief while Elizabeth explained how easily she had annulled her son's marriage.

When Mrs. Duncan had departed, Lynch called Hal Hammons and confirmed that Hammons had handled an annulment for Olga Duncan. After discussing the matter and feeling unclear about the attorney-client privilege, Lynch talked to Judge Westwick, presenting the case as a hypothetical situation.

In the meantime, Hal Hammons discussed the case with Judge Churchill, who had granted the annulment. Churchill recommended that Hammons talk to the district attorney about it. Hammons did so, however he did not divulge the names of the involved persons, again because of the attorney-client privilege. The district attorney told Hammons that he felt that privileged communications was not an issue in this case, but that he would feel more comfortable researching that point of law. Gustafson recommended that

Hammons bring the person he knew only as "a young lawyer" and his mother into his office to talk about the matter.

Meanwhile, Frank went to the offices of Judge Churchill to discuss the situation with him. Churchill recommended that Frank, as an officer of the court, either discuss the matter with District Attorney Gustafson or bring his mother before the court to answer to a charge of contempt. Churchill later asked Gustafson if the mother and son had come in. The district attorney, who still had no specific names, advised the judge that they had not.

Gustafson later pointed out that Hammons left for vacation during this time period and that nothing further was done about the annulment by any of the persons aware of it.

After learning of the annulment and discussing it with Hammons, Charles Lynch had occasion to bring it up with Frank when they happened to meet in court. It was obvious the young attorney was very upset that Lynch had gone to a judge about it. According to Lynch's testimony, Frank said that if Lynch had come to him he could have covered it up.

When Lynch suggested to Frank that such an action would be highly unethical, if not downright criminal by compounding a felony, the angry man turned on his heel and stomped off.

The next rebuttal witness called by Gustafson was probation officer, Lawrence Weitekamp, who had prepared the report on Marciano Esquivel recommending that he go to state prison. Weitekamp recalled a conversation he'd had on November 14 with Frank Duncan, discussing the report. Weitekamp stated that Frank had already obtained a copy of the report, which the attorney had picked up at his office the day before. The report was given to Frank by Clerk Alice Fraker, who testified next. She stated that Frank came to the office at 2:00 P.M. on November 13 and she provided him a copy of the report. Fraker stated she clearly remembered the incident, because the attorney was obviously mad at the probation officer's recommendation. She recalled that Frank called Weitekamp a "goddamn parrot" after he read the report.

Esperanza Esquivel was recalled to the stand. She testified that Frank had never communicated to her the recommendation in the probation report until the day her husband was sentenced, November 18. The defense tried to discredit Esperanza by asking if she had been charged with murder in this case. However, the question was withdrawn after objection by Gustafson.

The district attorney concluded his calling of rebuttal witnesses, hoping that he had cast considerable doubt in the minds of the jury about the truthfulness of Frank's testimony concerning the all-important date Frank had obtained the probation report.

When Judge Blackstock ordered the evening recess, both attorneys returned to their offices to write the crucial final summations, which were scheduled to begin the next day.

The Verdict

A judge knows nothing unless it's explained to him three times.
—Proverb

Roy Gustafson rocked back on his heels, his thumbs hooked in his dark-blue suspenders, while he delivered his summation. He was taking both the Duncans to task over the defensive front they had presented. Gustafson walked to the banister separating the spectators from the court officers, and pointed at Frank Duncan. His voice boomed, "There is one person who knows for sure who killed Olga and that is the man sitting right here. He knew there was only one person who could do that to his wife and that was his mother." The district attorney strode to the jury box. He placed his hands on the railing, his back hunched over, fixing each juror with his eyes. He continued, "In a way, he is to be pitied, because he is a product of this defendant. But I don't think that overrules the fact that he should have been man enough to refrain from going on the witness stand, or, if he did, to tell the truth."

Continuing his summation, the prosecutor displayed his strong feelings about Frank's professed love for Olga. "He testified how great he is with women. He's a ladies' man. He took a poor innocent girl from Canada, started her drinking. She was going with a flashy attorney and she came under his spell. His interest was not in the girl, but in his relationship with her. That is the type of man Frank is. It's obvious he never loved Olga. She loved him and she paid for it with her life. The marriage certificate, in truth and in fact, turned out to be her death certificate!"

Gustafson pivoted around and pointed at the Duncans. "He preens for the photographers, and so does his mother, but there is no solace for that girl who was found lying in a shallow grave."

Once again turning his attention to the jury, "Ladies and gentlemen, the evidence in this case proves her guilty beyond a reasonable doubt. It proves to a degree hardly shown in any court that Elizabeth Duncan is guilty! I ask you please, for the people of the State of California, to return a verdict of guilty."

Gustafson paused and looked at the jury and then strode back to the prosecutor's table. When he walked past the defendant, she hissed, "Son of a bitch!" at the surprised prosecutor. He took a seat, then looked in the direction of the defendant and asked, "Pardon?" Elizabeth sat staring straight ahead, her arms folded and her jaws locked. She ignored his question.

Earlier, at the conclusion of Mrs. Duncan's testimony, S. Ward Sullivan had made his strongest play for declaring a mistrial. During the defendant's cross-examination, Gustafson had begun to question her about her many marriages, over the strong objection of the defense. Sullivan had wanted to keep the marriages unrevealed to the jury because of their prejudicial nature. At the time of the questioning, Judge Blackstock had overruled the defense objection and allowed the line of questioning to continue.

The day after Gustafson had questioned Elizabeth about her numerous unions, he made a motion that they should not be part of the official record, and requested that the judge throw out the testimony relating to them. The prosecutor did this, he stated, because after thinking about it overnight, he decided that the marriage testimony was a "side issue" and not germane to the question of guilt or innocence. It is also likely that the prosecutor recognized the highly volatile nature of this testimony, and feared it could be used in a successful bid for a mistrial. The move to exclude the evidence infuriated the defense, which had fought to keep this line of questioning out in the first place. The judge granted the motion and the evidence was excluded.

In making his motion for a mistrial, based on the presentation of the marriage evidence by the prosecutor, Sullivan criticized Gustafson's courtroom tactics. Speaking outside of the jury's presence, he said, " . . . it was done for the purpose of debasing and degrading Elizabeth Duncan in the minds of this jury, by attempting to have the jury believe that a woman who would enter into various bigamous marriages would be more likely to commit the crime of murder." He further pointed out the obvious, "I think Your Honor will agree with me that though you struck the evidence and instructed this jury to disregard it, nothing that this court can do, and nothing that anyone else can do, can erase that from the minds of the jury."

Sullivan reiterated that he had gone into this trial with three prejudiced jurors, and that presentation of the marriage evidence was bound to affect the remaining nine.

Gustafson responded to the mistrial motion by pointing out that, although he had acted to exclude the evidence, he was well within limits in presenting it. This was based on the fact that the defendant had chosen to take the stand in the first place, something she was not required to do under the law, and had presented evidence, through direct examination, of her marriage to Frank Duncan, Sr. Since this area was first broached by the defense, Gustafson claimed that he had the right to impeach the witness on the issue of her legal marriage to Frank Duncan, Sr., and all others.

Judge Blackstock ruled quickly and, not surprisingly, denied the motion for mistrial.

On March 13, S. Ward Sullivan launched into his summation in an attempt to convince the jury of the innocence of his client. This famed defense attorney, who had won acquittals others thought impossible, was known for his skill in the area of summation. He thrust his argument upon the jury, often raising his voice to a shout as he attempted to mitigate the damage done by a well-presented prosecution case. Sullivan characterized the seven main witnesses who had testified against Mrs. Duncan as the "rogue's gallery of the Santa Barbara underworld." He also pointed out that the four who had testified to firsthand knowledge of the murder, namely Moya, Baldonado, Esquivel, and Short, were all accomplices as a matter of law, and that the jury could not convict on their testimony alone. He walked over to a blackboard and wrote a large X. He then wrote CAUTION above the X to remind the jurors that the testimony of accomplices in a crime should be viewed with extreme caution.

"You may believe every word of their testimony. But the law says you must reject it standing alone," he boomed, pointing at the board.

Sullivan characterized the prosecution's contention that Mrs. Duncan and her son had an unnaturally close relationship as an effort to create bias and prejudice towards his client. He stated, "They failed wholly in their attempt." Standing next to Elizabeth, and pointing toward Frank, he lowered his voice, and said, "This is only a mutual bond of affection and love between mother and son."

Sullivan continued, "I don't think Elizabeth Duncan is the first mother in history to object to the marriage of her son. I don't excuse Frank for not breaking away and creating a more normal relationship between his mother and himself." But, he pointed out, that certainly didn't make Elizabeth guilty of murder.

And finally, he thundered at the jury, piercing them with an intense look: "I'm going to ask you to return into this court with a verdict of not guilty!"

The jury's first vote, after nineteen days and 2600 pages of testimony, was to postpone deliberation until the following Monday. They wanted the weekend off. Prior to being released, Judge Blackstock gave them his sternest lecture about talking or reading about the case.

A refreshed panel returned to court on March 16 and listened to an hour and a half of instructions from the judge. Among the many jury instructions submitted by the two attorneys was the statement, "You are instructed that witnesses Barbara Reed, Diane Romero,

Rudolph Romero, Rebecca Diaz, Ralph Winterstein, Luis Moya, Augustine Baldonado, Esperanza Esquivel, and Emma Short are, if you believe from the evidence to a moral certainty and beyond a reasonable doubt that the crime of murder was committed, accomplices as a matter of law." Judge Blackstock, who made determinations about which instructions he would read to the jury, had agreed with the defense that Gustafson's main witnesses fell into that narrow area of law defining an accomplice.

Finally, the judge pointed out, "You are not partisans or advocates, but rather judges. There can be no victory, save in ascertainment of the truth." With these sage words, the judge sent the panel of eight women and four men into the jury room to begin their deliberation.

While the jury considered the fate of the defendant, Bob Holt moved among the newsmen in the pressroom, a wad of money in his hand.

"Are you in, Chuck, or what?" Bob asked a fellow reporter.

"In for what?" the man asked, hanging up the phone.

"We've got a pool goin'. The person who guesses closest to the time the jury is out wins the loot."

"Yeah, put me in. Let's see, I think they'll find her guilty in less then one hour and fifty minutes. Put me down for 1:50." The reporter dug into his wallet, and then asked, "How much?"

Bob checked his list of times to make sure the time hadn't been spoken for and then wrote it down on his sheet. "Five bucks will get you in," he advised the player. Holt took the money and moved on to the next reporter.

"It's a good thing we're not betting on her guilt or innocence," another newsman sung out, "because we couldn't find anyone to bet with her; she's obviously as guilty as they come!"

Holt counted the money before stuffing it into a coffee can. "Okay, guys, there's $85 at stake. I'll keep track of the time, with Mike's help. May the best man win!"

Frank Duncan, who was showing obvious signs of the stress that this long trial had created, was overheard making the comment that if his mother were found guilty, he would shoot either a juror or the judge. This information was quickly passed on to Mary Forgey, who alerted all the security personnel in the courthouse. Everyone stood by anxiously, awaiting both the return of the jury and the return of Frank, so he could be thoroughly searched.

Roy Gustafson, not one to second-guess what he considered his best effort, returned to his office to begin preparation for the penalty phase of the trial.

After four hours and fifty-one minutes of deliberation, and shortly before the judge was going to sequester the jury for the night, it was announced that a verdict had been agreed upon. Gustafson and Sullivan had returned to court to discuss the sequestering of the jury, and had only to await the return of the defendant, who was brought down from her jail cell.

The reporters scurried back to their seats, one of them with $85 in his hip pocket, just nine minutes away from the winning guess of five hours even.

Frank also returned prior to the reading of the verdict, but was denied access to the courtroom. He finally agreed to a search, but only after an adamant protest. No gun was found and Frank sat by his mother's side at the reading of the judgment.

Jury foreman Paul Gosney handed the verdict to the bailiff. The bailiff, in turn, passed it to the judge, who briefly read the verdict and handed it to his clerk, Bill Peacock. In a clear and concise voice that filled the hushed courtroom, Mr. Peacock read, "We the jury, impaneled to try the above entitled cause, find the defendant, Elizabeth Ann Duncan, guilty of murder in the first degree."

There was general pandemonium in the courtroom as some spectators cheered, while others clapped and stomped their feet. Reporters jumped from their seats and rushed out of the large doors, headed to the telephones. The judge beat upon his bench, demanding order and instructed the bailiff to evict the most unruly violators.

Elizabeth did not immediately react to the reading of the verdict, but her son did. A shaken Frank lowered his head and announced that the verdict was "like a death sentence." In a reversal of roles, his mother tried to comfort him and told him not to "worry too much."

Deputy Forgey escorted the convicted woman from the courtroom. While they waited for the elevator to return them to the jail, a curious Mary asked, "Elizabeth, if you had this to do over again, would you do the same thing?"

The convicted woman grinned at the deputy, thinking about her answer to this question. She then became deadly serious, the grin vanishing from her face. Her voice trembled, the hate reverberating in her words, "You bet I would. Nobody is going to have my Frankie—nobody!"

"Well, Elizabeth, I hope it was worth it to you."

"It was," came the cold reply.

When the elevator doors opened, Mrs. Duncan's voice softened, "You know, Mary, I'm very much in love with Frankie. If I can't have him, nobody can."

The deputy and the convicted murderess stepped onto the old elevator, which clanked and jerked its way to the women's jail. Ma gave Mary a knowing wink before she was led back to her cell.

Later, S. Ward Sullivan told the press that the convicted woman broke down in her cell, crying that she didn't know how the jury could have done such a thing, convicting an obviously innocent woman.

The jury was ordered back the next day to begin the penalty portion of the trial.

Frank Duncan gave an extensive press release that day. In the interview, he stated that he now faced a life filled with remorse that he hadn't done something to try to change the events of November 17. Although he had taken a considerable amount of verbal abuse from the prosecutor and the public alike, he stated that he wasn't ashamed of his actions. He also said that, in spite of what people had heard, he did not have an unnatural relationship with his mother. And finally, while twisting a Venetian blind cord around and around in his hands, Frank said, "The public will soon forget. I never will!"

The Penalty Phase

Is not marriage an open question, when it is alleged, from the beginning of the world, that such as are in the institution wish to get out, and such as are out wish to get in?
—Ralph Waldo Emerson, *Montaigne*

On March 18, the jury of eight women and four men returned to hear the prosecution present witnesses for the penalty phase of the trial. Gustafson hoped to convince the panel that they should send the convicted murderess to the gas chamber. In his campaign to do so, the district attorney called eleven witnesses to the stand. The parade of prosecution witnesses accused the defendant of a plethora of wrongdoings traveling back fifteen years into her past. These included falsely representing that she could inherit an estate in order to persuade a man to marry her, soliciting for an abortion, offering a witness money to testify, defrauding individuals out of their money in an assortment of schemes, failing to repay a loan, and using the name of a man she hadn't married in order to apply for a liquor license, and incest. While the prosecution admitted that all these past transgressions were far afield from murder, they did point out the criminal bent of the woman before them.

Among those who testified was Bettye Lou Brantley, an acquaintance of both Frank and his mother. She stated that in December of 1956, she drove Elizabeth from Oxnard to Stockton, California, to meet one of Mrs. Duncan's sons. According to the Brantley testimony, Elizabeth told her that "given time, she could have him doing just as she had Frank doing." Mrs. Brantley didn't understand exactly what her traveling companion meant until that evening, when (she testified) Mrs. Duncan and her son were "intimate" in a Stockton motel room that the three were sharing. Brantley stated that she was so disgusted by this event that she refused to drive Elizabeth back to Oxnard, taking her only to Fresno, where Elizabeth had to make other arrangements to get the rest of the way home.

Also presented to the jury were the two San Francisco police officers that had arrested Ma Duncan for maintaining a house of prostitution. The officers testified that they went to the massage parlor after being tipped off about the true nature of the business.

Officer William Wilson posed as a customer and bargained with the madam for the services of a woman. The deal was struck and the officer was led to a room with a bed. When Elizabeth brought a young woman to Williams, he arrested them both for the prostitution charge. Ma eventually served six days in jail for the charge, which was her only prior conviction.

After the prosecution rested, S. Ward Sullivan put his star witness, the defendant, on the stand. His tactic, in hopes of saving her from the gas chamber, was to elicit a feeling of pity for this woman, whom he hoped to portray as one of society's victims. He walked her through a life filled with turmoil and heartbreak.

Elizabeth Ann Duncan was actually born Hazel Lucille Sinclaira Nigh, in Kansas City, Missouri. The exact date of her birth is open to question, since at various times she indicated different dates on a wide assortment of legal documents. She testified in court that her correct birth date was April 16, 1904. Her actual birth certificate was never entered into the court record.

Hazel was one of two daughters and three sons born to her working-class parents.

When she was seven, the Nighs moved to the small mining town of Mogollon, New Mexico, which lies next to the Arizona border in the southern part of the state. Mr. Nigh worked in the silver mines in what is today a ghost town.

Hazel attended public school until the fourth grade, when she was forced to stay home to help care for her brothers and sister. She received no formal education past that point.

Mrs. Duncan's first marriage of record was to Dewey Tessier. However, the marriage certificate, dated August 24, 1918, indicated that, though she was just fourteen at the time, she had already been married. The bride's name was listed as Hazel E. Mitchell on the certificate. In court testimony, Mrs. Duncan stated that she did not recall ever being married to a person by the name of Mitchell.

Out of the union with Dewey, Elizabeth bore three children. The eldest child was Dorothy May Tessier, born on January 19, 1921.

The marriage to Dewey lasted a few months less than five years, or until the young Mrs. Tessier discovered that Dewey was "keeping company with other women." She left him and moved to Phoenix, Arizona, where she was forced to put the three children in an orphanage in order to go to work and support herself.

After learning where his children were, Dewey removed them from the orphanage and successfully hid them from their mother for a period of thirteen years. Elizabeth finally found them living in Abilene, Texas. Though she saw them occasionally, Elizabeth never reestablished close ties to the children.

In the meantime, on July 30, 1927, Elizabeth married a man by the name of Edward J. Lynchberg in Phoenix. Mrs. Duncan claimed she could not remember Mr. Lynchberg and attempted to explain why during direct examination.

"Do you remember ever going through a marriage ceremony with a man named Lynchberg?"

"No, I don't, I really don't."

"You can't recall that particular—"

"No, I certainly don't."

"Do you remember how many times you've been married?"

"No, I'm afraid to count them."

"In other words, you had some marriages you don't even recall."

"They didn't mean that much to me."

Mrs. Duncan's defense attorney then showed her a copy of the Lynchberg marriage certificate. Her response was, "No, I don't remember that. I must have been drunk or something. I don't know what else. If I done anything like that, I would remember the man."

Ma's marriage to Mr. Lynchberg was evidently short-lived, since she was remarried on July 13, 1928, to Frank M. Low, Jr.

It was during this time that Elizabeth gave birth to the only child that she would remain devoted to through the years: Frank, Jr.

Her relationship with Low lasted until the early part of 1931, when Ma left him because he beat her and "did not like his son." Although it was proven that Elizabeth never legally divorced Frank Low, she married Frank Duncan, Sr., for whom she would rename her favorite son. This marriage occurred on April 24, 1932.

This attachment, which was never a legal marriage, lasted the longest of the many unions Ma went through. During her time with Frank Duncan, she gave birth to Patricia Ann, who met an untimely death in a roller-skating accident in 1948. It was after this death that the threads of her relationship with Frank, Sr., began to unravel, due in part to Ma's increasing dependence on the drug Seconal. He eventually took a job overseas and, in 1951, he obtained an annulment on the grounds that they were never legally married anyway.

During her marriage to Frank, Sr., Ma found time to marry at least two other times.

On March 27, 1933, she married Frank Leslie Craig and, some seventeen years later, she entered into her seventh union with Joseph Gold.

While it was unclear if she ever legally terminated the union with Mr. Craig, she continued to use his name for many years after last seeing him.

Ma Duncan did obtain a legal divorce from Mr. Gold on November 19, 1951.

During cross-examination, Gustafson took the defendant to task after she stated that her marriage to Frank, Sr. was a normal relationship.

"And it was a normal relationship?" the district attorney quipped, sarcasm heavy in his voice.

I did . . . tell the jury that."

"Do you mean to convey the impression to this jury that it is a normal relationship for a wife to go out and marry somebody else during the time of a marriage?"

"I don't know what it is, but, anyway, I did it."

"Well, at any rate, this normal relationship that you had with Mr. Duncan, in the meantime you went out and married Mr. Craig, and then obtained an annulment of that marriage?"

"Yes."

"Is that right?"

"That's right."

"While you were maintaining this normal marital relationship with Mr. Duncan, you went out and got married to Mr. Gold?"

"Yes, well, yes. That was a few years, later."

"And then while you were still having this normal relationship with Mr. Duncan you went out and married Mr. Satriano?"

"Mr. Duncan wasn't in the picture at all when Mr. Satriano was married to me."

Elizabeth entered into a state of matrimony for the eighth time on December 15, 1951, when she wed George Satriano. Mr. Satriano, who was one of three husbands that the prosecution called to testify, married Ma for financial gain. When this didn't pan out, he divorced her some eighteen months later.

On July 28, 1953, Elizabeth Ann Duncan and Benjamin Young Cogbill were married in the County of Alameda, California. In this partnership, Elizabeth again appeared to be mixing business with pleasure. Mr. Cogbill set Ma up in business, establishing the "massage parlor" in San Francisco that resulted in the prostitution arrest.

She obtained an annulment of that marriage and remarried on January 6, 1954.

This time she married a twenty-six-year-old classmate and friend of her son. Like others of Ma's husbands, Stephen Simon Gillis entered into this union for financial gain and suffered for his indiscretion for many years to follow. Stephen Gillis was the second man called by the prosecution to tell his tale of woe.

Some time after her marriage to Gillis, Elizabeth met Louis D'Amato, a bus driver. Ma claimed to have been married to Mr. D'Amato on a trip to Las Vegas by a "one-legged justice of the peace." However, there was never any proof of this event actually happening. Mrs. Duncan testified that, after returning to the Ventura County area, she learned by calling his home and talking to his wife that Mr. D'Amato was already married. She filed for an annulment, but not until she had claimed a pregnancy by the cornered bus driver and demanded support money, which he never paid.

On August 10, 1957, Elizabeth married for the last time. Again she married a man many years her junior: Leonard Joseph Sollene, who was twenty-eight at the time. Elizabeth conned Sollene into matrimony with a promise of sharing $196,000 that she was supposed to inherit. This scam, which she had used many times before, centered on a large inheritance from a recently deceased husband, which she could only claim if she remarried. This marriage was never consummated, and Frank Duncan's obtaining of the annulment of the Sollene marriage, without his mother's consent, was the reason that Elizabeth Duncan attempted suicide on November 6, 1957, thus starting the series of events that would lead to the murder of Olga Kupczyk Duncan.

While the press had a heyday with the tales of her many marriages, the court officers attempted to make some sense of these affiliations. Her own attorney asked, "Why did you go through so many marriage ceremonies?"

She responded, "I don't know. I think I was seeking something, and I don't know what." Not unlike a black widow spider, she concluded by saying, "After I married them, I didn't want them at all."

The prosecutor thought he had the answer to what Ma Duncan was seeking. During cross-examination, he asked her, "You married all these people, you told the jury, because you were seeking something, but you didn't know what you were seeking?"

"That's right."

"Well, can you remember that what you were seeking was sex?"

"Perhaps that is it."

"And weren't you also seeking to have yourself married at all times to somebody so that if you became pregnant by someone else, you would have a husband to blame it on?"

"Indeed not!"

Roy Gustafson also theorized that her many marriages were an attempt to extort money from men by claiming pregnancy in order to collect child support. The prosecutor slanted the remainder of his case towards proving his hypothesis.

Bob Holt sat at his desk in front of his typewriter. While he typed away, he had to continually recheck his notes to ensure that he was accurately describing Ma's various husbands and the dates and conditions surrounding her marriages. He had also heard that there were other marriages, as many as twenty, but the prosecutor had not been successful in locating the marriage certificates for those, so they had not been presented to the jury.

After Bob had completed his story, he got up and began to walk to the editor's desk, proofreading his work while he walked. He stopped in mid-stride, shaking his head while he read, befuddled by the amazing story of this woman's life. He concluded that truth was indeed stranger then fiction and continued his trip to the editor's desk, where he placed the article in the in-basket.

Motive for Marriage

Question: "But you said to your counsel that you couldn't remember the number of marriages you had undertaken. Isn't it true that it is around the number twenty?"

Answer: "Oh, goodness, no! Twenty?"

Question: "Yes."

Answer: "Of course not!"

Question: "Well, we have already gotten ten certified copies."

Answer: "You will have to get ten more. Go dig them up!"

—Roy Gustafson questioning Ma Duncan, Thursday, March 19, 1959

The district attorney's efforts to completely discredit Elizabeth Duncan hinged upon the testimony of three of her ex-husbands. Each had one thing in common. They were men this woman had casually manipulated with her tales of instant wealth and a life of leisure.

The first of this trio of exes called to the stand was actually Ma's last husband, twenty-eight-year-old Leonard Sollene. Elizabeth knew the Sollene family prior to the marriage and she especially liked Leonard. She convinced the young man that she had an estate of $196,000, and that her deceased husband had included a provision in his will that she must remarry in order to claim the inheritance. This provision was inserted in order to keep her from "running around," after her husband's death according to Mrs. Duncan.

Sollene testified that he had thought Mrs. Duncan trustworthy and had believed her when she agreed to share the inheritance with him. Leonard had traveled to San Francisco with the oft-married woman, where they were wed. While in San Francisco, they stayed at separate hotels, but they did cohabitate briefly upon returning to Santa Barbara.

Within two weeks, Leonard realized that there was no estate. Unlike some of Ma's husbands, he was able to get the marriage annulled some two months later.

The district attorney next presented fifty-one-year-old George Satriano, who testified that he had met Mrs. Duncan at the Avalon Ballroom in San Francisco just prior to Christmas of 1951. She asked George if he cared to dance and the relationship started. That night, George happened to mention to his newfound friend that he was going to send his mother $25 for Christmas. As the typewriter sales-man admitted in court, " . . . in the course of an evening, she paint-ed quite a picture for me. She said, 'Why don't you marry me, and I will send your mother $1,000 for Christmas?' I was a salesman myself, and I was getting sold right along the line."

After Elizabeth stated she would set George up in business for himself, he did agree to marry her. This open court revelation brought laughter so infectious that Roy Gustafson joined in and even stern Judge Blackstock found himself stifling a chuckle. The judge quickly called a morning recess.

When the session resumed, Satriano revealed that, two days after meeting the smooth-talking woman, he did in fact marry her.

Mrs. Duncan had informed George that her recently deceased husband, who had been a corporate lawyer, had left her $100,000 in railroad stocks. In order to convince her new spouse of her wealth, she accompanied him to Crawford Office Equipment Company, George's employer, and offered to buy the business for $50,000. Fortunately, Mr. Crawford turned down the offer.

By March of 1952, George had resigned his job, hoping to live off his wife's wealth.

A month later, Mrs. Satriano entered the real estate office of A.P. Williams of San Mateo, a wealthy suburb in the San Francisco Bay area. After a day of shopping, she located an apartment complex that she especially liked. The woman, without betting an eye, wrote out a check for $50,000 as a deposit on the property. The realtor, after the check bounced, determined that Mrs. Satriano had only $125 in the bank. The prosecution contended that this real-estate deal was done to further convince George Satriano of her wealth. After four months of marriage, the suspension of his disbelief was beginning to sag. During the marriage, George was particularly proud of a new Cadillac that he purchased. It was the loss of a hubcap from this car that caused the breakup of what had grown into a stormy relationship. George was willing to buy a new hubcap, but his wife insisted that he wait for the insurance company to pay for it. When he disagreed, she tossed him out. Elizabeth later sued him for support and, upon winning in court, decided to take his "pride and joy," the Cadillac, which she couldn't even drive, instead of $50 a month in support money.

George soon became more than happy to give up the car after he received a phone call from a Mr. Filippo, a San Francisco private detective. George went to the man's apartment and heard a wire recording of Mrs. Duncan offering the private eye $500 to throw acid in George's face. After listening to this, George Satriano, who admitted in court he had never loved the woman, spent most of his time hiding from her until the divorce was final in July of 1953.

After presenting the Satriano testimony, the district attorney called the third ex-husband to the stand. It soon became apparent that twenty-six-year-old Stephen Simon Gillis was one of the most victimized of Ma's exes. Gillis was a classmate of Frank at Hasting School of Law in San Francisco. It was through his close friendship with Frank that Stephen became involved with Mother Duncan. The husky young man's liaison with her started in the fall of 1953, just after Elizabeth's annulment of the Cogbill marriage.

Gillis had talked to Mrs. Duncan only twice in person and the actual marriage was negotiated over the telephone. As Gillis testified in court, "She presented the situation as a sort of combined business transaction and social transaction. She indicated that there was an existing will, that there was a provision in the trust fund that she had to marry in order for her to collect under this trust, and that only her present husband at the time could exercise the release of the funds held in this trust."

He further described the arrangement: "She asked me if I would go through a marriage ceremony with her . . . (the marriage) would last anywhere from a year or two years . . . It could be dissolved . . . she wouldn't fight it."

The bottom line for the young law student, who often found himself in financial trouble, was an offer from Elizabeth of $50,000 to go through the ceremony.

When Gillis attempted to talk to his friend Frank about this upcoming agreement, Frank didn't believe him. He stated that he thought his friend must be joking, that such a marriage was just too farfetched even for his mother to take seriously. However, much to Frank's chagrin, his friend married his mother on January 6, 1954.

Frank was questioned in court about this event:

"Did you discuss the marriage with your mother after you found out about it?"

"I most certainly did."

"What did you say to your mother about it?"

"I was furious. I felt that it was the most humiliating thing that ever happened to me!"

And, to further show his displeasure, Frank Duncan never spoke to his former friend again.

After the marriage, Elizabeth wrote her new husband a check for $10,000. He put it in a bank in Loma Linda, but wasn't particularly surprised to learn that it bounced.

Within days of going through with this arrangement, the young man realized he had made a major mistake. However, he was soon to find out how grave a blunder he had committed as he tried to unweave himself from his wife's enveloping web.

Gillis wanted to immediately annul the marriage, but contrary to her promise, Ma prevented him from doing so by using direct threats. She informed the duped man that if he attempted to annul the marriage, she would see that he never worked as a lawyer. As he testified in court, "She would claim anything, in reality . . . she would claim I fleeced money out of her . . . that I committed assault and battery, that I intended to harm her son, and that I blackmailed her into marrying me."

In June of 1955, Stephen graduated from law school and worked for six months with the weight of Elizabeth around his neck. He served her with annulment papers in September of that year, but was informed that the proceedings were put on hold because his fifty-two-year-old bride was pregnant. The luckless man, knowing that he was not the father since he had never slept with the mother of his friend, decided to "get out of town." He joined the Marine Corps and shipped out to Quantico, Virginia, hoping to put this ordeal behind him.

However, while Stephen was at Quantico, his commanding officer received a letter from the attorney of Mrs. Stephen Gillis, indicating that she was eight and one-half months pregnant and destitute. Despite his protests, the Marine Corps forced him to send his wife $160 to help her buy food for herself.

What Stephen had yet to learn was the full extent Ma would go to ensure that she kept her young man on the hook.

On June 24, 1955, Ma and another woman showed up in the office of San Francisco physician, Edward J. Buckley. Elizabeth introduced the obviously pregnant friend to Dr. Buckley as her out of town sister, Mrs. Stephen Gillis. He examined the young woman and issued her a certificate stating that she was pregnant.

This certification of pregnancy, though it caused Stephen Gillis considerable problems for years to come, was also to trap Elizabeth in one of her most blatant lies during the course of her trial.

In July of 1956, Stephen Gillis left the Marine Corps and applied to take the bar exam. He soon found himself embroiled in a hearing before the state bar examiners, based on allegations made by his wife that he had fathered her child and abandoned them. In May, Elizabeth testified under oath before the tribunal that she had given birth to a baby girl on February 9, 1956, at Cottage Hospital in Santa Barbara. While she refused to divulge the name of the doctor who assisted with the birth or where the baby was currently living, she did state that the child's name was Stephanie Ann Gillis. As a result of Mrs. Duncan's statements about the child and other similar fabrications, the Board of Examiners denied Stephen the right to take the bar exam. Thus, almost two and one-half years after she had threatened to ruin his chances to become an attorney, Ma was true to her word.

Roy Gustafson, not one to miss an opportunity to impeach the statements of the stubborn woman, succeeded in having a transcript of this action entered into the record during Mrs. Duncan's trial. He then took her to task about the child named Stephanie during cross-examination on the afternoon of March 19. This proved to be one of the most flamboyant exchanges that occurred between the two during the trial. It started innocently enough when the district attorney asked Mrs. Duncan to name her children. She replied, "Dorothy, Betty, Dewey, Frank, Patsy, and Stephanie Ann."

"Who is Stephanie Ann?"

"Stephanie Ann Gillis."

"When was Stephanie Ann Gillis born?"

"1956."

"Where was Stephanie Ann Gillis born?"

"In Santa Barbara."

"At Cottage Hospital?"

"I didn't say at Cottage Hospital."

"I am asking you where she was born."

"She wasn't born at Cottage Hospital."

"Where was she born?"

"I am answering no more!"

At this point the court reporters' transcripts indicate in parentheses that the witness had raised her right arm from the elbow. The questioning continued.

"Does that mean stop?" the prosecutor asked.

"I am not saying anything more."

"Well, as a matter of fact there was no Stephanie Ann Gillis."

"There was a Stephanie Ann Gillis!"

"You haven't been able to bear a child for many, many years."

"You go right ahead. I am telling you what . . . I certainly did!"

"And this was in 1956, when you claim that you would have been fifty-two years old. Is that correct?"

There was an objection by the defense attorney, which was overruled.

The prosecutor, going for the jugular, continued. "As a matter of fact, you never had any child named Stephanie Ann Gillis!"

"I had a child by the name of Stephanie Ann Gillis."

"And that child isn't with your sister, is she?"

"That child isn't at the present time, no."

"And she never was with your sister."

"Yes, she was."

"Which sister?"

"I have only one sister,"

"Mrs. Morris?"

"Yes."

"And she had the child, Stephanie Ann Gillis?"

"For awhile, yes."

"At what time did she have that child?"

"I am not telling you about that because it is none of your business!"

"Who was the doctor that attended you?"

"Still up."

Again, the court reporter indicated that the witness raised her right hand.

"Still what?" the prosecutor asked.

"You know what I mean by that. You're a lawyer. You know what I mean."

"What do you mean by that?"

"You know what I mean."

Judge Blackstock then interjected, asking the witness, "What do you mean?"

"Fifth Amendment. I'm not saying anything."

The district attorney clarified her statement for the judge, who apparently did not hear her. "Fifth Amendment, she said."

Roy Gustafson then asked, "You don't want to incriminate yourself?"

"No, I don't want to incriminate myself."

"In other words, you don't want it proved you committed perjury when you went up to the bar hearing and testified to prevent Mr. Gillis from being a lawyer and lied and said that you had a child by him!"

While it was obvious to the packed courtroom who had won this exchange, it was not so obvious to the defendant, who sat with her arms crossed, refused to answer the question, and glared at the district attorney.

Stephen Gillis best explained Ma's influence over others when he stated in court, "She had a tremendous spell on everybody that she came in contact with, and no matter what lies she told, no matter how fantastic, it was believable."

But this woman now commonly referred to as Ma Duncan had met her match in District Attorney Roy Gustafson.

The Penalty is Fixed

A piece of graveyard fits everyone.
—Proverb

In what was considered an unusual move, Judge Blackstock allowed the defense to introduce psychiatric testimony in the penalty phase of the trial. S. Ward Sullivan, in presenting this evidence that is usually reserved for the sanity phase, knew that the only hope to save Elizabeth's life was to elicit a feeling of sympathy for his convicted client. He hoped to accomplish this by casting some doubt about her mental well-being.

Dr. Louis R. Nash, a court-appointed psychiatrist, was the first to testify. He had examined Elizabeth on three different occasions. During the course of his examinations, he had delved extensively into her background, through psychiatric testing and physical and neurological examinations. Dr. Nash also witnessed Mrs. Duncan's testimony each time she was on the stand. He concluded that the defendant had many personality disorders.

He stated, " . . . Mrs. Duncan has been a maladjusted individual. She has been an impulsive individual. She has been an egocentric individual. She has been an immature, emotionally constituted individual. She particularly has been unable to stand frustrations and she has been a person who has been unable to maintain her emotional equilibrium during major or minor stress. These findings add up to what is known in medicine as a personality trait disorder, more commonly called psychopathic personality." The doctor stated that this type of person would be characterized by the use of poor judgment in decision making, and would be a problem to herself and to society in general.

When asked, Nash stated that he had learned something of Elizabeth's sex life.

According to the psychiatrist, when Elizabeth met her future husband, Dewey Tessier, at age fourteen, she was intimate with him the first night and married him within a week. Nash stated that this relationship apparently set a pattern for her entire life, since she cohabitated with men as she met them. The doctor concluded that Ma Duncan was a pathological liar as well as a psychopathic personality, but admitted under questioning by the prosecutor, that she was not insane. However, the psychiatrist then said that it is not uncommon for individuals of this type to use society as a battleground. They are generally viewed as social misfits or sociopaths. But the standard for being judged sane—being in such a mental condition as to understand the difference between right and wrong—was met by the defendant. This conclusion sent a stir through the gallery.

During redirect examination of Nash, Sullivan brought up the possible effects of Ma Duncan's drug addiction on her personality. He asked, "And in your opinion, Doctor, would that have an effect on her mentality or ability to exercise good judgment?"

"Definitely."

"It definitely would? What effect would that be likely to have?"

"Any drug that has an effect on the brain that will cause sedation, such as barbiturates or alcohol, affects part of the ability of a person to think or to use the brain, affects their memory, affects their judgment."

To reinforce his previous point during re-cross-examination, Gustafson asked but one question. "Despite the fact that the taking of barbiturates might affect a person's ability to think, you nevertheless came to the conclusion . . . that, so far as Mrs. Duncan was concerned, at all times she had known the difference between right and wrong; she had known the nature and quality of all the acts which she had done?"

"That is true," was the psychiatrist's answer.

The defense provided its own psychiatrist, Dr. Brunon Bielinski, who testified to the possibility that Mrs. Duncan had suffered an organic brain disorder due to her long period of unconsciousness during the suicide attempt. However, he was not able to show conclusive proof other than the fact that Mrs. Duncan had a twitch in the palm of her hand.

To bolster his hypothesis, the psychiatrist testified that Mrs. Duncan had told him that Lincoln was the first president of the United States, Taft was president during the Civil War, and she didn't know the name of the country immediately north of the United States.

Bielinski stated that Elizabeth told him that she often heard voices, but had never before told anyone about them because she was afraid to. The psychiatrist also stated that he felt Mrs. Duncan's mental condition may have been worsened by the onset of menopause, the death of her daughter, a stroke, and a concussion she had previously suffered. Under cross-examination, Bielinski admitted he could find no medical records substantiating either the stroke or the concussion. When Gustafson suggested that the defendant might have fabricated some of the illnesses she told the psychiatrist about, Bielinski stated that he doubted that, because his many years of psychiatry enabled him to identify liars.

Gustafson finally got to the bottom line with the defense psychiatrist when Dr. Bielinski admitted that Mrs. Duncan, though a sociopathic personality, was sane under the meaning of the law.

Frank Duncan also testified in the penalty phase of the trial. Hoping to convince the jury to spare his mother's life, he concluded his direct examination with a stirring tribute to his mother. He stated, "She is one of the warmest persons I know. She can charm you out of your boots and she is generous to a fault. If I had a choice for a mother, as much as I have been humiliated here, I would still pick the same mother." Frank looked at his mother and smiled, causing Elizabeth to break down and sob.

After a recess, Gustafson asked Frank if he honestly felt that way, bearing in mind her activities in the massage parlor in San Francisco. An obviously agitated Frank replied, "Positively yes!"

After Frank had vacated the stand, Roy Gustafson launched into his closing argument, again producing a list of the many crimes that Elizabeth had committed. The list, which had grown to nineteen different violations, now included kidnapping, murder, and soliciting mayhem. He pointed out that the woman who sat before them had only ever been charged with two out of the nineteen crimes, showing her to be a very clever criminal indeed.

Gustafson stated that if the jury failed to bring back a death sentence in this case, the law should be written off the books. He further pointed out that a life sentence really meant only seven years in jail. The district attorney stated that, if the defendant ever got out of jail, even he would be in fear for his own life.

Continuing through his summation, Gustafson pointed out the obvious to the jury. He noted that it was common during the penalty phase of the process for relatives and friends to come to court as character references and to speak up for the defendant. What was wholly lacking, in this case, were those supporters. Only her son spoke for her character, even though she had two brothers and a sister in the immediate area. The defense could find no one else who would come forth to say anything positive about the life of this woman.

In his closing, in order to leave the jury with a strong message, Gustafson reminded the panel that Mrs. Duncan had contracted to have her own unborn grandchild killed.

Gustafson concluded, "Yours is not a pleasant duty. But I ask you that not one of you shirk it."

In S. Ward Sullivan's summation, he pleaded for sparing the life of his client, pointing out that *if* she ever did get out of prison she would be "an old, old woman." He reminded the jury that, although his client had done "a lot of weird things," she was still "a human being endowed with body and soul, made in the likeness and image of her Creator."

Sullivan continued, "Perhaps where Olga is now, if she could raise her hand and direct your deliberations, she would say: 'Don't take the life of Elizabeth. Spare her life. Put her where she belongs, away from society, in prison.'"

After the summations, the jury was given brief instructions by Judge Blackstock, who advised them that they might consider both sympathy and indignation towards the defendant when considering the verdict. The jury returned to the jury room to deliberate the fate of the convicted murderess. After only three hours and twenty minutes, at 9:20 P.M., they returned with the penalty fixed at death.

Judge Blackstock, who exercised his option to hear the sanity part of the trial himself, dismissed the weary jury with thanks from the people of the State of California for a job well done.

Prior to leaving, the jury, through the court, made it abundantly clear to the press that they would not consent to interviews. When pressed by Bob Holt to make some type of press release, the members of the panel stated that they would only talk to the press after the execution. However, in a commitment that became open-ended, the members of this jury never consented to discuss the dynamics of the deliberation process and stood good to their word, many until their deaths.

After the penalty was read, S. Ward Sullivan said that he would appeal the trial, stating that it was the greatest miscarriage of justice he had seen in his thirty years as a trial lawyer. He noted that there were many "glaring errors" in the case and reiterated the damage done to his client by the obviously biased and prejudiced jury.

Frank Duncan jumped on the bandwagon, rapping what he called the political ambitions of the district attorney, stating, "He intends to climb to some higher position over my mother's body."

The condemned woman commented that she had expected the death sentence, based on the "rotten deal" she had gotten the first time, due to the impaneling of a conspicuously prejudiced jury.

The sanity hearing was held on the morning of March 24, 1959. Judge Blackstock, noting the reports of the two psychiatrists who had testified in the penalty phase, stated that his findings were a "forgone conclusion," that the defendant was sane at the time of the commission of the crime.

On April 3, Sullivan argued for a retrial, trying for forty minutes to convince Judge Blackstock that his client had been unfairly convicted. In particular, he cited the change of venue issue and the predisposition of the jury as grounds for a new trial. Upon Sullivan's conclusion, Judge Blackstock denied a new trial and sentenced the defendant. He stated, "It is the judgment of this court that you be sentenced to die by the administration of lethal gas." There was no reaction from the condemned murderess.

That afternoon, the doomed woman was transported to Corona State Prison to await execution. She fielded a couple of questions before climbing into the back seat of the car for the drive to the prison. She stated that she had no idea if she'd like her new "home," since she'd never been there. She said that she didn't like the staff at the Ventura jail, other than Deputies Jeff Boyd and Mary Forgey. And finally she was whisked away, a hand in the air and an innocent half-smile upon her lips. Relieved to see her depart, the recently elected Ventura County Sheriff, Bill Hill, commented, "This is the moment I've been waiting for since I took office."

The Boys Head North

Juvenile delinquency starts in the high chair and ends in the death chair.

—James D. Murray, *New York World* and *Telegram Sun,*
September 8, 1966

The next of the trio to face the judicial system was Gus who pleaded guilty to first-degree murder and withdrew his plea of not guilty by reason of insanity. By doing so, he eliminated a need for a guilt phase of the three-tier system.

When Gus learned that a court trial on the penalty phase would be heard by Judge Blackstock, Baldonado, at the advice of his attorney, elected to have a jury trial to decide his fate.

The trial started immediately after the plea, with the attorneys eventually interviewing sixty-one jurors before they were able to agree upon a panel. The day after the jury was chosen, the district attorney presented his case, which incorporated only one hour and fifty minutes of testimony, in hopes of sending Gus to the death house.

Most of the testimony consisted of Gustafson reading Gus's grand jury confession, followed up with a reading of Baldonado's testimony in the Ma Duncan trial. After assaulting the defendant with his own words, the prosecutor put Sylvia Mary Butler on the stand to recount Olga's last few hours of life. At the conclusion of Nurse Butler's testimony, the prosecutor presented Coroner Virgil Payton, who identified the body and described the gravesite. When

Gustafson moved to present photographic evidence of the victim and the grave, he was prevented from doing so by the objection of John Danch, the defense counsel. Outside the presence of the jury, Danch argued that the photos were too gruesome to present and would unduly prejudice the jury. Judge Blackstock decided to allow photos of the victim taken in the grave, however he disallowed close-up autopsy shots of the victim's head wounds. During the testimony, Gus kept his head bent, and it sank noticeably lower when Gustafson read Gus's description of the actual murder. He looked up but once, when Gustafson demonstrated to the jury how the victim had been strangled. Gus quickly dropped his gaze, fixing his stare on a random spot on the table.

After the prosecution rested, the defense started a parade of witnesses to testify on behalf of the defendant. This included former employers, old school friends, and other acquaintances. The testimony elicited from these attestants was that Gus was a "happy-go-lucky sort of a guy" who was definitely a follower and not a leader. Most of these witnesses were very sketchy or forgetful about Gus's considerable criminal experiences when he was a youth. The Good Samaritan and schoolteacher, Onorinda Jones, who allowed Gus to live with her for a short time during his boyhood, testified that she remembered Gus as being "like most other children." When asked by Gustafson if most eleven-year-olds committed burglaries, the baffled woman admitted that perhaps Gus was a little different from other youngsters. She could not account for her poor memory as it related to the defendant's criminal record.

The defense presented testimony of Dr. Philip R. M. May, a local psychiatrist. His statements sounded surprisingly similar to that of the other psychiatrists who had testified in Elizabeth's trial. His final conclusions were that, while Gus was sane within the meaning of the law, he certainly had a sociopathic personality.

In the defense's strongest plea for sympathy, Gus's mother, Sophia, took the stand to recount the deprived childhood that her son had grown up in. This greatly affected the convicted murderer, who sat sobbing quietly and twisting a handkerchief in his hands.

When his mother also broke down on the stand, Judge Blackstock decided on a recess so all involved could compose themselves.

The defense next called Carmen Baldonado, who testified to her married life with Gus. She stated that they were married on December 28, 1955, and separated some sixteen months later. Carmen took the heat for the separation, saying it was mostly her fault because she was "jealous and too demanding." During cross-examination, Carmen stated that she was aware that Gus was dating other women, but that was okay because she was seeing other men.

John Danch then called Rabbi Joseph A. Gilbert, who was a staunch opponent of capital punishment. Danch hoped to mitigate some of the expected argument of the prosecutor, who had successfully used "an eye for an eye" and the Biblical right to retribution in his summation during Ma Duncan's trial. However, the prosecutor objected to the expected testimony and Judge Blackstock agreed, stating, "The objection is sustained, reluctantly. It is an interpretation of the Bible. One man interprets it one way, another the other. As a matter of law, this is not competent evidence."

Danch then called a Christian minister to the stand, but was met with the same sustained objection.

When the defense had concluded presentation of their evidence, Roy Gustafson launched into his summation. The prosecutor did use his "retribution" argument, saying that retribution is "a basic human instinct as strong as sleeping and eating." He characterized Olga's murder as "almost unparalleled in its cold-bloodedness," and demanded the jury send Augustine to death row.

In a thirty-minute summation, defense attorney Danch pointed out that, of those convicted every year, few are put to death. He then asked, "Is this one of the very few deserving the death penalty? This boy has had a hard life. He has had to struggle through some dark path that we don't even know about." Danch walked to his client and grasped him on the shoulder. Gus kept his head bowed, looking only at the table, "Is death the only solution we know? Is it the Christian solution? Is it the sort of solution that makes America great?" Danch thundered at the jury. He then sat down, his hand sliding down to Gus's forearm, squeezing it in reassurance.

After brief instruction, the panel adjourned to the jury room. One hour and fifty minutes and three ballots later, the jury of seven women and five men returned, with the penalty affixed at death. The jury was thanked by the judge and released. Augustine Baldonado was led away by court deputies, his wife and one of his children crying softly in his wake.

On April 14, Gus returned to court to hear Judge Blackstock pronounce, "You are sentenced to die by the administration of lethal gas." Gus briefly embraced his hysterical mother before returning to the jail to prepare for his drive north to San Quentin's death row.

Unlike his crime partner, Luis Moya sat proud and erect through the penalty phase of his trial. He affixed each witness with his gaze, smiling at those who spoke up in his behalf and busily taking notes when others testified against him. His attorney, Burt Henson, who had been very proactive in the press condemning the actions of the district attorney, was well prepared to put on a formidable case to save his client's life. Moya, like Gus, had already pled guilty to the first-degree murder charge.

Henson made a strong plea for a change of venue, citing the "day-by-day barrage" of publicity that was sure to prejudice the minds of the prospective jurors. However, as in his previous decisions, Judge Blackstock denied the request, reaffirming his confidence that the citizens of Ventura County would be able to differentiate evidence from publicity.

Roy Gustafson, anticipating a stiffer defense than in the case just concluded, and realizing that convincing a jury to condemn a twenty-year-old to death would present more of a challenge than his prosecution of Gus, diligently prepared the state's case.

Jury selection moved slowly, as the attorneys questioned each prospective juror closely. After interviewing seventy-one people, and after Henson had run out of preemptory challenges, the court finally settled on a jury of seven men and five women.

After a brief opening statement, Roy Gustafson read the testimony of Luis from the grand jury and Elizabeth's trial transcripts.

Gustafson's format then closely followed that of the previous trial, with Nurse Butler testifying to seeing Olga alive on the night of the murder, and Coroner Payton describing the grave and condition of the body. Photos depicting the crime scene and the victim were then presented to the jury.

Gustafson then called Detective Ray Higgins to the stand. Higgins played a tape-recorded confession that Moya had made the day after Christmas. Moya sat motionless, listening to his voice fill the courtroom for more than an hour. His family, having made the trip from San Angelo, Texas, sat quietly in the audience, listened attentively, his mother wiping away an occasional tear.

On April 23, the defense began to present their evidence. Henson requested permission to show a documentary produced by Los Angeles news commentator, Bill Stout.

The prosecutor objected to the film, so it was shown outside the viewing of the jury to determine its relevance. It walked the audience through each stage of the preparation for an execution, from the deathwatch to the final moment when the executioner recommended to the condemned, "Take a good deep breath and that will be the end of it." The final scene showed a hand clasping the end of the steel chair and going limp after the cyanide was dropped.

Moya sat through the presentation, his eyes glued to the screen. When the lights came on, the young man took a deep breath in an effort to relax.

Henson argued that since the jury was about to exercise a "Godlike function of deciding life or death," they should be allowed to view the film. The prosecutor called the motion picture propaganda and noted that it was produced as part of the television station's anti-death-penalty editorial policy.

Judge Blackstock agreed with the prosecutor, saying that after seeing the documentary he was convinced that it was not material to the matter at hand.

The defense then marched a host of witnesses to the stand to testify to the good character of the defendant. As in the defense of Gus, Moya's upbringing and the underprivileged circumstances of his youth were highlighted. In addition, Henson stressed Moya's newfound religious belief, calling to the stand the Reverend Floyd Gressett, who had convinced Moya to confess, but now found himself in the position of assisting the defense in keeping the defendant off death row. Gressett stated that he was sure that Moya's conversion was legitimate and not just playacting.

Eloise Gonzales, Moya's sister, also took the stand. She testified that she had received a letter from her convicted brother, expressing remorse and hope that, through his repentance, Olga and her unborn child would find salvation. Eloise also testified to the conditions of childhood poverty that all the Moya children grew up in, while slides were shown of their clapboard residence on a dirt street in San Angelo.

The defense presented testimony by a psychiatrist, who sounded very similar to the doctors that testified in the two previous trials. In a move that Henson objected to strenuously, Gustafson was able to get before the jury the fact that Moya's two co-conspirators, who had the same general psychological diagnosis, were sentenced to death in their trials.

Finally, Henson put his client on the stand. In a very low-key voice, the young man, who had appeared arrogant and cocky in his previous court appearances, now expressed great remorse for the crime. He looked directly at the jury and stated that, if he were allowed to live, he would devote the remainder of his life to Christ and religion. Luis noted that he found God on the night of his confession, kneeling on a cold concrete floor. "I had never bowed down on my knees to anyone. But here I was down on my knees to somebody I had never seen, but who I hope to see pretty soon. I am positive I have been forgiven."

Henson asked his client why he killed Olga. He answered, "I can't find any reason. It was just the money I was thinking about." He once again denied that he knew Olga was pregnant, because of the loose-fitting robe she was wearing that night.

During cross-examination, Gustafson had Moya recite his life of crime, noting that the defendant admitted to more than twenty-three different criminal acts. Moya also admitted that he had previously used references to God when he was steadfastly denying his guilt, an admission elicited to cast doubt in the minds of the jurors about Moya's religious sincerity. Luis also confirmed that he had frequently lived off the earnings of women who prostituted themselves to provide him money.

Both attorneys spent considerable time in their summations. Burt Henson's delivery centered around his defendant's deprived childhood, his tender age, his newfound religion, and the fact that Henson had heard "nothing but hate" since he had started this case. The hate which was directed towards his client was being fed by the police, the prosecutor, and the newspaper reporters, whom he likened to "carrion vultures" in their quest for "tidbits of hate!" In an attempt to make their verdict very personal, he explained to the jury that each one of them had the cyanide lever sitting next to them, and each must decide if they wished to pull the handle and kill his client.

Gustafson attempted to mitigate the defense's pleas for sympathy, pointing out that being poor as a child did not necessarily mean one had to turn to crime. He stated that the pictures of Moya's childhood were not unlike his own memories, because he had also grown up in poverty. He further noted that none of the other Moya children had turned to a life of crime like their sibling had.

The prosecutor expressed considerable doubt about the sincerity of the religious conversion the defendant said he had undergone. He strongly suggested that this conversion might disappear as quickly as it had appeared. And finally he noted, "You are not here to administer love, but to administer justice. Only the death penalty will most nearly balance the scales of justice in this case."

Following one-half hour of jury instructions, the panel adjourned to the jury room to discuss the verdict. After the longest debate of the three trials, some five hours and twenty minutes, the panel returned with a verdict of death. Like Elizabeth's jury, the panel refused to discuss any aspect of the case with the press, and quickly exited the courtroom upon their dismissal.

On May 7, 1959, Judge Blackstock formally sentenced Luis Moya. The judge, who before the Duncan murder cases, had never pronounced the death sentence, did so for a third time. In so doing, he stated, "If anyone imagines I have not thought about the case night and day and at midnight and at all times, they are mistaken. But if you are going to be a judge, then you have to judge." He continued by saying that the crime was the most revolting in the county's history and that the only factor that had come close to swaying him was Moya's tender years. The jurist then condemned Luis Moya to die by the administration of lethal gas.

Two hours later, Luis Moya drove north with Detective Ray Higgins and the Reverend Gressett to join Gus on death row. While en route to San Quentin, the trio traveled through the rolling cattle country south of the community of San Luis Obispo.

While they traveled, the condemned man gazed out of the car window at the spreading oaks and green pastures. He turned to Gressett and said, "Y'know Reverend, this is the first time I've really seen this countryside. I mean I've been through here before, but I never took the time to look at it."

"Well, it's sure nice country. God's country, I'd call it."

"Sure is." Luis fell silent, his eyes glued on the oak trees that buzzed past the car. He finally spoke again. "Will you do somethin' for me?"

"If I can. What is it?"

"After my death, will you see that my eyes—my—what part is it?"

"Corneas?"

"Yeah, my corneas. Will you see that they are donated to a blind child so someday they can see beauty in this world."

The comment and the compassion with which it was said surprised the pastor, who had come to know this man very well. "Well, Moya, that possibility is a long way—"

"Don't kid me, Pastor. I know what the score is. Will you help me with this? I'm asking you as a friend."

"Sure, Moya. If it'll make you feel better. I'll do my darndest."

"Thanks, Reverend." Luis's stare returned to the rolling cattle country while they continued their trip in silence.

With the transportation of Luis Moya to San Quentin, the press and people of Ventura and Santa Barbara Counties settled down to the more mundane occurrences of everyday life. Letters to Roy Gustafson and Judge Blackstock, which had come from all corners of the world, slowly decreased in volume. The people, knowing that the appeals process must run its course, waited patiently for the executions.

In the May 11 edition of the *Star Free Press,* a short article ran on the bottom of the third page. It stated that the Ted Mayr Funeral Home had attached the savings account of Olga Kupczyk Duncan, removing the total balance of $290 to cover part of the cost of her funeral. The story also noted that the funeral home had sent the ashes of the victim to her brother, William, in Canada.

Olga would not have a final resting place for years, her ashes being kept in the home of her brother until the death of her parents. Only then was she finally laid to rest, in the cradle of a grave, at a location kept secret by the members of the Kupczyk family.

An Escape Attempt

Trouble on the row!

—Sergeant Roy Kardell,
Condemned Row Isolation Sergeant
July 2, 1962, 12:20 A.M.

By the time Luis Moya and Gus Baldonado decided their best hope for survival was to break out of jail, all legal appeals had run their course through the judicial system. At every turn, Luis and Gus had met only disappointment, and their hopes to stay alive had grown dim.

Of the trio of perpetrators, Gus had the least hope for his legal appeals because he had only two legitimate issues. He took his best shot by bringing up the denial of a change of venue for the penalty phase of his trial. His main contention was that the pretrial publicity by the district attorney had hopelessly poisoned the jury pool.

However, the California Supreme Court decided that Judge Blackstock had not abused his discretion in this area. In reaching its conclusion, the court noted that 170,000 people lived in Ventura County and that "even if it be assumed that many persons formed opinions unfavorable to the defendant as a result of what was published, it does not follow that persons without such views could not be found to act as jurors."

The court further noted that it did not buy the defense argument that "those who had adverse opinions would be unable to set them aside and try the case fairly on the basis of the evidence produced in court."

Gus's only other appealable issue revolved around the introduction of parole evidence from an officer of the Board of Corrections concerning Luis Moya. In presenting this evidence, the prosecution had been attempting to show that persons convicted of crimes only do a small portion of their actual sentence. In one of Luis's previous cases, although sentenced to a ten-year term, he had been paroled after one year in prison. The court agreed that this evidence should not have been allowed, because Moya's prior offense was not first-degree murder. However, the court also determined, "We have concluded that it does not seem reasonably probable that in the absence of the error a result more favorable to the defendant would have been reached by the jury."

Luis also appealed the issue of change of venue, stating that the error was most egregious in his case because his trial was the last of the three. The court found no error in Blackstock's ruling, stating that Moya had not pointed to any new information for the court to come to a different conclusion than they had already reached in the Duncan and Baldonado cases.

Like Gus, Luis presented the testimony of the officer of the Board of Corrections as highly prejudicial. The court again concluded that the evidence did not unduly prejudice the jury.

Luis's next tactic was an attempt to use the exclusion of the testimony of Phillip W. Thatcher as an appealable error. During the trial, Henson had attempted to call Thatcher, a reformed ex-convict, to testify about the relationship between the acceptance of religion and the likelihood of rehabilitation. Inherent in this argument was a question about whether Moya's confession, which was prompted by Reverend Gressett's prayer session with the young man, had been voluntary.

The court quickly disposed of both arguments, deciding that there was no prejudice concerning the confession because Moya later came to court and testified to what he had previously con-

fessed. As regarded Thatcher's excluded testimony, the court concluded, "The effect of religious conversion upon rehabilitation is not
a matter sufficiently beyond common experience that the opinion of
an expert is required to assist the trier of fact." Therefore, " . . . the
court did not err in excluding Thatcher's testimony."

Luis's final effort was to claim error in allowing the introduction
of three photos of Olga's body covered in a thin layer of dirt and
lying in a shallow grave. The court indicated that, in its opinion, the
photos were actually far less gruesome than the facts of the killing
and the defendant's recitation of those facts during testimony in
open court.

These decisions of the California Supreme Court, which were
automatically appealed to the United States Supreme Court, were
handed down on March 11, 1960. The U.S. Supreme Court issued a
stay of execution on June 10, 1960, and then dismissed the writ for
certiorari of both defendants on May 22, 1961. Absent a last-minute
stay of execution by the governor of the State of California, the
killers' fates were sealed.

"Are you through yet?" Gus whispered to Luis, who was housed
next door in death row cell number 30.

"Shut up, Gus—let me get this done!"

"Hurry up and pass that blade over."

Luis continued to use the hacksaw blade, cutting through the
third bar while counting on the exercise time for the other death
row inmates to keep the guards busy.

When he was done, he slipped the blade to Gus, who had been
working on the bars for the last couple of days. Baldonado was nearly through the bars and just needed to finish up one more in order
to squeeze out of his cell.

A voice came down the row from the ringleader of this attempt,
Clyde Bates, prisoner number A43143: "Hey, Gus—you dumb
fuck—you're making too much noise! You're gonna get us busted!"

Gus, suddenly realizing that he was going at the bars too hard, lightened up with the saw. His will to escape, to take his one chance at ever seeing his twins again, was powerful. As he worked tirelessly, Gus thought back to the boys, whom he had seen only for a few brief minutes after they were born. He wondered what would become of his sons and what they would know and learn about him. He needed to see them again, if only for a few moments. He redoubled his efforts with the saw.

By a little after midnight on July 2, 1962, Luis Moya, Augustine Baldonado, and four other inmates had either sawed through bars or jimmied locks on their death row cells. They had armed themselves and were now prepared to put their plan into action and make their escape.

A few minutes later, Gus caught the attention of gunwalk guard, C. L. Deatrick, to inform him that his toilet wouldn't stop running. It was keeping him awake, Gus said, so he would appreciate it if Deatrick would take care of this annoying problem.

Deatrick exited his post and went into the service corridor to turn off the water, per proper procedures. While Deatrick was attempting to solve the plumbing problem, Gus repeatedly flushed his toilet to further distract the guard and prolong the time that he would remain in the service corridor. He finally yelled to Deatrick that the toilet was fixed, and the officer walked back toward the exit.

When Deatrick reached the exit, three inmates were waiting for him. The guard immediately attempted to jack a round into the shotgun he was carrying, but was struck a blow on the head by Moya, who was carrying a piece of iron bar. Deatrick went immediately to his knees. The shotgun and a handgun were removed from him without further resistance.

Inmate Manuel Chavez, A43144, who was awaiting execution for the murder of six persons in Los Angeles County, grabbed the handgun and proceeded to the office where Sergeant Roy Kardell was stationed.

Sergeant Kardell had just realized that Deatrick was overdue to check in. As he stepped out of his office to check on his partner, Chavez surprised him. The inmate told him, "Sergeant, this is it. Do as I say or I'll kill you. I have nothing to lose. Lie down on the floor."

Kardell later wrote in his report, "I hesitated, trying to figure out if I had a chance to take him. I decided to try to tackle him, and in leaning forward to do so, Chavez struck me with the revolver, knocking me to my knees." David Bickley, A67222, quickly showed up with the shotgun and threatened to "gut shoot" Kardell, who decided he had better cooperate.

What the inmates had failed to ascertain prior to the attempt was that the two death row guards had no keys to exit the Row. Their efforts were for naught, because overpowering the guards could not provide them with a way out. It was well understood at San Quentin that there was a "no hostage" policy, which meant that the life of the guards was forfeit. No prisoners would ever be released because they had taken a guard hostage. This was particularly true in the case of the correction officers who worked on the Row.

Knowing that it was time for the officers to call in with their count, Luis disguised his voice and made the call. Unfortunately for the escapees, Kardell had given them the wrong phone number, which raised suspicion on the part of the facility's operator. The operator alerted the watch sergeant, who called back, at which time Kardell was able to blurt out, "Trouble on the Row," before the phone was snatched from his hands.

Luis Moya, who was standing closest to Kardell, snarled, "You really messed us up. Now we're going to have to kill you!"

Kardell, who in spite of his dire circumstances was not intimidated by the young murderer, responded, "Well, we all have to go sometime."

Fortunately for Deatrick and Kardell, the inmates were not able to carry out their threat because of the fast action of the guards responding to the sergeant's warning. Within a very short time, fifteen officers with shotguns, Thompson submachine guns, and gas were in position to assist their comrades. Several went onto the roof area over death row and fired so many rounds of gas that they ran out of ammunition.

Additional guards were readying themselves for an armed assault on the row just as the assistant warden shouted, "Cease fire!" Luis Moya had grabbed the phone and negotiated a way to give up.

The inmates who had joined in the escape attempt were fit company for Moya and Baldonado, for they had cut a wide swath of murder and mayhem through the state of California. Chavez and Bates were crime partners who were responsible for the deaths of six people in Los Angeles County when they set fire to a nightclub.

Willard Winhoven, A61663, was a career criminal who was up on a number of burglaries and four attempted murders. He finally made the big time when he committed murder and was sentenced to death.

On July 14, 1961, San Quentin had received inmate David Bickley, A67222, for five counts of robbery and one of murder. Bickley's case was on appeal, but there was little hope that he would evade the executioner. During the escape attempt, Bickley, who had grabbed the shotgun from the gun guard, told Kardell, "I've shot a cop before and if I gut shoot you, well, you don't die right away." In a response similar to his words to Moya, Kardell responded, "Well go ahead, I've lived a pretty good life anyway."

After their surrender, the inmates were taken into custody, strip-searched, and rehoused into isolation cells. It was, as one of San Quentin's administrators noted, "a satisfactory conclusion to the insurrection on the Row."

A thorough investigation of the escape attempt revealed that the inmates had managed to make a total of thirty separate cuts on the bars over a three-day period, and had almost been successful in reaching the outside world by cutting the window bars above cell number three. While the blades were never recovered because they were flushed down toilets, Luis Moya told the investigating officers that he had used a hacksaw blade that was one inch wide by five inches long. He also told officers that they "did not intend to kill anyone unless we absolutely had to," which is probably the reason that Deatrick and Kardell were not murdered outright.

While neither Deatrick nor Kardell were killed by the inmates, Deatrick spent three days in the hospital with head injuries. A number of procedural changes were made on death row, including relocating the gun walk officer, lightening the workload of all officers so they could keep a closer eye on activity on the Row, and requiring more frequent inspections of the cell bars.

All six inmates involved in the escape attempt were given twenty-nine days in isolation. However, three days after the event, Luis Moya and Gus Baldonado were given a new execution date of August 8, 1962, so in view of this they were returned to their regular cells.

Luis, in a manner typical of him, tried to have the last word about this event. In a story the *San Francisco Examiner* carried on July 11, 1962, he complained to the paper about San Quentin's reaction to the escape attempt. In particular, Luis remarked that the tightening of security after July 2 was going to cause "the lid to blow off the Row."

The same article printed the reaction of Warden Fred Dickson, who made a classic response: "If those guys think they're going to run the Row—well, they've got another think coming!"

Awaiting Death

Mrs. Duncan was very friendly, receptive, and appreciative of our interest in calling upon her. She expressed again the conviction that she was not guilty, and that the State would not take her life. She has gained strength and comfort from the visits of her sister and son, and was confident that he would still find a way to save her life. When asked about the Sacraments, she replied that her priest has administered Holy Communion whenever she requested it. She seemed content with the present and shared no fears for the future.
—Chaplain Davis, Chaplain's Report, July 16, 1961

The California Institute for Women (CIW) in Corona was well prepared to receive Elizabeth Duncan. While they had not had a death row inmate since the Mountain Murder Mob gun moll Barbara Graham, who was executed in 1955, the prison staff had certainly had experience with the likes of Ma Duncan. Upon the arrival of the convicted murderess, they quickly processed her and placed her into segregated housing, well away from the general population. Other than the visits of her son and sister and her interactions with the staff, Elizabeth would spend the rest of her life devoid of human contact.

Immediately, the administrators of the women's prison had to deal with numerous requests from the press to interview the notorious killer. But it soon became apparent that Ma was in no condition to continue her romance with the media, having suffered a psychotic break within a week of her arrival at Corona. In response to her psychosis, and in order to evaluate her mental condition, prison psychiatrist G. W. Shannon visited Elizabeth on April 9, 1959. Dr. Shannon began his report as follows.

I spent one hour, from 11:00 to 12:00, talking to Mrs. Duncan. When I unlocked the outer room, she was shouting at the top of her voice, was very angry and agitated, and demanded all sorts of attention. This tirade continued for about two or three minutes while I sat down without comment. Soon she quieted down and gave me a chance to introduce myself.

She seemed grateful to have someone to talk to. She made many complaints about her treatment and that she had no water. I pointed to the sink and she said, "Well, there's no ice." I pointed out to her that she was hardly in a position to be demanding of specials, that ice was not available, and that she would have to accept things as they were.

In the course of the conversation, she did at times agree that she was getting good treatment and that she understood that there were certain rules and regulations over which the local employees had no control, and that as a condemned person, she would have to abide by the rules.

Mrs. Duncan is at times quite hopeful and positive that she will not be executed. She volunteered the information that over $47,000 had been spent in her defense, as well as a five-carat diamond ring. She is looking forward to a visit from her son in a few days, and says that he is all that she has to live for.

The prison psychiatrist went on to note that, during their conversation, Mrs. Duncan frequently stopped, looked aside, and listened intently, motioning for the doctor to keep quiet. She was evidently hallucinating and, to his direct question, said that there were people fixing pipes and she wondered when they would stop working on them.

During the evaluation, Dr. Shannon also gained some insight into how Elizabeth viewed her co-conspirators and fellow convicted murderers. He noted her saying that she was sure the two boys were innocent and that she was going to do everything in her power to see that they were not involved. She said that she did not hold any grudge against them for testifying against her. She also volunteered the information that she had known both of the boys because her son had defended them in a narcotics trial.

About Olga, Dr. Shannon's report says: "She . . . makes no effort to hide the fact that she held her daughter-in-law in utter contempt and had great hatred for her. She looked upon her as a scheming woman who quit work as soon as she had succeeded in marrying the son, and she violently opposed the marriage on the basis that her son could not afford to keep a wife."

Frank, the immutable defender of his mother's actions, was quick to assign blame upon hearing about her bizarre behavior at CIW. He told the psychiatric staff that his mother's conduct was due to the heavy sedation she had been under while incarcerated in the Ventura County Jail. Elizabeth's son told the psychiatrist that the jailers had facilitated his mother's addiction to Seconal by providing up to eight pills each night.

Dr. Shannon accepted this as the truth and reported that Mrs. Duncan had received very little in the way of sedation since her arrival in Corona. He concluded that it seemed evident that the auditory and visual hallucinations, which were prominent on Friday, Saturday, and Sunday, were the results of overmedication and then the subsequent withdrawal of the barbiturates.

The concern over the sedation of Mrs. Duncan would again become an issue in a last-minute appeal filed by Frank and attorney S. Ward Sullivan. In this desperate attempt, the defense team tried to convince the California Supreme Court that, because she had been heavily drugged during her trial, Elizabeth had been unable to cooperate in her own criminal case. The court refused to grant a hearing, stating that the new information did not rise to a claim of a significant constitutional question.

In the meantime, Elizabeth, now finally "cured" of her drug addiction, actually became quite agreeable with the prison staff responsible for her welfare. Perhaps because she no longer felt herself to be under a microscope, she grew cooperative in providing the officials at the state prison further insight into her complex being.

In an interview with psychiatric staff, Elizabeth confirmed that she was born in Kansas City, Missouri, on April 16, 1904. Her father, Archie Gilmore Nigh, worked in construction, as a bookkeeper, and finally as a chiropractor in the course of his life. Her mother, Inez Irene Caldwell, remarried after Archie Nigh's death and moved to Santa Barbara, where she ran a convalescent home for thirty years.

Ma remembered considerable conflict in the Nigh household, although she never said that she was physically abused by either of her parents. She had apparently felt left out because of the close relationship between her mother and Elizabeth's youngest brother, James. When talking about their later-in-life relationships, Ma stated, "She gave everything to James, bought him his business, and when she died, left everything to him." According to Elizabeth, James and his wife "were jealous of my standing in the community and of my home. But I used to give his wife my clothes and she'd accept anything from me. Now they have a beautiful home. Mother bought it for them."

Elizabeth said she had started school in Bisbee, Arizona, when she was six years old, but that her formal education was short-lived because, when she was fourteen, her mother would no longer allow her to attend school. She was expected to stay home and care for the younger children, a task the teenager found disagreeable.

At age fifteen, "in order to get away from home," Elizabeth met and married Dewey Tessier, "the only man I ever loved." Three children were born of this union and the children's fates apparently had a great impact on how Elizabeth came to view her relationship with her son, Frank. After Dewey left her for another woman, Elizabeth felt unable to support the children and placed them in an orphanage in Phoenix, Arizona. Dewey eventually gained custody of his children. Upon learning this, Elizabeth "had a complete nervous breakdown. I was very nervous, couldn't sleep. I was shaking." Ma spent sixty days in a rest home before she was able to resume a semblance of normal life. Following the breakdown, she had minimal contact with her children.

Elizabeth admitted to other mental breaks. At fifteen, she had learned that her husband had molested her younger sister. In response, she had attempted suicide by means of an overdose of laudanum and she was admitted to a hospital for an overnight stay.

At twenty-four, Elizabeth had met and married Frank Lowe, Frank's natural father. Lowe, who was an attorney, "drank a lot and had ulcers. We got along, but he slapped me. He used to slap Frankie around, too. We were married for four years and lived in Washington, DC. I left him when he spit on me!"

During that marriage, when Frank was two years old, Elizabeth recalled, "I went completely off my base and was put in an institution in Washington." She remembered that, while in the institution, she had laughed uncontrollably, had hoarded money and food by hiding both whenever she got an opportunity, and had tried to refuse to relinquish little Frank when he was allowed to visit her.

In her personal history statement to the prison authorities, Elizabeth went into a detailed account of her failed marriages. When her marriage to Frank Lowe had dissolved, she said, " After that, I started getting married one time after another. Some of the men Frank (her son) knew about; some of them he didn't."

Noting one thing all the men she'd married had in common, Ma stated, "As a matter of fact, almost all the men lived with their mothers. I'm never one to be jealous of a mother. I know how it feels to have a son."

Elizabeth's bottom line for the many relationships she entered into was best summed up in her own statement to a court-appointed psychiatrist: "If you marry me, you'll be sorry! I act so sweet, but I don't mean it. I fool them. When I'm alone with them, I can't stand it!"

Mrs. Duncan was meticulous in her personal appearance, in which she seemed to take pride. She was also proud of the fact that she had provided Frank with significant support while he attended law school. During that time, she had worked as a companion to a wealthy elderly lady, and this was her son's primary means of support.

It was also during that time that Ma was arrested in San Francisco for keeping a house of prostitution. She minimized her involvement by stating that she was just doing a favor for a friend and had thought the establishment was a legitimate massage parlor. Ma was sentenced to a year's probation for the violation. In her account of her personal history, she denied any other brushes with the law, although her rap sheet showed two further arrests in San Francisco for passing bad checks and an additional arrest in Santa Barbara for petty theft.

Elizabeth readily admitted that for many years she had been addicted to Seconal. She said she had purchased up to two thousand of the tablets at a time, and that she'd had a large stock available on the night of her life-changing suicide attempt. She delivered a discourse about how she had come to be in her current predicament. In her own words:

> Frank told me he was through and told me to move. I was despondent and took the sleeping pills, and for three days I was unconscious in the hospital. Olga met my son there and I found out that he married her on June 20, 1958.
>
> Her name was Olga Kupczyk, I think. I didn't approve of the girl. I didn't like her. She looked a lot older than thirty. When Frank brought her to me, I was shocked. She just stared at me. I didn't like her. I thought Frank brought her there to spy on me, to see if I was okay after I tried to commit suicide.
>
> I got the annulment. I went to the lawyer and appeared in court at Ventura. I said that I was Olga. Charles Lynch was the attorney. He's the racketeering lawyer in Santa Barbara. I told him I wanted Frank to be free. Then I called the Salvation Army and told them I wanted a man to work for me. Winterstein came, and I told him what I wanted and he agreed to pose as Frank. The lawyer said that it

would be legal. Frank was living at home at the time. I'd asked him to get the annulment, but he wouldn't.

He didn't tell me she was pregnant. I don't know whether that would have made any difference or not. I just didn't want her in my family. I didn't want Frank to leave me. She would call me up after they were married and threaten me. She said I was a crazy old bitch. I told Frank about it, but she kept calling me. Later, we didn't bother each other at all. I didn't know until I read in the paper after she disappeared that she was pregnant.

They said she was killed on November 17. Frank reported her away. He thought she'd gone away. He was worried, and so was I. Then they arrested me and took me to jail on December 13 on the annulment charge. I thought that she'd be back. I thought she'd gone away to frighten me and to frighten Frank so that he'd come and live with her. I didn't have anything to do with it. Here I sit in jail for some Mexican's lies. If it wasn't all for prejudice, I'd never have been convicted.

When asked to explain why so many people had testified against her, Elizabeth responded that most of them were Mexicans, that Mexicans had a tendency to stick together, and that therefore their testimony was biased.

Ma's life at Corona soon settled into a routine. Her complaints generally revolved around the lack of company because of her solitary confinement status as a condemned inmate. She spent her days watching television, and was quick to boast that she had never read a book in her life. Much of each day was spent writing long, affectionate letters to her son, reading true story magazines, or looking forward to her brief periods of outdoor exercise. She often complained of migraines and continually attempted to get Seconal by saying she was unable to sleep at night. This claim was not borne out in the comments of staff members who noted that most nights Mrs. Duncan slept soundly, with no need for nighttime medication.

Elizabeth's numerous psychiatric exams reflected common themes. They described a woman of average intelligence (her IQ was determined to be 95) who displayed no evidence of mental illness or psychosis. Her condition was generally deemed to fit best into the category then known as character-behavior neurosis, which might today be compared to a sociopathic personality disorder. It was noted that throughout her life her pattern had been one of emotional immaturity and an infantile response to reality consistent with her education and intelligence.

By July of 1962, Mrs. Duncan's only hope for life rested with California Governor Edmund G. Brown, who was known not to favor the death penalty. "My mother gave me life," Frank Duncan pleaded before Governor Brown on July 11. "I am going to ask you to give her the rest of her life." While Frank begged for his mother's life, S. Ward Sullivan, who realized that the chances for commutation were bleak, filed unsuccessfully for a writ of habeas corpus over the administration of drugs in the Ventura County Jail.

Governor Brown accepted the reasoning of newly elected Ventura County District Attorney Woodruff Deem, who had concluded, "Nothing can refute the fact that this was a killing for hire, boldly done, brutally accomplished on a woman who was about to give birth to a child."

By July 31, 1962, Frank Duncan had given up all hope of saving his mother. In an emotionless letter, he wrote to J. O'Connor Mortuary, 455 Valencia Street, San Francisco: "Pursuant to a telephone conversation of this date, this letter is your authorization to remove from San Quentin prison the remains of Elizabeth Duncan after the execution of said body therein. This will authorize you to have our permission to remove said body from said place and to prepare the body for disposition thereafter. Thank you for all the considerations given this matter."

Ma Duncan's three-and-one-half-year wait to meet the executioner was rapidly drawing to a close.

The Executions

The California Executioner keeps banker's hours. He never kills before ten o'clock in the morning, never after four in the afternoon.
   —Caryl Chessman, *New York Post,* May 3, 1960

The door to cell 39 slammed open and Luis Moya stepped into the wide corridor.

He was met by two deathwatch guards, who quickly shackled him with a belly chain, pinning his hands to his waist. After they had shackled him, one guard sang out, "Dead man walkin'," the traditional notification that an inmate was taking his last walk from the cell block. Then the chatter started: "See ya, Louie" ... "Take care" ... "Be seein' ya around" . . . and, finally, "I'm right behind you, pal," from another death-row inmate whose time was rapidly approaching.

Luis ambled toward the birdcage, the domed entranceway constructed of bars, which allowed access to Death Row. He shuffled slowly, so he could banter with the men he was leaving behind for the last time. He had come to know them well, for all had in common the knowledge that they too would one day take the death walk down this corridor.

"Hey, Clyde!" Luis yelled to the six-time murderer from Los Angeles.

"Whatcha want, you sorry son of a bitch?" the convict called back.

"We gave 'em hell, didn't we?"

"Yeah, we did sure as shit . . . " His voice trailed off. "S'long, Junior."

Luis looked at one of the guards and whispered, "Let's get outta here. I'm not so hot at good-byes." A sob was heard coming from one of the cells as Moya made his way down the block.

The door slammed behind them as they stepped onto the elevator that took them down from the fourth floor to the deathwatch cells on ground level.

Luis Moya and Augustine Baldonado would spend their last night in these cells located next to the death chamber, under the constant monitoring of five guards. The deathwatch guards, as they were called, would cater to their every reasonable request prior to their appointment with the executioner. Directly outside the two adjoining cells were a record player and a radio. The guards played whatever music the two wished to hear.

They also kept them fully supplied with tobacco and hot coffee. When they were asked what they wished to eat, both men opted for a light dinner, planning to make up for it in the morning with a large breakfast.

The condemned men spent the night silently. Even Gus, who had become the death-row jester, had run out of jokes. They both dozed fitfully and listened to the music.

At 9:00 A.M., the large breakfast they had ordered was brought in on stainless steel food carts. Gus took one look at it and found that his appetite had deserted him.

"You gonna eat this shit," he asked Luis in the next cell.

"Yeah, sure, why not?"

"I don't know . . . it don't look that good. Y'know what, Louie? I'm scared, man!"

"Sure, Gus. But we gotta hold it together. I'm with you all the way. We gotta do this with pride, man . . . " His voice trailed off.

"Yeah, I know . . . with pride. But pride ain't gonna save my ass."

"No, but at least your family will have somethin' good to say about you someday: 'He went out like a man.'"

"Well, I never thought it'd end like this. Remember all those times you said 'Stick with me?' It didn't work out so good, did it Louie? Maybe at the last . . . "

"Fuck that, man! You're the one who ratted, not me!" Luis shouted. "I just wanna get this done. I wish they'd strap me in that motherfucker right now! Just do it!" Luis got up and kicked his cell door, bringing the response of one of the guards.

"Having an attack of nerves?" the guard asked. He'd seen the toughest of men come unglued during the wait.

"Naw, get lost!"

"Whatever," the officer looked in on Gus, then left.

After the guard had departed, Gus ventured, "Maybe I'll try some of these eggs." He picked up his fork and began to move them around his metal tray.

At 10:15 A.M., one of the deathwatch guards stuck his head in the door and announced, "The old lady is gone."

"Good," was the response from Luis.

Elizabeth Ann Duncan, CIW#3249, dressed in a pink-and-white-striped prison smock, her hair pulled back in a tight bun, had walked unassisted into the octagon-shaped death chamber. She looked briefly at the witnesses, noting that her son was not among them.

"I am innocent. I want to see my son," she said as they strapped her into the metal chair marked with the large letter "K." No one knew Frank's location, so they didn't answer her. While making final preparations, the executioner explained to her that if she took a deep breath it would be over quickly. She did not respond to his advice, obviously disappointed that she was unable to say goodbye to the only person she ever loved, her son Frank. At 10:04 A.M., the executioner lowered the cyanide pellets into the acid.

Elizabeth took a deep breath, gasped once, and her head thudded back against the hard steel chair. At 10:12, the prison doctor, listening to the stethoscope that extended into the death chamber and was taped over her heart, pronounced the fourth woman executed in California dead.

While his mother was taking her last breath, Frank, with his new wife, Elinor, was in San Francisco at the United States Court of Appeals, attempting to get a last-minute stay of execution. The judge who heard his motion stated that he was unable to find any basis for granting a stay and had not done so.

After the announcement of Elizabeth's death, Luis called to the guard. "I want to talk to Floyd Gressett. Would you send him in?"

Reverend Gressett was ushered in and the two men began to pray. Gus, who had never embraced a religious belief, listened quietly to the murmuring coming from the cell next door.

At 11:00 A.M., the warden came into the cell area and announced to both men that their eleventh-hour judicial appeals had been denied. This left only the hope for clemency from Governor Edmund (Pat) Brown. Though Governor Brown was known to be anti-death penalty, he had suffered serious political effects after he had vacillated in another high profile case. Governor Brown, after reviewing the killer's case, said that he was "unable to find circumstances" sufficient to interfere with the imminent executions.

By this route, the defendants had reached their day of reckoning.

At 12:50 P.M., one of the deathwatch guards opened the cells of the waiting men.

They were directed into the nearby sergeant's office, where the stethoscopes were placed over their hearts prior to their donning white shirts.

While Gus was buttoning his shirt, he said, "I'm sorry for what I said before, Louie. I just lost it for a minute."

Luis looked up at his longtime friend, a lump forming in his throat. "Shit, man, that's okay. I mean, I understand." He finished tucking in his shirt, and walked over and embraced his older friend. "Are you gonna hang tough?"

"Yeah, I got it together now," Gus replied, returning the hug.

"Well, I'll see ya in the hereafter, Gussie," Luis said when one of the guards indicated that it was time to go. Gus swallowed and nodded his head. He could not speak.

The men walked to the chamber, skirting the witnesses. Gus recognized his brother, who was crying softly. He told him in a cheerful voice, "I'm all right." But his brother was unable to control his weeping.

The men were strapped into the chairs marked "A" and "B" within the green chamber. They talked with each other in a joking manner to keep their nerve up. At 1:05 P.M., the executioner pulled the red-handled lever and the cyanide tablets were lowered into the sulfuric acid. Gus commented, "It's down," referring to the lowering of the tablets. Before the pungent, sickening-sweet odor enveloped the doomed men, Luis made eye contact with Reverend Gressett. His lips formed the words, "Goodbye, Reverend." His head then slumped forward on his chest.

Gus sought out the eyes of his brother-in-law, Lawrence Roman. He said, "Go see my kids." Baldonado's body braced against the restraints and he slumped forward, held in the metal chair only by the straps. By 1:15, both were pronounced dead by the prison doctor.

Though Luis was not successful in willing his corneas to a needy child, his body was shipped to Stanford University, where it was used in research by medical students. Gus's body was released to his family and he was buried in Thousand Oaks, California.

Frank Duncan took possession of his mother's remains. Her burial place, like that of her victim, is known only by her family.

Olga as a young lady.
(Photos courtesy of Jody Nigh.)

Olga as a young adult.
(Photos courtesy of Jody Nigh.)

Olga and her mother, at nursing school graduation.
(Photo courtesy of Jody Nigh.)

The vehicle used to kidnap Olga, in the city impound.

Back seat of vehicle used to transport victim.
(Photos courtesy of the Santa Barbara Police Department.)

Officers exhuming Olga.

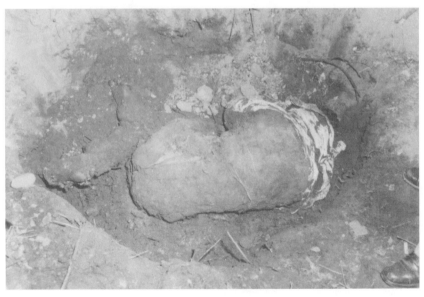

Olga's body in the grave.
(Photos courtesy of the Santa Barbara Police Department.)

Ralph Winterstein.
(Photo courtesy of the Santa Barbara Police Department.)

Frank and his sister, Patsy, as children.
(Photo courtesy of Jody Nigh.)

Frank, Hazel (Ma's given name), and Patsy.

Hazel (Ma Duncan) circa 1940.
(Photos courtesy of Jody Nigh.)

Ma Duncan and her sister, Helen Morris.
(Photo courtesy of Jody Nigh.)

Frank Duncan with his mother, Elizabeth Ann "Ma" Duncan, in 1959.
Frank, an attorney, helped to defend his mother when she went on trial
for hiring two thugs to murder his pregnant wife.
*(Photo courtesy of the Department of Special Collections,
Charles E. Young Research Library, UCLA.)*

Confessed to Duncan Slaying – December 27, 1958.
Luis Moya, left, and Augustine Baldonado, confessed kidnappers and slayers
of Mrs. Olga Duncan, talk outside of the Ventura Grand Jury Room.
(Photo courtesy of the Department of Special Collections,
Charles E. Young Research Library, UCLA.)

Tender Moment – January 14, 1959.
Attorney Frank Duncan receives a kiss on the cheek from Mrs. Elizabeth
Duncan. *(Photo courtesy of the Department of Special Collections,*
Charles E. Young Research Library, UCLA.)

On Trial - February 17, 1959.
Elizabeth Duncan and her son, Frank, foreground, listen intently
as attorney S. Ward Sullivan, center, questions jurors.
*(Photo courtesy of the Department of Special Collections,
Charles E. Young Research Library, UCLA.)*

Ruled Sane - March 25, 1959.
Ma Duncan clasps hands of attorney S. Ward Sullivan, center, and son
Frank after being found sane in daughter-in-law's murder.
*(Photo courtesy of the Department of Special Collections,
Charles E. Young Research Library, UCLA.)*

Elizabeth Duncan in her younger years.
(Photo courtesy of Jody Nigh.)

Elizabeth "Ma" Duncan in her jail cell.
(Photo courtesy of the Department of Special Collections,
Charles E. Young Research Library, UCLA.)